Historical and Critical Essays

The author. Sterling Professor of French at Yale University, HENRI PEYRE is a member of the American Philosophical Society and of the American Academy of Arts and Sciences, the holder of some twelve honorary degrees from American colleges and universities, and former president of the Modern Language Association and of the American Association of Teachers of French. He has published hundreds of articles and more than thirty books, most recently *The Literature of France* (1966), *The French Novelists of Today* (1967), and *The Failures of Criticism* (1967). Studies of Sartre and Valèry will appear in 1968.

Historical and Critical Essays

BY
HENRI PEYRE

Acknowledgments for permission to reprint copyrighted
material appear on page 283.

Manufactured in the United States of America

FOREWORD

IN THE spring of 1967, I had the honor to be invited by the University of Nebraska to deliver the Montgomery Lectures at that University. The general subject was history and literature in France in the last century and in our own. The lecturer's intent was to stress how much history had gained through being allied to literature, not only in power of appeal and in beauty of expression, but also in philosophical import and as prophecy. Literature, on its own side, at a time when it was periodically tempted to retreat from the turmoil of the world and from its growingly democratic audience (with art for art's sake; esoteric symbolism; the solipsism of Proust, Gide, Cocteau; the cult of "nil" in Mallarmean poetry, in the antitheatre and the "new novel") had been enriched through being bound up with history and with those political and social events which are the history of to-morrow. The second lecture dealt more particularly with the singular power which French historians and philosophers of history had possessed of creating, or spreading, three of the most potent myths of the modern world: race, nationalism, and the cult of the Revolution.

To those two lectures, given here in a revised form as the first two chapters of this volume, are added a number of essays published earlier; some of them had been the themes of talks to classes which I took while lecturing at the University of Nebraska. They range from topics in comparative literature (how the modern French have viewed ancient Greece, English literature, Shakespeare) to the relations of French literature with religion, with the preparation of the French

Revolution, with Napoleon. Others touch on the perennial force of romanticism; others still are concerned more directly with the American scene, observed by a French author who has, for over thirty years, been associated with academic life in this country: the responsibility of mass media in a democracy, the search for excellence and leadership in education. A final one interprets the message of two contemporary French novelists and moralists who have long cast a spell upon American college youth. Through the variety of the themes treated or broached here, the lifelong concern of an author who stubbornly refused to separate the study of the past from the understanding of the present and from hopes for a better future is, I trust, apparent.

My stay at the University of Nebraska was made stimulating as well as pleasant through the kindliness of many colleagues and the responsiveness of the faculty, students, and friends of a remarkable University. My very special thanks go to Dean and Mrs. James C. Olson, to Professor D. E. Allison, to Professor and Mrs. Reino Virtanen. To them, this volume is gratefully dedicated.

HENRI PEYRE

Sterling Professor of French
Yale University

CONTENTS

Historical and Critical Essays

1 | HISTORY AND LITERATURE IN CONTEMPORARY FRANCE

THERE ARE individuals as there are nations which thrive on crisis and never rejoice more gleefully than when they can, as doctors, lean over the sickbed of an art or of a literary genre to declare it moribund or, as moralists, depict that perilous condition as a challenge. French criticism counts an especially large group of such mournful prophets who have announced that painting, music, the theatre, the novel, the essay were dying, as good manners, clarity, and common sense had already done. Ever since the middle of the present century, the most loudly lamented crisis has been that of creative literature, which has been profusely advised to make way once for all for the "human studies" (more and more, the adjective "human" is being severed from literature and reserved for social, anthropological, and historical disciplines). Being thus assailed as anachronistic and lacking in appeal to men and women who live in an industrial and technological civilization is, naturally, nothing new for poetry, which has regularly responded to such detractors by becoming bolder and more obscure. The theatre is likewise accustomed to being vilified as dragging behind other branches of literature and aiming only at commercial profit and at entertaining—and often failing in both ambitions. The onslaught on the novel, relegated to the position of an expression of and a tool of the bourgeoisie and doomed to disappear with it, is a more recent occurrence.

Fiction is far too pliable and resilient a literary form to succumb so easily. In spite of many endeavors to constrain it to acquire a form

1

and to become a closely textured art, it has stubbornly retained the privilege of remaining formless. Every newcomer with a vision of his own molds it anew and resurrects it from the ashes to which it was doomed. But there are phases, in the motley vicissitudes of fiction and of other branches of literature, during which they yield in vitality to other means of expression and to another type of imagination. For over a century and a half in France, in Britain, and to a lesser extent in Germany and in America, history has been the rival of what is commonly called "creative literature." Or rather, it has defied the restricted conception of literature which seemed to exclude historical writing and grant a higher estate to invented or imaginary genres. Academic syllabi and the prejudices of the teaching profession have perpetuated that exclusion of history from the programs of literary studies. Short stories by Mérimée, Daudet, Maupassant; plays by Alexandre Dumas father and son, by Emile Augier, and their present-day successors (Anouilh, Ionesco) destined to an equally certain and prompt demise from fashion; sonnets by Nerval, Baudelaire, Mallarmé; and a few works of fiction have become the monotonous staple nourishment of thousands of pupils and students in French classes outside France. But the authors who actually molded the French character, who inspired or governed many of its political and social reactions, who were read by French children and reread by adults, were often either novelists who had claimed to be the historians of a society (Hugo, Balzac, Zola), or historians. Augustin Thierry, Guizot, Michelet, Tocqueville, Renan, Taine, and their twentieth-century successors provide just as much literary enjoyment as the finest stylists among imaginative writers. They had a greater appeal to the masses of readers in France and created or spread the myths by which the country tried to live: patriotism, nationalism, race, revolution, progress or decay, sanctity of the people, or advocacy of an elite. There is much folly in history and not a little treachery among those "cunning passages, contrived corridors and issues" denounced as history by T. S. Eliot's "dry man in a dry month" in "Gerontion." Still there has been much more of an obsession with decrepitude and sordidness in novels and plays of the last two centuries, hence a more one-sided or distorted portrayal of life at the very time when Western Europe and America were displaying such heroic energy in changing the world. History affords a truer picture not only of the past but also of the minds of men and women who attempted, from the past, to learn how to bring about a more satisfying future.

The pages which follow are a plea for a much larger place to be given historical writing in the teaching of the humanities in general and of literature in particular. Our contention is that too much of literature lately, in the leading countries of the West whose books reach a sizable audience, has become defeatist and masochistic. Defeatist, for it hardly dares tackle the momentous issues which anguish modern man: misery, war, inequality, responsibility for the plight of the underprivileged countries or classes, rehabilitation of love as transcending sex, the search for a new approach to the discredited myth of progress and for a poetical and constructive alternative to the temptation of war. Masochistic, because the best authors who practice literature today appear to do so with a bad conscience. They are constantly ready to revile it, to demonstrate the inadequacy of language to convey any emotion or thought, to deny literature even the mere possibility of a content other than descriptive. Criticism has followed suit. It has turned into a very technical game of analysis of symbols, metaphors, structure, and other secrets which only the sophisticated specialists can decipher for a few of their hyper-intellectual students. The impact which the lives of the artists, their relations with their times, the story of the throes of creation of a work of art, might have on common men and women is altogether neglected. Implicit in much of modern criticism and teaching of literature is the conviction that it should imitate the exterior appearance of scientific method or, even more specifically, the measuring, dissecting, and combining devices of engineers. A few analytical minds among college students may revel in that pseudo-laboratory atmosphere. A great many, however, in American universities as in those of Europe, are discouraged by the inhumanity of studies thus understood; they are driven to social and historical studies, or simply to disgruntled rebellion and apathy. They look elsewhere for expression of the enhancement of life, of idealism, of keener insight into themselves which the young have not ceased to yearn for. Ludicrously remote from us sounds the triumphant proclamation of the American who, almost exactly a hundred years ago, announced that "viewed today, . . . the problem of humanity all over the civilized world is social and religious, and is to be finally met and treated by literature" (Walt Whitman, in *Democratic Vistas*).

Among the many valid definitions of man, two stand out which are relevant to our concern: that he is a creature with a past, endowed with memory, hence anxious to record that past and to master it; that he is also the animal which knows that he must die, and therefore struggles against time and creates, in the hope of leaving some traces of himself behind, or, as a modern Frenchman has put it, a tiny scar or dent on this earth. Not all nations nevertheless have had a history in the sense in which the Greeks and the Romans, the creators of historical writing, have provided models of historical writing to the moderns. In that sense, the nations of Africa can hardly be said to have had a history before the arrival of the Europeans. In other cultures, those of Asia in particular, the pace of history has in no way been comparable to that of Western nations, which have become anguished by the frightening process of acceleration of history since the emergence of nationalism and the impact of several technological revolutions. A relatively young country like the United States would seem to have especially valid incentives to read into and about the history of the nations which have most deeply influenced it: not having a very long history itself and not inclined to much reverence for the past, it should, in its educational institutions, pursue the development of historical imagination, so that its cultured citizens may be more than the citizens of one age and of one country. Moreover, its attitude toward other nations has altogether changed from the avoidance of foreign entanglements to an unavoidable but ominous concern with all that happens on the globe; it therefore has to take over much of the legacy of other nations, to appropriate their past and to pursue their achievement in its own original manner.

The two opposite requirements of modern education are probably the acquiring of scientific techniques and the deepening of a sense of history. In the first realm, that of science and technology, a knowledge of the past is a superfluity; the origins of chemistry, of surgery, of the internal-combustion engine, of aeronautics, need not preoccupy the students of science overmuch; many of them look with disdain upon anything published in scientific journals over three years ago. Paradoxically, the gigantic strides taken by science, multiplying a thousandfold man's power to alter his environment, have not enabled modern man to match the intellectual security which his predecessor enjoyed until the eighteenth century, or approximately the time when the Western world began feeling dissatisfied with the present and with itself and turned nostalgically to the past. Neither Petrarch nor Raphael, neither Ronsard nor Ben Jonson ever wished he might have lived in Greece or in ancient Rome; they absorbed what they could of antiquity in order to put it to good use. With the advent of a more relativistic perspective, however, the men of the Enlightenment envisioned an indefinite improvement of institutions and of the human mind, freed from superstitions and from the shackles of injustice, and at the same time dreamed of the pagan past with regret. The historian Peter Gay has analyzed with much detail that obsession of the age of Gibbon and Diderot with pre-Christian myths and ancient republics in *The Rise of Modern Paganism* (New York: Alfred A. Knopf, 1966). Ever since, history, as opposed to the severance of technology from the past, has become the other cynosure for the moderns. All humanistic disciplines have, with delight in the Heraclitean flux or with laments over the triumph of relentless and irreversible time, placed themselves within the perspective of history. Few are the thinkers, from Kant, Hegel, Fichte, down to the Marxists and the Existentialists, who have not attempted to formulate a philosophy of history.

That has not gone without mishaps. Few fields of speculation are strewn with more lamentable failures than that of philosophy of history, to which, after Vico, the Germans and the French in particular were drawn. Hegel, who lectured on that ambitious subject at the end of his career, is said to have expressed his cautious skepticism in the sentence, The only thing we learn from history is that we never learn anything from history. Paul Valéry, in far more destructive tones, derided the havoc wrought upon politicians, generals, and philosophers by their obsession with precedents which were not applicable to novel and unpredictable conditions. He branded the cult of history as the cause of the mental inertia of the nations of Western Europe, ready to submit to being controlled by some American commission.

Obviously, every situation is a new one and there is no trace of an eternal recurrence in human affairs. The past can hardly be expected to provide a solution to a problem which is set in new terms. Speculations on the past do not account for what is occurring now; it is rather the present which throws some elucidating light on the past, through displaying the remote consequences of some decision made long ago. Hence the constant renewal of the face which history offers to us, and the need for every generation to rewrite history, as the present is projected over the past like a cipher to flash new meanings to an observer who almost becomes an experimenter. Still, the need of the human mind to trace analogies is not altogether unfounded. There are some elements in common between one economic crisis and another, one war and another, one revolution and another. Those who invoke past precedents (the Terror, the curbing of internal strife, the workers' riots of June, 1848, the Commune of 1871) most earnestly are in fact not the nostalgic conservatives, but the revolutionaries of Russia since 1917 or of Mao's China. A few broad processes are at work in countries and behind situations otherwise dissimilar. A knowledge of history may cramp adventurous leaders by reminding them of the limitations which their equally rash predecessors eventually encountered. It may also encourage a different sort of originality, through eschewing errors committed before. In any case, as J.-J. Rousseau, who was not lenient to history, put it, "The ability to foresee that some things cannot be foreseen is a very necessary quality." In contrast to the heady beverages imbibed by some scientists and technicians today, naïvely boasting that 90 per cent of the scientists and probably 95 per cent of the engineers who ever lived on our planet are alive at the present time, the study of history may well bring, among a few other graces, that of modesty.

It took nothing less than the two chief upheavals of the modern world—the French Revolution and romanticism—to renovate history in the nineteenth century. The great writers of the Enlightenment in France have many a claim to our gratitude: they introduced sociology into history (Montesquieu); formulated, and attempted to follow in its historical unfolding, the idea of progress (Turgot, Condorcet); and they launched the history of civilization as the alternative to the history of sovereigns, wars, treaties, and of events. Voltaire was one of the first to point out the weakness of what the French have since come to call, not without some condescension, "l'histoire événementielle." He is one of the progenitors of the history of civilization. But only when the imagination of the men of the years 1820 to 1848 had been aroused by the desire to identify themselves with other men and other ages, and was inflamed at the same time by liberal passion in politics, did French history reach its great creative age. In that field as in others, the influence of momentous events like the Revolution and the Napoleonic epic affected in depth not those who had participated in those historical crises, but those who were only children when they happened and who looked back with awe or with wonderment, when adults, upon the giants who had preceded them.

Chateaubriand is an enigma for those who were not born to the French language and who remain impervious to the rhetoric and to the pose which, in their detached eyes, mar his writings. It has never been easy for the readers from other nations to understand why he meant so much to the young enthusiasts of 1800–1830 in France. His only undisputed masterpiece, one of the greatest books in the French language, the *Mémoires d'outre Tombe*, had not then appeared: the "Breton enchanter," as his compatriots like to call him, was only carried to his tomb, on a wave-beaten reef off the coast of Saint-Malo, after the French had effected a revolution and crushed a Paris uprising in July, 1848. He left his greatest book as his appeal to posterity. The much earlier *Génie du Christianisme* (1802) contains much childish reasoning; it upholds a strained and unprovable thesis and yet it remains an epoch-making book, one of the three most significant expressions of European sensibility (the other two being the *Divine Comedy* and Goethe's *Faust*, according to no less an authority than De Gaulle). It is read nowadays, and it is readable, only in fragments; but such is the fate of many revered volumes—of the *Aeneid* and the *Faerie Queene* and probably the *Divine Comedy*. The impact of the volume, which, for the general public, rediscovered the Gothic cathedral and, incidentally, Homer and Virgil, and the impact of a prose epic even more seldom read in its entirety, *Les*

Martyrs, determined the historian's career of Augustin Thierry and, through him, of other nineteenth-century French historians. For several decades history in France was to be romantic history.

After a reaction, between 1880 and 1910, which attempted to make history austerely scientific and advocated objectivity and impersonality as the historian's duty, it is no undue generalization to contend that the brilliant school of historians (who are at the same time writers of uncommon talent) in France at the present time (1930 to 1968) is again permeated with romanticism. The man whose presence is felt behind many practitioners of historical disciplines today is Jules Michelet, perhaps the most authentically romantic of all the French writers of the first half of the nineteenth century. More perhaps than the historians of any other nation except Arnold Toynbee in Britain, French historians passionately believe in the need, and in their own ability, to provide a synthesis of the knowledge of past civilizations. The *Revue de Synthèse historique* is the title of the journal, and of the group, which more than any other left its imprint upon historical writing in France after World War I. More also than most historians except the British, the French cling to the notion that history should be written with liveliness and grace and should reach not only other historians, but the public at large. In a collective volume of more than seventeen hundred pages of the Pléiade series devoted to *L'Histoire et ses Méthodes* in 1961, one of the most solid French historians of today, Irénée Marrou, the editor, concluded: "History, man's knowledge of man, is made for men; the scholar does not have the right jealously to monopolize its possession; he must impart it to other men, his brothers."

The trend has thus been to put an end to the divorce which too long kept history apart from other disciplines: ethnology, demography, sociology of cities, agrarian sociology, religion, literary and art history. One of the most perfunctory portions of big collective histories such as the *Cambridge Modern History* and three or four French ones (Lavisse, Halphen et Sagnac) was the chapters devoted to the men of letters and the artists. A few lines each, uninspired and dry and clearly secondhand, dealt summarily with Michelangelo or Velasquez or Corneille or Mozart. In what relationship did those men stand to the setting of their age, to science and engineering (in the case of architects or musicians), to social conditions, to religious beliefs? The question was ignored. Art apparently was merely an extraneous affair, hardly representative of the spirit of the age or heralding a new spirit of revolt against the prevailing conventions. The movement, inspired in France by Michelet, to which Lucien Febvre gave a new impetus in this century, led a large group of historians to attempt a descriptive analysis of the sensibility of an age. Georges Duby and Robert Mandrou have thus composed the most intelligent history of French civilization of earlier centuries and have written other volumes on more modern times. A number of other social historians such as Charles Morazé, Beau de Loménie, C. E. Labrousse, Jean Lhomme have probed into the concept and the growth and alleged demise of the bourgeoisie in the last two hundred years. Louis Chevalier has provided a method for urban history and a bulky model for such a study in his volume *Classes laborieuses et classes dangereuses à Paris* (1960). Marc Bloch, the most dynamic personality among French historians along with Lucien Febvre and, since his death under a German firing squad in 1945, perhaps the most influential predecessor of recent scholars, Albert Soboul; Georges Lefebvre, the renovator of studies on the Revolution; Raymond Aron and Irénée Marrou of the Sorbonne; Fernand Braudel at the Collège de France, are only a few of the great historians whom other nations envy.[1] Three of the finest stylists in modern France, all belonging to what may be called the same family of minds, with Chateaubriand, Nietzsche, and Barrès as their inspirers, all passionately read in the present decade, are also historians: one, De Gaulle, is a memorialist of the recent events "quorum pars magna fuit"; the others, Elie Faure and André Malraux, are

---

[1] The London *Times Literary Supplement*, often more perspicacious in its treatment of history outside England than it is of literary scholarship, has repeatedly proclaimed its admiration for the present school of historians at work in France—both for the scope of their syntheses and for their manner of writing. It has deplored that the compatriots of Gibbon and Maitland have become "content to write heavily and clumsily, accepting the worst German models instead of the best French. . . . No historian is worth his salt who has not felt some twinge of Macaulay's ambition—to replace the latest novel on the lady's dressing table. . . . The historian has to combine truth and literary grace; he fails as a historian if he is lacking in either" (August 25, 1950).

historians of art, conceived as a universal activity of the spirit. Not a few of the most significant achievements by professors of literature have consisted in the exploration of broad concepts, beliefs, ideals, or myths: the idea of happiness in the eighteenth century (Robert Mauzi) or the concept of nature (Jean Ehrard).

The first requirement of history is that it ally poetry with truth. The word for history in Greek, and in Sanskrit before Greek, stemmed from a verb close to "veda" and to "oida" which suggested to know, to examine and therefore to see with clarity. The substantive which, in several languages but not in the German "geschichte," came from Greek connoted information or knowledge secured from inquiry. At no time, however, was history reduced to a mere accumulation of facts, not even with the Benedictines, the Bollandists who collected the *Acta Sanctorum*, Mabillon or Lenain de Tillement, modest collectors of knowledge in a century (the seventeenth) which counted no other genuine historian. Even in the early years of the twentieth century, when J. M. Bury in Cambridge combatively asserted that history was a science, no less and no more, and Charles V. Langlois established a method to banish boldness and any unproved hypothesis, the latter wisely acknowledged that "to know is nothing; one must understand." Unfortunately, such prudent, slow-moving, half-blind history aping science proved to be no more scientific than the writings of Michelet or Carlyle, and it was too forbidding, bristling as it did with notes and references, to be readable. It disregarded one of the most acute needs of modern man, who finds little poetry, properly speaking, to his taste or readily enjoyable: the need for the poetry of history.

Emery Neff, a professor at Columbia University, wrote a volume entitled *The Poetry of History* which, like Edmund Wilson's *To the Finland Station* (1940), dealt in great part with French historians of the nineteenth century. The word "poetry" was naturally used in a broad sense: that of a dynamic interpretation of events, of the forces at work behind events, and of individuals who make history. It does not connote mere adornment, still less a prettification which would be a falsification. History thus conceived and vividly written could indeed prove to be the only genuine successor to the epic in modern literatures and the only equivalent of what a few great films on wars, revolutions, the birth or the death of a nation, the conquest of other worlds, might be. It deals with heroes in an age when the theatre and fiction have too resignedly bid farewell to heroes; but it also displays collective forces embodied by those men who understand them and attempt to control them; and it inevitably finds, or lends, a significance to the senseless or disorderly appearance of events. Like a tragic epic, much of history thus written is a fight against destiny which envisions an ultimate purpose in the succession of incidents, as did the Greek epics and the few Christian ones of any worth.

Facts are naturally not disregarded in such histories; but all facts lie inert and hardly meaningful until they are interpreted. The worship of facts and the collection of them with no hypothesis or motive behind such patient drudgery have seldom proved fruitful. They have greatly slowed the advance of the social sciences which, in America in particular, indulged in that reductionism too long. The overestimation of paltry new documents or new facts unrelated to a governing idea has often been a source of distortion in history and biography, while an original interpretation of the already known facts or existing data would have perhaps opened a newer vista. The Greeks had placed history under the sponsorship of a muse, Clio, as they had the other arts. *Clio* was the title chosen, not only in France by Charles Péguy, a passionate critic of the scholarship which rejoices in the false security of blinkers, but also by a scrupulously exact English historian, George Macauley Trevelyan, in an essay first published in 1904 and as a book in 1930. The celebrated Cambridge Regius Professor did not hesitate, when the current of historical studies in his country ran otherwise, to advocate the marriage of history and poetry. "At bottom, the appeal of history is imaginative," he asserted. "Truth is the criterion of historical study; but its impelling motive is poetic." And again, in lines which Emery Neff chose as the justification for his title: "The poetry of history does not consist of imagination roaming at large, but of imagination pursuing the fact and fastening upon it. Let the science and research of the historian find the fact, and let his imagination and art make clear its significance."

The debate between advocates of the strictest objectivity in the historian and those who consider that requirement impossible and in any case harmful will always divide the worshipers of Clio. Ever since it has become the custom to detect the prejudices of his class in every man who thinks and writes, modern psychologists have pictured Thucydides, once revered as the most scientific and detached master of history among the Greeks, as the mouthpiece of his own social group. One of his ablest and most recent commentators, M. I. Finley, has joined others in blaming Thucydides for making history a form of Hellenic tragedy and for actually abandoning history in his anxiety to give it a political meaning. Cicero coined the striking formula to define the historian's duty: "Ne quid non veri audeat, ne quid veri non audeat"; "Let him have the courage to say nothing which he believes to be untrue and dare say all that he believes to be true." But he himself was a committed man and, like many orators pleading a case, he was adept at bowing factual truth to his purpose. The distorted picture afforded by Tacitus of the age of Tiberius and Nero (according to Gibbon, the happiest era of peace and security enjoyed by the world) does more credit to his literary genius than to his freedom from the prejudices of a Roman aristocrat. Indeed, his famous statement promising solemnly to write history "with neither anger nor passion" has been belied, not only by him, and of course by Michelet and Carlyle, but also by modern writers with a keener awareness of the requisites of science. When the German historian Mommsen was nearing his fiftieth year, in 1866, he encouraged a favorite student of his to compose a thesis stating blandly: "Historiam puto scribendam esse et cum ira et cum studio" ("I believe that history should be written and with anger and with passionate enthusiasm"). José Ortega y Gasset, who reported the detail in an essay translated in the *Partisan Review* of December, 1949, added: "There is no naivety greater than supposing that *ira et studium* are incompatible with 'objectivity.' As if objectivity were anything but one of the innumerable creations for which we are indebted to the *ira et studium* of man!"

The present trend among the European historians is certainly to deride the claims to objectivity, even to impartiality, in their predecessors. The famous assertion of Benedetto Croce that "all history is contemporary history," meaning that no historian can ever forget his own time and place, and searches, consciously or not, for the relevance to his own age of a moment of the past, has become trite. Croce himself, when he thus summed up his spiritual testament, on the eve of World War II, envisaged history as the history of liberty and, as the Italian title of the work went (in 1938), "as thought and action." He implied that his compatriots might stand up and be counted as protesting against the sterilization of Italian intellectual and moral life through Fascism. That judgment is fraught with perils for which wise liberal thinkers may watch, for it might serve to legitimize the rewriting of history by Fascists, Communists, nationalists, and internationalists. It has been interpreted with some laxity by Edward Hallett Carr, the author of one of the many recent volumes entitled "What Is History?" (1962); his favorite approach would no longer be to determine gropingly the past "wie es eigentlich gewesen" ("as it really took place"), in Ranke's rash words, but to ask the question, Whither? Where did it all lead? Has it served what each historian takes to be the march of history? The underlying view of history and of life behind such assertions is similar to that of Hegel, who argued that all that happens is the inevitable unfolding or working of the Idea becoming real. A supine acceptance of facts and even a resignation to the supremacy of might as making right was the eventual and woeful consequence. The historian's task is not, after all, to pick the winner in an eternal struggle of forces between which a choice should be made on moral grounds, and to bet on that winner even if he tramples our own moral ideals and our sense of justice under foot. E. H. Carr naturally knows better and has proved it in the works he wrote during the direst years of World War II for his country. His most meaningful contention is that the pseudo-impartiality of the historian's bowing to facts is a more dangerous fallacy, because it will not admit the inherent fallibility of such respect for the factual. "Facts," he writes, "speak only when the historian calls on them; it is he who decides to which facts to give the floor, and in what order or context."

Such views had already been held, and been lived up to with rich results, by nineteenth-century French historians. The whole rebirth of history, with Augustin Thierry, originated with political involvement in the present, that is, in the liberal attitude of the youth of 1825 reinterpreting the Revolution as an uprising of the oppressed lower classes and wishing that the movement be pursued. Ernest Renan, who admired Thierry as the father of modern French history and as its victim (he lost his eyesight while still young through his intensive research), formulated with felicitousness the value of imagination and of some passionate involvement for the historian. His essay on Thierry, collected in *Essais de Morale et de Critique* (1859), offers his most eloquent definition of the duty of a historian:

> The imagination, which exclusively erudite historians proscribe with their anathemas, often stands a better chance of finding the truth than a slavish fidelity, which is content with reproducing the early accounts of the chroniclers. . . . History is not one of those studies which the ancients termed "umbratiles" [relegated to the shade], for which industriousness suffices. It concerns the most fundamental issues of human life. It demands the whole man with all his passions. Soul is as indispensable to it as it is to a poem or to a work of art, and the individuality of each writer should be mirrored in it.

With the same benign catholic sympathy, Renan used to repeat that he alone has the right to devote himself to the history of a religion who has first believed in it before scanning it with the scrutnizing gaze of disbelief. He applied the same precept to the story of his life when he related some incidents or moods of his childhood and youth with urbane charm: "One must only write about what one loves." That was not a timid Victorian reluctance to face the brutal realities of existence, but a systematic method of sympathy and empathy in the historian which enables him to understand, to explain, and to forgive more than the relentlessly severe upbraider of Christianity like Gibbon, of the inevitable but deplorably ominous triumph of democracy like Tocqueville, of the Revolution and its aftermath like Taine. Love is not necessarily less discerning than indifference. Max Scheler, the acute German psychologist and philosopher, lodged a vehement and not unwise protest against "the specifically modern view according to which love blinds us, instead of making us clear-sighted."

A hundred and eighty years of accelerated history in France and in Western Europe since 1787 (the date many moderns assign to the true beginning of the French Revolution) have taught us the impermanency of all scholarship, and in particular of all history which is not a perduring work of art. Every generation is justified in living up to Goethe's bidding in *Faust*: "Erwirb es, um es zu besitzen" ("Earn that heritage of your fathers, in order to possess it"). It faces issues of its own, and all the experience of its elders is of scant avail in ever new predicaments. It poses its own questions to the past, or it asks the same questions in a new guise. Under the impact of the forces which weigh upon him or of the circumstances which hem in his eagerness to act freely, the modern historian of antiquity will direct his especial attention to the class struggle in Athens, the agrarian revolts and the uprising of the slaves in Rome, the beginnings of technology in the Middle Ages, the struggle of the bourgeoisie for administrative influence with Colbert. Tocqueville likewise looked in America for a possible alleviation of his melancholy forebodings on the ascent of the masses in Western Europe. Others, more recently, have utilized their study of a chosen period of the art of the past as a jumping board to foster their own creativity. Scholarship in that context can, instead of remaining a barren detachment from the problems which face us, be converted into the most inspiring spur to creation. The rediscovery of Egyptian art or of archaic Greek, of Negro masks from Central Africa and of Romanesque sculpture has thus powerfully stimulated architects, sculptors, decorators of our own century. The shock of novelty is more thrilling in the presence of those long forgotten art works than it could ever be with products of our time; the imitation of those exotic survivals from the shipwreck of centuries is less enslaving than that of works of the generations which immediately preceded our own.

Plato, Aristotle, the Sophists and the Cynics, and other thinkers in antiquity before Polybius, in the second century before Christ, did not consider they had enough of a perspective or an adequate context for comparison to sketch a philosophy of history. From St. Augustine to Bossuet, and even down to those great religious minds of the present day (Arnold Toynbee, Herbert Butterfield, Albert Béguin), the central movement of history was the unfolding of a revelation and of obscure ways of God to man preyed upon by a decline of his civilization and sickened by its "discontents," as the Freudian phrase terms them. With the surge of a relativistic perspective, at the time of Locke, Fontenelle, and Voltaire, the Western mind undertook to accept the constant flux of human affairs. The clinging to an absolute valid for all men of all countries, the conviction that a plateau had been reached by the subjects of Louis XIV, or by those of Queen Victoria, or by the favored land of the United States in 1920–1929 and by the later demagogues with the "we never had it so good" slogan, ceased to be attitudes clung to by the more reflective minds. Ever since the earthquake of the revolutions (American, French, and, with less positive an outcome, Flemish, Rhenish, Swiss), men have entertained dark forebodings about the future. A "Grande Peur" which recalls that of 1789 spread to the West after the Bolshevik victory; it has taken on a new hue and color since, as Russian Communism has become progressively respectable, but it is no less insidious in us. Fear of racial riots in America and South Africa, fear of underdeveloped peoples elsewhere who are as ready for desperate destruction as for working out their own salvation, fear of overpopulation, of nuclear self-slaughter, impregnate the sensibilities of the West today, as we draw near the year 2000, somewhat as other and less earthly dreads preceded the end of the first millenary of our era. Philosophies of history are one of the avenues along which many thinkers have roamed since Hegel and Comte, hoping to derive from the consideration of the past some direction toward which the future might march. It is doubtful that at any time since that of the Old Testament there have ever been so many eager minds (scientists, statesmen, engineers, even more than dreamers and poets) passionately crystal gazing at the next few decades. "If you can look into the seeds of time,/ And say which grain will grow and which will not." The bidding of Banquo to Macbeth has become that of many a modern thinker.

The English-speaking countries seem to have been more successful than the Latin and the Slavic ones at keeping clear of those metahistorical speculations. In Spain, and in Russia to a much greater extent, it may be said that all philosophy has revolved around philosophy of history. There is hardly a single thinker in those two countries who, instead of envisaging metaphysical issues "sub specie aeternitatis," did not center his reflections around the essence of Spain or the destiny of holy Russia. For all nations, no doubt, "the love of history is inseparable from self-love," as the statesman Henry St. John (Bolingbroke) hinted early in the eighteenth century in one of his *Letters on the Study and Use of History.* Philosophy of history provides ingenious reasonings by which to justify one's claims to being a chosen people.

Like all general and highly fanciful speculations on the national character or on the mission of a people or on what may constitute, at any given time, the "Zeitgeist," or spirit of the age, any attempt to detect laws at work behind the history of any human group or of any culture is doomed to being torn down by opposing endeavors. American history, true to Tocqueville's dictum that the people of the United States are more addicted to general ideas than their cousins from England, has been seduced by a succession of monist explanations of the energy of their compatriots: the ever receding challenge of the frontier, their ethnic diversity, the material security of a "people of plenty," their migratory restlessness. Each key opened a number of locks, or led to the semi-artificial casting of locks which the key would ideally fit. No such unitary explanation could be valid for the longer and more chaotic history of European nations. But, in the eighteenth and nineteenth centuries, the temptation to discover a rational pattern in the vicissitudes of the past became overpowering. Conspicuous breakdowns of ambitious and frail towers have not dampened the audacity of the twentieth-century historians. Oswald Spengler has been refuted a score of times; Arnold Toynbee has been uncharitably dealt with by Hugh Trevor-Roper and by A. J. P. Taylor. Neither will fail to count rivals among his successors. "Every nation's true Bible is its history," Carlyle peremptorily declared. Of reinterpreting Bibles there is no end.[2]

---

[2] The English themselves have written often and with fascination on the philosophy of history as it blossomed in other countries. A long and well-informed volume on the subject by a pastor, Robert Flint, *The History of Philosophy [of History] in France and Germany*, appeared in Edinburgh in 1874. Friedrich von Schlegel had a volume of philosophy of history, somewhat undistinguished, *Philosophie der Geschichte*, as tomes XIII and XIV of his *Complete Works* (Vienna: Klang, 1846). But Herder impressed his own age, and no lesser minds than those of Kant and Goethe, with his famous *Ideen* (*Ideas on the Philosophy of the History of Mankind*, 1784). Herder was translated (from an English

The invasion of every branch of knowledge, in the nineteenth century, by the momentous idea of development altered the perspective of mankind. The question on the lips of every individual, which soon became that of many an ethnic group, was, How have I become the one that I am? Is there a pattern in me according to which I am to become, even more fully, the one that I am? Can I govern my future and the future in general through disentangling the law of my being and obeying it, as Bacon enjoined us to command nature through obeying it? A rationalist postulate underlay all such efforts, even when they turned into mystical assertions which flew in the face of many facts. The embarrassing view that chance may reign supreme in the affairs of men and that the absurd, joyfully acclaimed by Schopenhauer and Camus, is an obdurate wall against which we beat our heads, has been at some time or other entertained even by hardy optimists. "Possibly there is no more sense in human history than in the changes of the seasons or the movements of the stars," remarked Sir Lewis Namier.

Nevertheless, the need of the human mind is to observe similarities and recurrences, to connect unrelated facts, to look for causes and weigh consequences, and, generally, to superimpose a satisfying rational pattern upon chaos and nonsense, and to hope dimly that some of the revolting stupidity or cruelty of history may not be duplicated by the future. The German sociologist Georg Simmel, long before the absurdists of our time, had noted: "Historical science will not be a resurrection of the past, for all the works of life are absurd, but an effort to endow with a meaning what had none." Hence the forging of myths by nineteenth-century historians: three of those myths—nation, race, and revolution—will form the subject of the following essay.

---

translation) by a speculative and ardent Frenchman, Edgar Quinet, in 1825, and that work of his and others (on Hebraic poetry) impressed Ernest Renan powerfully in his youth. Much of Renan's life work aimed at substituting history for philosophy. History, he wrote in his *Essais de Morale et de Critique* (1859), "I mean the history of the human spirit, is the true philosophy of our time. Every one of us is what he is by virtue of his system in history." An excellent selection of modern essays (chiefly by English and German authors) on the subject is Hans Meyerhoff's *The Philosophy of History in Our Time* (New York: Doubleday–Anchor Books, 1959).

Immense hopes were aroused in the romantic age by that sudden emergence or resurgence of history. None expressed them with more messianic warmth than Michelet. The newly won sense for, and knowledge of, the past were to serve as a lever to upset a present which was deemed unsatisfactory, and to build a better future. History was the training ground for statesmen and politicians: Guizot, Thiers, Tocqueville, Louis Blanc, Lamartine graduated from history to an active political role (short-lived for the last three) and served as ministers in one or more cabinets. The tradition has been continued in France: Jaurès was even more remarkable as a historian than he was as a philosopher; Herriot, Daladier, Bidault, Soustelle, Joxe, even Pompidou and De Gaulle and the unorthodox and often unhistorical art historian, Malraux, were trained in historical disciplines. "History is past politics; politics is present history"; A. E. Freeman's famous dictum is taken to heart by our contemporaries. The doctrine of "engagement"—urging thinkers and authors to commit themselves to participate in the battles of their time and no longer to enjoy the benefits of a political regime without either defending it or improving it—was not invented by the Existentialists. It was believed and practiced by the Saint-Simonians, by the militant Catholic reformers such as Lamennais, by the several socialist prophets of the years 1825–1848.

A reaction followed which advocated the haughty refuge of art for art's sake. After another wave of social commitment which followed the Franco-Prussian War of 1870–1871 and accompanied the naturalist trend in fiction, another withdrawal into pure, ethereal art and rarefied symbolism followed. The alternating phases of involvement and disengagement will probably continue, in France at least. In the years 1960–1968, after the acclaim which had hailed Existentialist doctrines, a contrary trend toward resignation, toward the negation of man's ability to free himself from the shackles of determinist structures, and toward aristocratic loftiness, appears to be asserting itself. Gaullist France has been alleged, too hastily probably, to be depoliticized and apathetic. But, in France as in Russia, more so than in any other Western country, literature and politics, history and the concern in the present have too long been welded together. No amount of prosperity or of propaganda is likely to sever their links. The redressing of past injustices (conspicuous in historical accounts or novels on the massacre of the Albigenses, in new volumes of the Dreyfus Affair), the imaginative appeal, as always more potent with the retrospect of twenty or thirty years, of the Spanish Civil War, of the Resistance, of the martyrdom of the Jews, of the unequal fights in Africa and Asia between the mechanically stronger powers and the former colonies, are likely to make the literature of the 1970's a literature inspired by politics and by history. It stands to the credit of the most dynamic thinkers among the French—Bergson, De Gaulle,[3] Malraux, Teilhard de Chardin—that they have adopted it as their motto to think as men of action and to act as men of thought.

Sir John Seeley's aphorism has thus lost little of its appositeness after three quarters of a century: "Politics are vulgar when they are not liberalized by history. History fades into mere literature when it loses sight of practical politics." The lesson derived by the modern French, modernizing their country as they had not attempted to do since 1860 and bulging with national pride, from the philosophy of history which their thinkers like to indulge, is not one of defeatism. Rather it is an appeal, from Catholics and atheists alike, to persuade man that the forces of night (blood, wars, sex limited to its brutal manifestations) need not today reduce man to mere "sound and fury signifying nothing." In a little known text, a review of a novel by Louis Guilloux in the weekly *Marianne* on November 20, 1935, André Malraux, not yet a world figure and not yet a politician professing heroism, penned these noble words:

> The greatest art is to take the chaos of the world and to transform it into consciousness, thus to make it possible for men to be masters of their fate: Tolstoy, Stendhal. Next comes the art of choosing one's chaos, of imprinting one's own mark upon it. Thus we may make men out of mere

[3] The frequent assertion of journalists that De Gaulle is a rigid Cartesian, imprisoned in his own logic, is contradicted by his whole life, his empirically devious politics, and his writings. As early as his *Edge of the Sword*, published in French in 1932 and translated by Gerard Hopkins in 1960 (Criterion Books), and throughout his life, he gave his highest praise to Bergson, and to the philosophy which submits that "the only way in which the human mind can make contact with reality is by intuition, by combining instinct with intelligence."

…e what may be saved from the most paltry of lives, through
them in the greatness in them, of which they had remained

…istortion to depict the nineteenth century, the greatest in its
…ievement lived by mankind, as an age of optimistic cant or of
…hope in the ultimate triumph of one class, in the five or six
countries which regarded themselves as the Western world. The
expectations aroused by the accession of the masses to some form of
democracy and by the sweeping away, through the Revolutionary and
Napoleonic wars, of the litter of feudalism carried the first half of the
century forward in a splendid *élan* of faith. Once the attempts to
supplement the political and the industrial revolutions by a social one,
in 1848–1849, had collapsed, that chimerical belief in imminent
progress was dealt severe blows. Throughout Europe, the first decades
of the second half of the century (1850 to 1875 or so) were an era of
disappointment and of pessimism. Religion was under attack from the
new historical sciences, the new geology, and evolutionism. The
benefits of industry were called in question. The idea of progress,
which had once been presented as a law, aroused doubts and objections in many minds. History, the queen of an age which, after Hegel,
seemed to have renounced metaphysical systems, abdicated many of
its ambitions. It no longer was absolutely convinced that the future
could be foretold from our contemplation of the past. Renan, who
had left unpublished a big manuscript of his twenty-fifth year,
L'Avenir de la Science, the most idealistic proclamation of faith in the
historical and philological disciplines ever written, smiled at history
as "a poor little conjectural science." Michelet, who had gloriously
assigned as a goal to history "the integral resurrection of the past"
and who had identified himself with the people in their uprising
against misery and injustice, allowed melancholy to displace his
enthusiasm. In a moving preface to his volumes on the Renaissance,
in 1855, he cast a sad backward glance on the hopes once aroused by
history, viewed as the handmaiden of politics and the guardian of
freedom. History had been degenerated into a source of barren
passiveness. The past was cramping any thrust forward and paralyzing
inventiveness:

History was to vivify us; it has, on the contrary, made us la
us to believe that time is everything and that will power amc
little. . . . History is the story of the soul and of original the
fecund initiative, of heroism, heroism of action and heroism of cre.
. . . We have conjured up history, and here it is, everywhere around .
We are besieged, stifled, crushed by it. We go forward bent double under
that burden. We no longer breathe, we no longer invent. The past is
killing the present.

Michelet's appeal was, instead, to trust again "man's unconquerable will," in the Miltonic phrase, and to eschew entering into the future with backward steps and with one's gaze fixed behind. Some years later, a thirty-year-old professor of classical philology who had already devoured most of the works left in the Greek language, Nietzsche, included, in *Considerations Out of Season* (1874), a long essay on "The Use and Abuse of History for Life" ("Vom Nutzen und Nachteil der Historie für das Leben"). He vituperated against his own ilk, historians who use the past in order to justify the present and who do not know how and what to forget. Their worship of history does not lead, as it should, to action, that is, to forgetting many things in order to accomplish one. A courageous historian should muster the courage to break up the past. The motto of history ought to be "Memento vivere," and not "Memento mori." What is greatest in the past alone need detain us.

You can only explain the past by what is highest in the present. . . . The unrestrained historical sense, pushed to its logical extreme, uproots the future, because it destroys illusions and robs existing things of the only atmosphere in which they can live. . . . We need history in order to live and to act, not in order to find in history a convenient means to avoid life and action, or to excuse a selfish life and a low and cowardly action. . . . The message of the past always is an oracle. It is well understood only by those who are the builders of the future.

The holder of the chair of classical philology at Basel was henceforth to become the prophet of the next century, on the threshold of which he was to die, in 1900, his reason long gone; his ominous predictions received fulfillment with an era of irrationalism, of wars, and of revolutions. The French, for whom he had always reserved his highest praise, more than the English and his own countrymen, whom he equally despised or derided, have endeavored to live—dangerously indeed—up to Nietzsche's message. Their imaginative writers with a passion for history (Montherlant, Malraux, Elie Faure, Teilhard de Chardin) and their less impassioned historians[4] have heeded the Crocean dictum that "the deed of which the history is told must vibrate in the soul of the historian."

[4] Benedetto Croce's sentence occurs at the beginning of his *Theory and History of Historiography*, as that collection of essays is entitled in the English edition (London: Harrap, 1921). Among those French historians are Raymond Aron, *Dimensions de la Conscience historique* (Plon, 1961); Philippe Ariès, *Le Temps et l'histoire* (Monaco: Rocher, 1954); Eric Dardel, *L'Histoire science du concret* (Presses Universitaires, 1946); Joseph Hours, *Valeur de l'histoire* (Presses Universitaires, 1954); Henri Irénée Marrou, *De la Connaissance historique* (Seuil, 1955), and a methodological essay, "Philocritique de l'histoire et sens de l'histoire," in *Actes du sixième Congrès des Sociétés de Philosophie de langue française* (Presses Universitaires, 1952); Paul Ricœur, *Histoire et vérité* (Seuil, 1955); and Pierre Henri Simon, *L'Esprit et l'histoire* (Armand Colin, 1954).

2 | THREE NINETEENTH-CENTURY MYTHS
RACE, NATION, REVOLUTION

THE RANCOR with which the word "romantic" and much that it denotes are often derided in our own age stems in part from our envy of the unfettered optimism which lay behind the façade of melancholy and despair of the romantics. The first half of the last century would not concede that anything was impossible to man, leaning upon the long past which he had retrieved from inert oblivion and using it as a jumping board into the uncharted future. Social, political, economic forces were to be marshaled by post-revolutionary man. Immense new possibilities were opened by the industrial revolution.[1] History would serve as a dynamite to explode superstitions and zealous reactionism. It would project man forward above the hitherto

---

[1] The French effected their industrial revolution considerably later than the British, but they were the first to coin and to use the phrase, according to a scholar, Anna Bezanson, in the (English) *Quarterly Journal of Economics* of 1922. The eminent English historian, then at Oriel College, Oxford, George Norman Clark, in a lecture given and published at Glasgow (Jackson & Son) in 1952, traces the use of the world "revolution" as applied to industry to a French Chamber of Commerce in 1806. A French writer coupled the adjective "industrial" to the noun "revolution" in 1827, and the economist Jerome Adolphe Blanqui sanctioned the use of the phrase "industrial revolution" in 1837. John Stuart Mill used the phrase eleven years later. A gifted historian, inspired by Marxist views, has attempted, somewhat rashly, to couple the French Revolution and the industrial revolution as parallel, the second following the first around 1820: E. J. Hobsbawm, in *The Age of Revolution, 1789–1848* (London: Weidenfeld and Nicolson, 1963).

cramped and shrunken human condition. Michelet, Lamennais, Fourier, Comte, all far more deeply romantic than the poets and the dramatists to whom the French romantic movement is often limited, were all intent upon extending further the bounds which had restrained the human creature. Even among the poets such as Lamartine, and later Hugo, the expansion of man into a centaur, a superman, or a demigod became a dream occasionally entertained. It was Musset, in his most declamatory poem, "Rolla," who expressed most strikingly the yearning of the young century, as he also voiced its gnawing self-doubts in his no less declamatory prose *Confession d'un enfant du siècle*: "Qui de nous, qui de nous, va devenir un dieu?"

There lurked doubts, however, amid such rash hopes; and the cult of history had already met a few dissenters who, like James Joyce's Stephen Dedalus a century later, probably whispered to themselves: "History is a nightmare from which I am trying to awaken." None of the men of 1800–1848 could altogether close their eyes to the justification for the excesses of the Revolution which Danton, Saint-Just, or David had found among the legacy of ancient history. Once again, in France more than in Britain or Germany, since the cleavage with the past had been infinitely more brutal in France, historians and their readers, disdaining empiricism and over-wary myopic limitation of their gaze to one segment of the past, undertook to envisage huge global ideas as resulting from the consideration of the past, and favored to influence men in their march forward. We call "myths" those vague, seductive "idées-forces," in which emotions, desires, the will to believe, the literary presentation of half-truths thus multiplied tenfold in their appeal, have more of a share than reasoned and coldly logical demonstrations. Those myths testified to the persistence of a religious need in an age which had attempted to shake off the remnants of traditional faith. Indeed, racism, nationalism, and revolutionism, as it might be styled, are very close to being the three most potent para-religions or pseudo-religions of our own age, in this respect as in many others the pursuer of the work of the nineteenth century.

Racism has led to such nefarious excesses and has proved such a monstrous force for evil among the most cultured Western nations that it has become difficult, since World War II, to view its assumptions dispassionately. The French would hardly take pride in being credited with having originated that superstition. If they were guilty of gross anti-Semitism just before and during the Dreyfus Affair, and not immune from it under the Vichy government, they have, on the whole, not indulged the same prejudice of possessing a racial superiority as have the Germans, or the compatriots of Cecil Rhodes, or the inhabitants of the newer republic in which Negroes, Jews, Indians were long discriminated against. However, in the history of the myth and in the history of nationalism, they occupy the central position. Today some of their best anthropologists have had the courage not to ignore the subject of the diversity of cultures only because such a theme has been put to diabolical use by a neighboring land. An American historian of French origin, Jacques Barzun, has given the most convenient and the liveliest account of the history and present position of the question of racism in a 1937 volume, revised and republished in 1965, *Race, a Study in Superstition* (New York: Harper and Row). He had preceded it with a scholarly monograph on the many theorists of race in France before the Revolution, *The French Race* (Columbia University Press, 1932). Our debt to those two volumes, in the pages which follow, is gratefully acknowledged.

Due perhaps to the geographical situation of the country, astride of three different seas, a meeting ground between North and South and the "land's end" reached by successive migrations of nomadic tribes from Central Asia and Eastern Europe, France is the country in which speculations on the theme of races (racial purity, ethnic and linguistic parallels, superiority of the Gauls or Celts over the Germans and of Latin culture over Germanic) have been the most active for the longest time. More strangely still, the myth of the superiority of the Germanic, Nordic "races" and of the Anglo-Saxons owes more to Frenchmen (Boulainvilliers, Augustin Thierry, Gobineau, and others) than to English and German authors. Three quarters of a century ago, a large number of Frenchmen appeared to be ready to subscribe to the thesis that the Anglo-Saxons were, through some decree of fate or of history, a stronger, more energetic "race." A book (a very shallow one, to say the truth), entitled *A quoi tient la supériorité des Anglo-Saxons*, by Edmond Demolins (1898), popularized, and distorted, views which had been put forward with more nuances by Taine, Taine's disciples or readers like Paul Bourget and Emile Boutnuy, and Taine's nephew, André Chevrillon. By 1960, the wheel of fortune, or of intellectual fashion, had turned; and one might even surmise that, in De Gaulle's posthumous papers some day, a manuscript may be unearthed imperiously stating the reasons for "the inferiority of the Anglo-Saxons"!

Ethnologists and anthropologists do not agree on many propositions of the young and highly hypothetical disciplines. On one point, however, there would seem to be few divergencies among them: that France constitutes a more diverse synthesis of the "races" of Europe than Italy herself or than Germany or Holland or Russia. Dolichocephalic and brachycephalic types have been inextricably mixed; Celts and Ligurians probably made up most of the early inhabitants, but almost nothing is known about them. If anyone could be bold enough to put forward a quantitative conjecture in a forest of darkness, that of a number of ethnologists would be to the effect that more than three fourths of the Belgians and perhaps two thirds of the French stem from Celtic and Germanic stocks (Burgundians, Lombards, Alamans, Saxons, Visigoths, Cimbrians), while more than half of the inhabitants of Germany originated from Slavic and even Finnish stock. Those of the French who have liked to boast of their Latin origins may have been right if they alluded to the language which, owing to the Church but also to the advantages of Roman law and administration, the inhabitants of Gaul adopted; but it is not likely that more than twenty-five thousand so-called Roman soldiers ever settled in Gaul, and those were not accompanied by their wives, so that they soon married local women. How "Roman" or "Latin," otherwise than in language and perhaps culture, were those handfuls of conquerors is another question mark, when we bear in mind that, as Hugh Trevor-Roper recalled in *The Rise of Christian Europe* (New York: Harcourt, Brace and World, 1965), some of the most "Roman" of Roman emperors—Aurelian, Diocletian, Constantine, Justinian— were, as we would call them today, Yugoslav, and Theodosius was a Spaniard. There is obviously no uniform process in history through which the invaders and conquerors either radically modify the culture which flourished before them (as the Spaniards have done profoundly in several countries of the New World) or are absorbed into that culture (as many migrating groups and individuals have been to a remarkable degree in China and in France). Legends are much too easily spread by passing travelers: the dark stock, which often struck visitors to the Netherlands, where the rest of the population conforms more closely to the so-called Nordic, or Germanic, type, used to be glibly attributed to the Spaniards who once ruled the country; but anthropological research has discovered that those dark-haired and dark-eyed people long antedated the arrival of the Spaniards.

To unravel the mysteries which shroud that notion of race is beyond both our intent and our competence. It is clear that we are all today in a state of sensitive and horrified revulsion from the hideous excesses to which a misinterpretation of racial myths drove the German people, galvanized by Hitler, Goebbels, and Rosenberg. But the surest way of forestalling the recurrence of such crimes is not to express our horror, to fail to realize that every nation has beginnings, or germs, of what fructified abominably elsewhere, and to refuse to look history squarely in the face. No amount of shrugging our shoulders in the presence of the silly confusion which loosely equates race with people, nation, culture, language will discredit the interchangeable use of some of those words by all but strict minds, distrustful of semantic chaos. Few of the vehement disclaimers of biologists are of much avail when they warn us how meaningless is the color of the skin or that measurement of the skulls, dubbed dolichocephalic or brachycephalic, implies literally nothing concerning the quality of the brain encased in the skull bones. Common sense will always notice that peoples are unevenly gifted for scientific or for abstract thinking, for the arts, for statesmanship, for war, for organization, or for industry. History affords scores of instances of the profound mutations undergone, some rapidly, others slowly, by the same people: the Germans during the nineteenth century; the inhabitants of "merry England" becoming Victorian England and having oscillated earlier between Puritanism and paganism; the Russians; the Americans; and the Chinese under our very eyes since 1920. But forecasting those metamorphoses before they occur is a more tantalizing task than explaining them after they have taken place. A great French historian, Camille Jullian, prefacing a volume by a Celtic scholar, Henri Dottin, in 1916, did not hesitate to state: "The question of race . . . is the most important question in the history of nations."

Julius Caesar was the first to generalize on the national and ethnic features both of the Gauls, fickle and inconsistent, and of the Germans, warlike and scornful of soft living. The country which Caesar conquered and Romanized was later (at the end of the fourth century A.D.) invaded by a Germanic tribe, the Franks, who had probably come from Thuringia and Hungary. Tacitus went further, asserted the purity of the Germanic "race," described their physical appearance, and praised their spirit of equality, their frugality, and their control of their emotions. He launched the myth of the superiority of the Germans as conquerors over the peoples (the Gauls) whom they had conquered and even over the Romans, whom they had several times beaten and whom Tacitus, late in the first century A.D., branded as decadent under the tyranny of evil emperors.

Much later, a French nobleman, Count Henri de Boulainvilliers, who was born in 1658 and died seven years after Louis XIV, proud of his class as was the memorialist Saint-Simon and resentful of the progress of the bourgeoisie under Louis XIV and Colbert, undertook historical research to support his thesis that the nobility stemmed directly from the Germanic Franks, while the French masses descended from the Romanized Gauls. Those noble Franks had raised the country to its peak of power and excellent administration with Charlemagne. Decline had then set in. Far more curiosity for the Middle Ages and zest for antiquarian research into the French past was evinced by men of the Renaissance (like Chancellor Pasquier) and the Classical Age in France than is often realized; the nostalgia for the early centuries of Carolingian rule, then of the first Capetians, was intense among the nobility, who resented the ascent of the middle class, and among the liberals who discerned the flaws of absolutism and yearned for a revival of the old Estates General. Montesquieu, who penned the finest definition of freedom to come out of France before the Revolution and who inspired a number of the ideas in *The Federalist* and in the American Constitution, and a smaller number of the early revolutionaries in France, cannot be called a racist. But he stood close to Boulainvilliers in several respects and admired the

Franks. The simplicity of the laws of the barbarians aroused his enthusiasm. He hailed their victory over Roman laws, as the Germanic Franks imported into Gaul a form of government from which that of Great Britain eventually evolved, having thus been "devised in the woods." Voltaire, who was grossly and brutally unfair to Montesquieu, tried to puncture some of the chimerical balloons flown by the great sociological historian, who could blend with his search for the laws of history and of jurisprudence a fanciful capacity for illusion. Voltaire believed in the progress achieved by civilization and the deliverance from prejudices too strongly to fall for the praise of the barbarians of Clovis and Charlemagne. The controversy went on between the partisans of the honest and pure Germanic ancestors of the French and those of the Romans who had brought them their laws and language and had captured their fierce conqueror as the defeated Greeks, in Horace's line, had once captured Rome herself. On it was grafted the debate between Celt and Latin, when a little more became known about the Celts, in the nineteenth century. Late in that century and early in ours, two great French historians, Fustel de Coulanges and Camille Jullian, returned to the fray with much more solid documentation and reasoning cogency, arguing that much less in the institutions and culture of old France was due to Nordic influences than had been contended by the advocates of a Germanic racism. Both were convinced they were impeccably objective, Jullian (who came from southern and Roman France) with subtlety, Fustel with more rigidity. The latter, when his students one day interrupted one of his brilliant demonstrations with applause, cut them short with the famous words: "Do not applaud me, gentlemen. It is not I who speak. It is simply history which is speaking through me."

The nineteenth century, spurred on by the widespread curiosity for all origins (Herder, the Grimm brothers, Percy's *Reliques*) and for the Ur monuments and remnants of each national culture, contemplated with rapture the long vistas opened by the speculation on races. Chateaubriand, an inveterate devotee of classical antiquity who nevertheless undertook to demonstrate the esthetic fecundity of the Christian faith, tried to reconcile his admiration for Homer and for the organizing genius of the Romans with his awe in the presence of the Germanic forests, among whose pillars of trees the Gothic cathedrals were supposed to have originated; he praised "the impetuosity and the mysticism of the Gauls." But the chief claim to an eminent place for Chateaubriand in the history of racism lies in his having fostered the vocation of Augustin Thierry, jointly with the author of the Waverley Novels (who also indirectly determined the vocation of Ranke in Germany). At the age of thirty, after having pondered over the need for the French Third Estate to reassert its claims opposed by the Bourbons, he called upon the parallel of England. The underprivileged agrarian populations enslaved by the Frankish conquerors had failed to receive their due from historians, he contended. Much might be discovered about them in old chronicles, in local traditions, and more might be surmised from the example of Britain. There the conquered populations which made up, as he supposed, the original stock of the country, conquered by William the Conqueror and despoiled by him, had gradually reasserted themselves. They had recovered freedom and offered models of it to Europe. In that colorful masterpiece of prose, highly romantic in a noble sense, *History of the Conquest of England by the Normans* (1825), Thierry presented English history as a dramatic duel between two races. So masterful and vivid is his narrative that it provided their view of the history of those centuries to generations of Frenchmen, including the playwright Jean Anouilh when he composed his drama on Thomas à Becket. The notion of race as the underpinning of history was, through that volume and others by Thierry (his *Récits des temps mérovingiens* [1833–1840] were for decades a classic for the youth of France), disseminated through history textbooks in Europe.

Augustin Thierry had a younger brother, Amédée, who was even more widely read at the time, although he has not retained a respected position among historians. In a volume which long sold among a vast public, *History of the Gauls* (1828), he characterized two groups, or "races," of Gauls: the Celtic Gauls, alleged to be "remarkably intelligent" (no adjective flatters the French more) and the Kymri, or Germanic Gauls, apparently less alert but more pragmatic. Amédée Thierry produced a deep impression on an English doctor residing in France, W. F. Edwards, who in 1829 published in French a fanciful and dogmatic volume, today discredited, *Des Caractères physiologiques des races humaines considérées dans leur rapport avec l'histoire*.

He distinguished in modern France between the descendants of those two parallel but diverse "races" of Gauls, and thought he could do so from anatomical criteria: the shape of the head, chins, stature. Since he spoke with scientific assurance and appealed to science to support his theories, that English doctor was for many years to be taken very seriously by ethnologists, anthropologists, and biologists.

Jules Michelet's fame eventually eclipsed even that of Augustin Thierry, even though Thierry, blind before the age of thirty, continued his research and his publication and was universally respected until he died in 1856. In one of the most admirable pages of prose, learned by heart by all French schoolboys, the 1869 preface to his *History of France*, Michelet characterized the intent of his work and dramatically recounted the circumstances, during the July (1830) Revolution, in which the vision of France with her whole past and the life of her masses aroused against tyranny had imposed itself upon him. He then had resolved to base history upon geography, physiology, economics (what men eat and drink, their ecology), but, above all else, upon the psychological and mystical will of a people to be itself. "Man is his own Prometheus." Repudiating all determinism and reducing the factor of race, whose role had been grossly exaggerated, Michelet wanted to detect, at the root of history, "a moral fact of huge import and underrated up to now: the powerful working of self upon self, through which France had molded her own living organism."

Yet the great romantic historian, the only man in the last century in France along with Hugo and Zola who was able to portray masses in motion, had been, in his younger days, sensitive to the enticements of the racial characterization of nations, and of the different French provinces. His ambition in his youth, in those years around 1830 when nothing appeared too colossal to daunt the energy of the romantic giants of France (Michelet, Hugo, Balzac, Delacroix, Berlioz), had been to compose nothing less than a universal history. His inspirer and the chief influence on his ideas was Vico. He completed a part of that great project, a *History of Rome*, published in 1831, which as late as 1898, in the *Revue des Deux Mondes* of April 1, was warmly praised by a distinguished specialist and urbane writer, Gaston Boissier. While concerning himself with the analysis of religion, of institutions, and, after Polybius, venturing generalizations on the philosophy of history, Michelet also resorted to the notion of race to account for the qualities which enabled Rome to triumph over the other "races" of Italy. He was then under the impact of Niebuhr's *Roman History*, which had made much of the conflict of races; the struggle of diverse races lent itself superbly to Michelet's conception of history, which was to bring the past back to life, hence not to dead formulas and desiccated narratives, but to a drama. His strong moral sense, however, soon induced him to revolt against the determinism which race tends to impose upon men. His history was primarily a struggle against all fatalities.

At the root of the facile generalizations on the subject of race lies the most puzzling issue of world history: Why do civilizations and nations rise and fall? Why do cultures degenerate while others gain vigor? Why have music, sculpture, poetry, drama, philosophy, higher mathematics prospered in certain lands at certain times and not elsewhere? Not one, but a diversity of explanations will, and should, always be adduced to try to answer those enigmas. Cyclical theories will be ingeniously proposed; economic, religious, moral factors will be variously stressed. Wary scholars who have been repelled by the preposterous and nefarious theories put forward in Nazi Germany and who stand in majority on the liberal side of most racial issues today in the United States, South Africa, and Europe have, since 1945, kept shy of any terminology implying a value judgment on the inequality of races or of cultures. Still they are, again and again, led back to the admission that diversity of creative gifts does exist, and that setting the hundreds of cultures, nations, peoples or "races" in the world on an equal plane can only amount to a pious lie which does disservice to research. Claude Lévi-Strauss, one of the greatest and most liberal anthropologists of our time, stated his position firmly and tactfully in a booklet sponsored by UNESCO, *Race et Histoire* (1952). He refused to shirk the question which occurs to many anxious minds: "If there do not exist innate racial aptitudes, how is it explained that the civilization developed by the white man should have accomplished such enormous progress, while those of colored peoples have stayed behind, some halfway, others with a lag of thousands or tens of thousands of years? We cannot claim to have resolved, by a negative answer, the problem of the inequality of human *races*, if we do not also consider that of the inequality, or of the diversity, of human *cultures* which, in fact if not in right, is, in the public mind, closely bound up with it." Less charitably, and with the gift of a scathing polemist, Lévi-Strauss rebuked one of his critics, Roger Caillois, in "Diogène couché," in *Les Temps Modernes* (No. 110, March 1955, pp. 1187–1220).

Any mention of the inequality of cultures (the modern euphemism replacing what was understood a century ago by the loose term "races") arouses the twinges of a bad conscience in the French. The phrase was popularized as the title of a big, confused, abstruse yet epoch-making book by Count Arthur de Gobineau (1816–1882), *Essai sur l'Inégalité des races humaines* (1853–1855). The French, especially after the national shame which afflicted many of them after the outburst of hatred of the Dreyfus civil war, have tried hard to contend that Gobineau's influence was felt chiefly in Germany, where a Gobineau society was indeed established; they hinted that their apostle of Nordic superiority had hardly been taken seriously in his own country. Such, however, is not exactly the case, as has been shown by Jacques Barzun in his book on *Race*. A careful study of Gobineau's fortunes with his contemporaries and successors, in France and in other countries, is still to be written.

Gobineau was no maverick and even less of a fanatic. He was one of the most cultured of men, a literary critic of talent, one of the finest letter writers and essayists of the last century, an extraordinarily perspicacious observer of Asia, and a better linguist than most of his compatriots: he knew German well; he wrote to Tocqueville a series of acute analyses of Swiss politics and character when he was sent to Switzerland as Minister of France; he learned Iranian when he was stationed in Persia; and he was gifted with a rare comic sense as well as with a brilliant style. He reached full manhood at the very time when the romantic enthusiasm of the French was flagging, around 1848, and a new myth—that of decadence—was replacing the faith in progress which had sprung up with renewed vigor after the Revolution. He thought he observed signs of decadence everywhere around him in the society which Balzac was describing as controlled by greed and lust. He was the ambitious son of a noble but impoverished family, was aware of his intellectual superiority over the bourgeois of Louis-Philippe's time, and entertained foolish delusions about some remote Nordic ancestors whom he ascribed to himself, on the flimsiest evidence. Democracy and revolution were his bête noire. Paradoxically, he served the materialistic Second Empire, then the democratic Third Republic, most of his life in diplomatic positions in Greece, Persia, Brazil, and Sweden. Paradoxically also but understandably, his very hatreds granted him a clear-sightedness often refused to placid and benign travelers prone to finding wonderful anything that is exotic. On the Orient, which he interpreted with a perspicaciousness praised as second to none by a British viceroy of India, Lord Curzon, he remarked: "When we Europeans have gained control of Asia, like young men from aristocratic houses, we shall have there an 'intendant' who will inculcate upon us the vices which we still lack and who will reduce us to penury." Like a number of his compatriots, among others another aristocrat from western France, Barbey d'Aurevilly, he was an anti-Christian Catholic; and Nietzsche might, if he had needed inspirers, have borrowed from him a number of his views. Gobineau was entrusted by Tocqueville, for two thousand francs a year, with a research job on the state of moral doctrines in the nineteenth century. He soon tried to convince his employer, an agnostic who clung to his Christian heritage, that there was nothing in the Gospels which could not be found in Socrates and Plato or in Alexandria, that there was nothing sacred about suffering, and that the fear of God may have kept a few timid souls from stealing a loaf of bread, but prevented very few from committing murder or slaughtering their enemies in wartime.

In 1848, Tocqueville, Foreign Secretary for a time, appointed Gobineau as his Chief of Cabinet, then started him on his diplomatic career as envoy to Switzerland. The older statesman and philosopher learned much from the young rebel, whom he liked and admired, but whose doctrines were repugnant to him. Gobineau tried hard to prove to the observer of American democracy, then (in 1855–1856) at work on his even more remarkable volume L'Ancien Régime et la Révolution, that he disliked the reign of the masses as much as Tocqueville did. Tocqueville balked at such logic, or perhaps at such candidness. His letters, in their epistolary exchange, are wiser than Gobineau's, but also more timid and less brilliant. Tocqueville maintained that Gobineau's fatalism, resting on the conviction that the mixture of races carries with it ineluctable decrepitude, doomed men to discouragement and inertia. Gobineau, replied from Teheran on March 20, 1856:

> If I am a corrupter, I am one who uses corrosives and not perfumes. . . . I do not say to people: you have excuses, or you should be blamed. I say to them: You are dying. . . . Your autumn is doubtless still more vigorous than the decrepitude of the rest of the world, but it is an autumn.[2]

With more determination than any of his predecessors, from Boulainvilliers to Augustin Thierry and to Guizot, Gobineau endeavored to establish his theory of decadence on the ill effects of the mixture of races. He popularized the myth of a once pure Aryan race, which had become Semitized in part, hence bastardized. Obviously his views, expressed at great length, with many confused digressions, were totally unscientific even for his own age. They had seemed, but only in the eyes of bad philologists, to be strengthened by the still recent discovery that the Indo-European tongues all had belonged to one primitive family and their earliest specimen had once been spoken in the uplands of India—as if one could ever equate language and race! The peremptory, pre-Nietzschean aphorisms of the French Count were clearly uttered with a sense of showmanship: "All that is not Aryan is born to serve," or "We do not come from the ape, but we are rapidly getting there" (as quoted by Jacques Barzun). Gobineau has since been refuted over and over again. But even those who multiply objections to his flimsy system cannot help being fascinated by his talent, which has been likened to that of an epic poet. One of the most ardent disseminators of the theories of that scorner of the Semites was a friend of Proust, a Frenchman of Jewish

---

[2] One is reminded of the line of Baudelaire's sonnet, "L'Ennemi," which was to be the tenth piece in *Les Fleurs du Mal* published the following year (1857) while Gobineau was in Persia, "*Voilà que j'ai touché l'automne des idées,*" which has served as a title to a study of decadentism by Renato Poggioli. In a broader context, see A. E. Carter, *The Idea of Decadence in French Literature, 1830–1900* (University of Toronto Press, 1958), and Koenraad W. Swart, *The Sense of Decadence in Nineteenth Century France* (The Hague: Nijhoff, 1964).

origin, and of Robert Dreyfus. One of the most rapturous praises of Gobineau's brilliance, blended with many reservations on his ideas, was by a liberal and generous doctor, one of the most universal minds of modern France, Elie Faure, in *Trois Gouttes de sang* (Malfère, 1929).

Gobineau has since been branded as a culprit in one of the most horrifying utilizations of ideas, or myths, by men wielding power and skilled at making fanatics out of their compatriots. That is a patent exaggeration and a misguided view of the way in which intellectual influence is exercised. Influence only bears fruit on a soil ready to receive the seeds, and in that specific case, there were many factors in German history (ethnologic, economic, intellectual, including the lack of independence and of the courage to be heretics among scientists and scholars, the poisonous mixture of South German or Austrian romanticism with Prussian organization, etc.) which disposed millions of people to adopt crude anti-Semitic slogans. It is probable, though not certain except from Nietzsche's sister's testimony, that Nietzsche read Gobineau. But Richard Wagner, who impressed Hitler far more than Nietzsche ever did, discovered Gobineau's writings, took a fancy to the man in 1876, invited him to Bayreuth in 1880–1881, and eventually dedicated the bulk of his prose works to the French Count. Wagner had, when unsuccessfully trying to establish himself as a composer in Paris, been jealous of some Jewish composers (Mendelssohn, Offenbach) who had become the public's favorites there. He wrote an ugly anti-Semitic pamphlet, "Jewishdom and Music." A number of Wagner's admirers also became Gobineau's enthusiasts, like Ludwig Schemann, who in 1894 founded the "Gobineau-Vereinigung." Then and since serious German writers have placed Gobineau high above Nietzsche. One of the warmest devotees of Wagner was the scion of a celebrated English family, Houston Stewart Chamberlain. That son of a British admiral was educated abroad, wrote his books first in French, then in German. He married a daughter of Wagner and in 1899 published his *Grundlagen des XIX Jahrhunderts*, translated into the author's native language only in 1910 as *The Foundations of the Twentieth Century* (London: John Lane). The volume sang a paean to the purity of races; it decreed most of modern history to have been a continued lapse into chaos because of the mixture of races. Salvation would come from the regeneration of mankind through the Teutonic "race" (under which he generously included Scandinavians, Celts, and some pure Slavs). "The importance of each nation as a living power today is dependent upon the proportion of genuinely Teutonic blood in its population." Christ was a pure Aryan. The Jews always were idolaters and "the most irreligious people in the world." We know what was made of that farrago of preposterous assertions by Rosenberg, Goebbels, and Hitler. But long before then (Chamberlain died in 1927), Kaiser Wilhelm II had adopted Chamberlain as his inspirer. In 1901 (December 31), the German ruler effusively thanked Chamberlain for having revealed their mission to the German people: "To be God's tool for spreading German culture. . . . Dear Mr. Chamberlain, you have been chosen by God to become my ally in the struggle of the Germans against Rome and Jerusalem. . . . I slap my big sword to declare myself your faithfully grateful friend. Wilhelm, Emperor and King." Gobineau, who had a keen sense of irony, would have been aghast if he had then been alive. He had been disturbed enough when, just prior to the Civil War, southern segregationists invoked his book, which had reached them in an English translation.[3]

The myth of race may have been exploded once for all, but the notion will not easily disappear from history. Many were the men in England, in the closing years of the last century, who were enticed by doctrines distinguishing between Celt and Saxon, Anglo-Saxons, and others: Bishop Stubbs; A. E. Freeman, the historian of Anglo-Saxon Britain; John Richard Green; and, of course, Cecil Rhodes. Paul Bourget, Charles Maurras, among the French, and earlier Viollet-le-Duc, had been impressed by Gobineau's theories and subscribed to parts of them. The influence of that very seductive French writer may

---

[3] Strangely enough, Nazi racial thought claimed another inspirer, along with Gobineau and Chamberlain: the anthropologist Vacher de Lapouge, a Frenchman who was born in 1854 and who had taught at the University of Poitiers. He was the author of *Les Sélections sociales* (Thorin, 1896) and *L'Aryen, son Rôle social* (Fontemoing, 1899). The Germans remembered that little-known racist mystic when they occupied France in 1940, imposed his books, and promoted one of his descendants to a high academic chair.

also have been felt by greater personalities—those of Renan and Taine. But strong personalities have a way of assimilating and of transforming an influence to the point of making it hard to recognize.

Gobineau claimed, or hinted, that Renan had borrowed some of his views. They did meet between 1855 and 1859, but Renan, six years younger, was already much more advanced as a scholar, a member of the Institute; and Gobineau was then flattered by any attention paid to his doctrines by the Semitic philologist and historian of religion. The one significant letter in Renan's correspondence addressed to Gobineau (dated June 26, 1856) contained apologies from Renan, who had not yet reviewed the Count's volumes on *The Inequality of Human Races* (and never did). He paid the author compliments on his talent, warned him that few persons in France would understand him, then diplomatically added:

> France believes in race very little, precisely because the fact of race has been nearly obliterated in her. . . . I cannot say that I agree with you on all points. . . . The factor of race is immense at the origin, but it constantly loses its importance and, as is the case for France, it disappears altogether. Is that a decadence? . . . There are so many compensations! Setting apart the altogether inferior races which, if intermingled with the great ones would merely poison the human species, I envisage in the future a homogeneous humanity . . . in which all memory of diverse origins will be lost. . . . Will such a civilization be inferior to that of aristocratic ages in an absolute manner? I hesitate to decide on that.

In spite of moments of pessimism when he felt out of tune with the technological civilization of his time, Renan refused to believe that a state of decadence would of necessity ensue from the mixture of races taking place as greater mobility developed. But he felt bold enough, at the beginning of his career, to sketch a psychology of the Semites, and to the end of his life, he contrasted that with the character of other "races," or groups, such as the Celts and the Greeks. His life work, indeed, rested upon firm notions of the different characters of those three "races." Before he could have read Gobineau, in a volume on the *Origin of Language* written in 1848, then in a learned work on the general history of Semitic languages, first published in 1855, but composed and offered in an earlier version in 1847 for an Academy prize, Renan had boldly generalized on races. In the very first chapter he asserted that races were not equally gifted and submitted that he was fully ready to admit that

> the Semitic race, compared to the Indo-European one, really represents a lower combination of human nature. It has neither that loftiness of spiritualism which India and German lands alone have known, nor that feeling of moderation and of perfect beauty which Greece bequeathed to neo-Latin nations, nor that delicate and deep sensibility which is the dominating feature of Celtic peoples. Semitic consciousness is clear, but not vast; it understands unity marvellously, it does not know how to attain multiplicity. Monotheism sums up and explains all its traits.

Elsewhere the historian had coined the memorable formula, the desert is monotheistic (with only one force presumably prevailing there—the sun or the wind or the sand). He denied the Arabs and the Jews both art (music excepted) and philosophy.

Such assertions are patently contradicted by facts. Not only have there been many outstanding philosophers, painters, and sculptors who were Jewish, but both the early Israelites and the pre-Islamic Arabs were polytheists. In the 1855 preface to the *History of Semitic Languages*, Renan added reservations to his dogmatic assertions, warning that "statements on races must always be understood with very many restrictions; . . . the primordial influence of race, whatever immense share must be granted to it in the movement of human affairs, is offset by a host of other influences, which at times seem to control or even to stifle that of the blood altogether." His generalizations on the Semites could, he acknowledged, be valid only for a minority of "pure Semites," whose contact with alien races had been held to a minimum. Nevertheless, several times in his writings and particularly when, as a relief from his historian's labors, Renan indulged philosophical essays and fantasies, he recurred to the negation of natural equality, both among men and among races. In 1860, in an essay on "Metaphysics and Its Future," he slipped in a sentence which aroused the indignation of a number of orthodox and self-righteous Christians: "One has, of God and of truth, what one is capable of and deserves. I see no reason why a Papuan should be immortal." More blandly still, in his *Philosophical Dialogues*, he wielded the threat of an irretrievable decadence of the human species as a possibility. "The absence of sane ideas on the inequality of races may bring about a total decline." Again: "The principle most hotly denied by the democratic school is the inequality of races and the legitimacy of the rights which the superiority of races bestows." In the preface to the same work (composed, it must be added, after the crisis of despondency brought about by the French defeat of 1871 and the destruction wrought by the Commune), Renan even stated: "Men are not equal, races are not equal. The Negro, for instance, is made to serve the higher purposes wanted and conceived by the white." He inserted a parenthesis, however, to specify that slavery was in no way justified thereby.

Such assertions (and they are not isolated in Renan's writings) clearly belie the legend which pictures the thinker as a dilettante, fond of nuances to the extent of leaving none of his affirmative statements ever unmodified by over-subtle reservations. He was convinced that different ethnical groups are unevenly favored with the gifts of the intellect; that the government of the world would eventually be invested in superior beings, scientists, who might be the possessors of secrets too complex for the vulgar. History has since justified some of those prophecies. But he also trusted "man's unconquerable will." In 1882, in a lecture which has become a familiar anthology piece, read in all French schools, "What Is a Nation?" he defined nation, not by community or race or of language, but by the will of groups to continue achieving a common accomplishment in the future. In an even more significant address in 1883, "Judaism as Race and Religion" (both are collected in *Discours et Conférences*), he laid the greatness of Israel to the fact that, thanks to its prophets, a local and narrowly national religion had become a universal one. Then, tracing the progress of that religion around the Mediterranean Sea, he showed that most of the persons who had adopted it (some were thereby prepared to welcome Paul's predication later and became Christians) were of other "races" than the Jewish, or than Semitic, ones. Many Hellenes and many Romans (Juvenal was indignant over it) became converts to Judaism. In Abyssinia, in Arabia, in Gaul, in Southern Russia where millions of Khazars adopted it around the ninth century A.D., many people were converted to Judaism. It may be that since, they have, through the influence of the environment, of similar mores, come to look like one or another of the so-called Jewish physical types. The notion of a "race-résultat," slowly developed, should thus be substituted for the imaginary purity of pristine races.

Here indeed is the crux of the matter which sets Gobineau apart from other historians who resorted to the notion of race, such as Renan and Taine. Gobineau, to be logical (he attempted to be, amid innumerable contradictions and unproved assertions), had to deny or to omit the impact of the "milieu." For if, through the climate, the environment, the adoption of similar ways of eating, being educated, working, members of the black or yellow or Semitic or other races gradually become like the peoples among whom they live, the whole fabric of race as the great explanation of the achievement and of the decadence of cultures falls to the ground. Elie Faure, while rapturously admiring the ethnical poem of his fellow Gascon, Gobineau, even contends that all that is fecund in art, science, government has happened in lands where races were intermingled (Asia Minor and then Greece, Italy, Western Europe, North America). The theory, indirectly stemming from reservations to Gobineau's thesis, might be called a racism in reverse. We have a remarkable semantic study of the word "milieu" (*medium* in Latin, *ambiente* in Italian, *circumstancia* in Spanish, "environment" as Carlyle coined it in English, "habitat," etc.) in several tongues by Leo Spitzer, in *Essays in Historical Semantics* (New York: Vanni, 1948). Unfortunately, we are without a parallel study on the semantic metamorphoses of the word "race," diversely derived from *radix* (root) and from *ration* (type), the latter being the more probable. Few of the men who have used the term have cared to propose a precise definition of it. Taine, who popularized both "race" and "milieu," borrowing the latter from Balzac, certainly did not.

The triad "race, milieu, moment" (meaning either, or both, momentum, or acquired speed, and the instant of a certain emergence in time) has been popularized by Taine's eloquent critical manifesto, the preface to his *History of English Literature* (1864). It has aroused many objections; the strict determinism which was, wrongly, read into it has been refuted often. Taine's letters and other, and much more subtle, prefaces by him to the three successive volumes of *Essais de critique et d'histoire* have repudiated determinism. Simply (he was praised for it recently both by Harry Levin and by Edmund Wilson in this country), Taine "rid us once for all of the uncritical notion that books dropped like meteorites from the sky" (Levin). Race was prudently defined by him as "those innate and hereditary dispositions in man . . . which usually accompany marked differences in temperament and in body structure." Less prudently, he added that there are naturally varieties of men as there are breeds of horses and bulls, some brave and intelligent, others timid and limited. But he stressed the climate, the environment, the political circumstances, and even the response to history's challenges more than he did the hereditary factor. The first two chapters of his *History of English Literature* did rashly generalize on the Saxons and the Normans. But Taine was well aware of the vagueness of any explanation through the factor of race when he came to individuals—Shakespeare, Swift, Byron. Among the millions who belonged to the same race, one happened to be endowed with talent or with genius. Taine always insisted that history is primarily an art and that "creative imagination is its handmaiden." To Sainte-Beuve's objections, in a letter of May 30, 1864, he replied:

I have endeavored to portray individuals. . . . They are individual although they belong to a group, because that group (or class) itself is made up of individuals. They are none the less spontaneous for being ruled by general laws, because laws only work through individuals.

Debates on the importance of hereditary factors in history have not been closed with our outraged realization of the monstrous harm caused by racism. Henry Stuart Hughes sadly and rightly remarked in 1962 in his volume *Contemporary Europe*: "Nothing in the decades before 1914 did more to break the fragile but still perceptible links of European culture than widespread and uninformed theories of national and racial differences." True enough. But the enigma persists of why certain ethnic or cultural groups (the Polish Jews being the prime example) are far more richly gifted for art, letters, science than other Europeans (after all, the French Huguenots, the Irish Catholics, the Armenians, and other groups in Russia or on the Iberian Peninsula were also pressured or persecuted or dispersed). Inequality of gifts or diversity of ability can hardly be denied. The purpose of history should be to teach us how to correct natural inequality through equality of rights and of opportunities, and how to marshal the valuable diversity of European, Asiatic, South American nations for the greater good of mankind as a whole and the increase of our zest for living.

The 1919 Treaty of Versailles, in several respects, especially through setting up several countries in Central Europe where the Austro-Hungarian Empire had signed its own death warrant in starting the war after Sarajevo, marked the highest point of nationalist victories in Europe. It was prepared to a large extent by the historians whom Lloyd George, Woodrow Wilson, and Clemenceau had gathered around them. The era which followed echoed with remorseful denunciations of nationalism by historians and political scientists and the pious wish that the principle of interdependence, serving as a basis for a European federation, might be substituted for the principle of nationalities, whose application had left Europe at the mercy of nationalist demagogues. Some cynical disappointment has set in since World War II: journalists and politicians still rail at the nationalism of leaders of other countries as anachronistic. They often ignore, or fail to notice, their own. But few dauntless optimists dare to expect that nationalism, as a force, has ceased to be effective in the atomic era. English scholars, such as Barbara Ward in her *Nationalism and Ideology* (New York: W. W. Norton, 1966), politely or haughtily upbraid De Gaulle for being intoxicated with history, living either in the past or in a remote and unreal future; they denounce the mixture, most unpalatable to empirical sages of the British Isles, of politics and ideology, and continental European nationalism, as festering the body politic.

Others, while deploring the Balkanization of Africa, the controversies between Flemish and Walloons, the fights over Kashmir, Tibet, Israel, express their doubts that vituperations on the part of the big powers will be effective in dissuading young nations from repeating their mistakes. The *Economist*, in an article entitled "The Dynamo of Nations" (July 11, 1964), remarked resignedly: "It is not particularly surprising that there should be those willing to demonstrate that if, like the toad, nationalism's exterior is ugly and venomous, it hath yet a precious jewel in its head." It acknowledged nationalism to be, "at bottom, a highly developed sense of community," and that, in Hungary and Poland in 1956–1957, national solidarity was a humanizing and liberalizing influence. It perfunctorily formulated the hope that Arab nationalisms might turn toward a larger federation and that the Latin American nationalisms might some day dispense with the scarecrow of the United States to achieve a meeting of minds and of interests. But the melancholy conclusion read: "For the moment the shock therapy nationalism brings to new nations can hardly be dispensed with."

In America, one of the most mature and farsighted periodicals dealing with foreign affairs, the *Bulletin of Atomic Scientists* (June 1964), welcomed a thoughtful communication signed "Gustav Ichheiser" which shook some of the complacency of political scientists. It asked: "Is nationalism really outmoded?" It answered: "In consequence of certain historical developments, it has become and is likely to remain for a long time the most dominant cultural form and most elemental force of our age." The author went on to discriminate sharply between the "conscious nationalist," who knows that he is one and is therefore not dangerous (De Gaulle being the model and being exonerated as forward-looking, since nations will continue to see issues from their national point of view), and the unconsciously nationalistic America, which, it was contended, "tries, without being aware of it, to impose its own nationalistically inspired ideas and ideals, its own brand of nationalistic design upon the whole Western community of nations."

Debating the pros and the cons of a force which has become more dynamic than any religion, upbraiding the new nations of Africa or Asia which are repeating the errors committed by the Western nations and balking at uniting into larger federal groupings is of little avail. A score of books have appeared in English on nationalism; they all point out the role of history in fostering the growth of that "idée-force," and to the powerlessness of history now to undo what has been done. Herder was probably the prime mover, in the eighteenth century, when he expatiated on the folk spirit and on the spiritual principle underlying national cultures. He was, however, not partial to the Prussians, and was more in sympathy with the Slavs than with his own compatriots. Herder died in 1803, before the Napoleonic

Wars which lay at the root of German unification. Another German, Fichte, after having hailed France as the embodiment of liberty and culture, became an advocate of nationalism and of German leadership in his famous *Reden,* or *Addresses to the German Nation* of 1807–1808. He rested his claims on the authentic "purity" of the German language as contrasted to others in Europe.

Still, as was the case for racism, nationalism found its home in France and became most influential through French historians, Michelet chiefly, and through the spread of their mystical cult of the French soul to thousands of teachers and millions of pupils, wherever French history was taught. A tenuous distinction has been offered repeatedly between patriotism and nationalism, one being laudable, the other radically evil; but such a distinction remains artificial and confusing. *France, a Nation of Patriots* was the title of one of the several volumes on nationalism by Columbia professor Carleton Hayes, who subsequently became American ambassador to Madrid. The word "patrie," coined by sixteenth-century French poets, arouses a vibration in French ears and hearts which is perhaps not exactly matched by what "das Vaterland," "la patria," "the mother country" may connote in other cultures. A geographic mystique (France as a perfect hexagon, the temperate land par excellence); religious associations (France the eldest daughter of the Church, the cult of Joan of Arc); the fervent respect for a long history which stressed the Crusades, St. Louis, the commoners fighting with the king at Bouvines in 1214; the claim of being the true heir to ancient Rome and Greece all contributed to making French nationalism a form of religion.

But it was chiefly the Revolution, the brutal declarations of foreign powers which threatened to stifle the young republic, the rise of the people to arms and their victory at Valmy with the slogans "Vive la nation" and "La Patrie en danger" (1792) which launched nationalism on its sweeping conquests in the nineteenth century. The Revolution effected in France a national unity and a centralization to this day without parallel in Europe; it imposed the national language above the dialects, a common education, a new conception of a national army, and of wars fought with and on passion and *élan.* The fears and the opposition of Prussia, Austro-Hungary, England, at times Russia, to the new French regime, and the uprising in the Vendée added

impetus to that nationalism. Hegel formulated a lesson which statesmen have since taken to heart (and which the opponents of the
Russian, Algerian, Egyptian, Chinese revolutions have chosen to
disregard): "Nations divided against themselves conquer internal
stability through external war." Strangely enough, Hegel himself and
other Germans provided the most delirious ideology, or rhetoric, to
inflate the nationalism of the French. "At every age, that people is the
master," decreed Hegel, "which embodies the highest concept of the
Spirit." Fichte had been similarly confident that France was, through
her revolution, the torchbearer of history and that to become French
would constitute an honor second to none. Anacharsis Cloots,
Prussian-born, offered the French legislative assembly in 1792 a
project for doing away with all local governments in Europe and
replacing them by a single nation with a single capital, Paris. "Any
resistance to the universal instinct clamoring for the Rights of Man
for all of mankind must be opposed."

Michelet never went so far. His love of France as the incarnation of
all that is generous and noble rested on his identification of himself
with the people of France and with the Revolutionary masses. But
although he distrusted England, fed on meat and ale and not participating like France in the sacrament of bread, aristocratic and suspicious of foreigners, he never conceived his patriotism narrowly. Like
many historians and political thinkers of his time, he stood for the
liberation of the Poles (he wrote a warm but lucid little book on *La
Pologne martyr*) and of other minorities in Europe which had not
conquered nationhood. The more narrow French nationalism,
blending hatred of foreigners with cynical advocacy of self-interest,
came after Michelet and often turned against him. It found its
prophets in De Maistre, Comte, Le Play, Gobineau, then in Bourget,
Barrès, and Maurras. Its sad outcome became conspicuous when
most of those nationalists espoused the anti-Dreyfus cause in the last
years of the century; a number of their successors, distrustful of the
Third Republic, sided with Vichy in 1940, denying the very patriotism
which had been the better part of their doctrine.

The formidable task facing historians today is to instill into their
readers and into future generations the urge to transcend what is
narrow and negative in nationalism—economic self-sufficiency;

incitement to war; finding Europe's mission in shortsighted distrust of the super powers and of motives for federation on higher unity, in denial of the values offered by other foreign nations rather than in fruitful rivalry. The march toward such a goal is gradual and slow: much has been achieved already since 1950—in fact, more than in the previous five hundred years. But undervaluing the force of nationalism in Asia, Africa, Europe, or even in North America could only be conducive to a brutal awakening to realities.

A regrettable fact is that, in countries like France, Germany, Italy, where doctrines and philosophies are paramount and no political party can long do without at least a semblance of supporting ideology, there has been little, if any, political doctrine of genuine value inspired by the parties of the left. Karl Marx thought and felt as a German, even as a Prussian, and approved of Bismarck, as did another socialist, Ferdinand Lassalle. Proudhon, in France, and Georges Sorel later, believed in authority and in violence. Jaurès, Léon Blum, Herriot never proposed a striking doctrine in support of internationalism, nor did any of the historians who inspired the French leftist parties, and certainly not the philosophical essayist Alain. Meanwhile, the conservative and nationalist doctrines of the right could boast of historians and systematic thinkers who impressed the French elite, and spread to the masses. Nationalism in France took on a new vigor after the defeat of 1871, thanks to the schoolteachers and the spread of universal education. Democracy reinforced it and disseminated it. Illusions like the one which tried to contend that wars are machinations of evil tyrants luring the masses to battle have been woefully dispelled. No monarchy of old, probably not even Napoleon's Empire, would, or could ever, have demanded and obtained from the French masses the insensate slaughters of Flanders, Verdun, and the Somme and the slow and nearly sure martyrdom of war in the trenches.

The socialists, then the Communists have had to acknowledge (they have done it *in petto*, if not loudly) that nationalism, and neither socialism nor Communism, comes closest today to being the modern religion. It alone can dispose of ritual, flags, slogans, communal singing, and torrents of eloquence, and require blind and fanatical obedience. All the politicians who began by being socialists or even Communists—Millerand, Péguy, Laval, Doriot in France, Mussolini,

Pilsudski, Stalin, and several of Hitler's henchmen—turned to nationalism—often of the most arrogant and demagogic brand—in order to retain their hold on the masses. It took them little time to realize that there is more xenophobia, more naïve patriotism, and more pride in their national mores and even in their national culture among farmers clinging to their plot of land and workmen in factories than among the more sophisticated middle and upper classes. The Communist theoreticians and leaders in France have in fact proclaimed that "the transferring of national responsibilities from one class to another"[4] was an essential feature of our age and that the proletariat was ready "to assume the national destinies" of France, once considered the privilege of the bourgeoisie. The stubborn patriotism showed by a number of Communist rank and file as well as by some of their leaders and their poets such as Aragon and Eluard would seem to confirm it.

"In America, men have the opinions and passions of democracy; in Europe, we have still the passions and opinions of revolution," Tocqueville remarked in the second part of his *Democracy in America*. French historians and moralists have been fond of coining lapidary aphorisms on the theme never very remote from their minds and hearts, and around the word which is surrounded with a halo of sanctity, or of sacred horror, for them: Revolution. The man who has, from 1958 on, presided over the destinies of culture and art in France and whom some brand, mistakenly he contends, as a counter-revolutionary, had, in one of his early novels, *Les Conquérants* (1928), an exclamation which has set many a French heart beating: "Revolution! All that is not it is worse!" The mystical Joan of Arc or Antigone of modern France, a martyr to her own intransigence, Simone Weil, remarked more ambiguously: "Revolution is the opium of the people." Very few have been, in the course of the last century, the French historians, even the most convinced "counter-revolutionaries" among them (the term was invented by one of the noblest martyrs of the Revolution, Condorcet) who were not secretly

---

[4] The phrase is by the Communist leader Maurice Thorez in a preface on Marxism and culture to Jean Fréville's *Sur la Littérature et l'art* (Editions sociales, 1936).

proud of the French Revolution—even Taine, who tried hard to undo its far-ranging effects; even Renan, who, having long deplored the Revolution, concluded at the end of his life that since it was so maligned by foreigners and Frenchmen alike, it must be secretly envied by them and was probably the greatest of the French achievements.

No other myth certainly can match the glamor and the explosive force of contagion of that one. The word is repulsive to most "Anglo-Saxons," since it implies change, not by consent and agreement to disagree, but by violence; a rapid, and not a patiently gradual, method of replacing the past by something different; inevitable, but at times indiscriminate, sacrifice of lives and destruction of property; and a profound change in the distribution of property. Exasperation with injustice and a passionate belief that the future can be made preferable to the present naturally help foment a prerevolutionary mood. That enthusiasm only temporarily blinds the architects of change to the old truth that all revolutions begun on liberal slogans have in the end been followed by a stronger army, a stronger police and an authoritarian regime, able to cope both with the counterrevolutionaries on the right and those who, on the left, refuse to put an end to the revolution which has succeeded. Still the myth glows and glitters. Historians add to its brilliance and tragic seduction; Carlyle himself has served the revolutionary cause in the minds of many of his young readers. The French upheaval of 1789–1799 outshines all the other revolutions in modern history. Alone, to this day, it fascinates the Chinese, the Africans, and the Latin Americans. One of the great if naïve causes for surprise of the generous and law-abiding Americans who attempt to interpret their country abroad is their realization of how ineffective the model of the American Revolution remains for other lands: its sole action was through its share in promoting the French events of 1789. English historians who have lauded the wisest of revolutions, in their eyes, that of 1688, will not even attempt to hold up its example to nations less gifted in the art of compromise. "The English," the American "anatomist" of revolutions, Crane Brinton, noted, "have, for the last century and more, been insistent that their revolution is unique—so unique as to have been practically no revolution at all."

Some of the earliest enthusiasts for the French Revolution among thinkers and writers were found, not in Paris, but elsewhere in Europe. Blake planned a poem, "The French Revolution," in seven cantos, and completed only one, in which the Archbishop of Paris and the Governor of the Bastille were scathingly treated. Wordsworth's enthusiasm during his first visit to France in July, 1790, then his thirteen months' stay at Blois, when he hailed "France, standing on the top of golden hours,/ And human nature seeming born again," has been recorded in *The Prelude*. He changed his views later, with the Terror, as did Coleridge, who in 1798 confided to verse his "Tears in Solitude" at the prospect of a French invasion of England; but the future conservative thinker, in his fine 1807 poem "To William Wordsworth, on the Night After His Recitation of the *Prelude*," was fired by his friend's memory of the glorious dawn,

> When France in all her towns lay vibrating, . . .
> . . . .
> Amid a mighty nation jubilant,
> When from the general heart of human kind
> Hope sprang forth like a full-born Deity.

None however matched the delirious joy with which several Germans hailed the outburst of freedom in France. Klopstock, not up to then much drawn to France, overflowed with praise for the people who were accomplishing that Revolution, adding that their Germanic blood accounted for their revolutionary fervor. Kant, even after the Terror, remained an admirer of the momentous accomplishment. In his last work, in 1798, *The Conflict of Faculties*, he repeated that the Revolution was, in its essence, moral: "It revealed, in the depths of human nature, a possibility of moral progress which no politician had suspected before." Hölderlin composed a "Hymn to Freedom" in 1793 and later celebrated Rousseau, the decipherer of the signs through which God speaks to us, the eagle who had heralded the storm. Schelling and Hegel planted a tree of freedom at Tübingen when the Bastille fell. Hegel bowed in rapture before that reconciliation of the ideal and the real, "heaven having come down on earth." In his *Philosophie der Weltgeschichte*, he salutes "the wonderful sunrise" and insists that "the French Revolution is an event of world history," not just of the French. Fichte proclaimed that his *Doctrine of Science* belonged in certain measure to the French nation, for to that nation he owed the stimulation in him of the energy needed to understand the ideas which filled his great work. More than Kant or Hegel, he wished to act upon his ideas and to consider the Revolution in France not just as a manifestation of "the Idea," but as a historical fact. He even praised regicide, and he was eyed with suspicion by the German authorities when, militantly, he published in 1793 his *Contributions (Beiträge)*, "proposing to rectify the judgment of the public on the French Revolution." The wildest and most touching of those Germans who became more French than the French was Anacharsis Cloots, the most idealistic of dreamers, "the personal enemy of Jesus Christ," as he came to be called when he advocated a lofty ethics without religion; that strange Prussian stands with André Chénier, Lavoisier, Condorcet (who took poison before his head could be cut off), and Le Pelletier de Saint-Fargeau, among the most deplorable, because they were the noblest, of all the victims of the Terror.

While their revolution was being enacted, the French, otherwise occupied, had little leisure for celebrating it in verse or ascertaining its import for world history. Their romantic movement came with a lag of some thirty years after those of Germany or England. Two early and ambitious philosophers of history alone, in 1797, three years before the eighteenth century ended, published confused treatises on the events just lived through; one was Chateaubriand, back from his American voyage, living in London as a penurious émigré, accumulating historical parallels and secondhand erudition in his confused *Essay on Ancient and Modern Revolutions*; the other, also from the nobility and a subject of the King of Savoy, was Joseph de Maistre. He was French at heart and in his culture, and in one of his letters, that foe of the Revolution uttered the cry: "Long live France, even if republican!" In his *Considerations on France*, published in Lausanne in 1797, he pictured the Revolution as an immense and impersonal force, relentlessly driving men on. In sentences reminiscent of Burke, whom he had read, he declared: "It is not men who lead the Revolution, it is the Revolution which employs men." Later, just after his death in 1821, a volume by

Joseph de Maistre, who had represented his sovereign at the court of Russia, appeared, *Les Soirées de Saint-Petersbourg*. It was to impress the men of the nineteenth century enduringly (Baudelaire called De Maistre a "master of his thought") and even the reactionaries of the twentieth. De Maistre asked there the torturing question which many a religious conscience echoed, Why does God allow such cataclysms to occur, and a blood bath like the Terror? The Count's reply was that there is a virtue of atonement in the shedding of blood. It is a divine law that the blood of the innocent redeems the guilty; Christianity rests on that foundation stone. War is inexplicable otherwise; it is divine, since it is a law of the world. "The earth, soaked with the blood of men, is an immense altar." Men do not revolt on that sacrificial battlefield. The *Te Deum*, that prayer which ascends to the Lord of the Hosts after many foes have been slaughtered, is the most splendid of hymns, "a divine dithyramb." The executioner who has just broken the bones of or crucified the guilty comes home full of a religious joy. God welcomes him in His bosom; he has fulfilled His designs.

It took a very extreme and fiercely logical conception of Christianity to espouse De Maistre's doctrines, but there is a Jansenist and Jacobin trend in the French which made some of them responsive to those probings into God's oblique ways of manifesting His will in history. Alfred de Vigny protested, or had Christ protest, in the long monologue attributed to Christ questioning God's obstinate silence, in his poem "Le Mont des Oliviers." But a growing number of Catholic thinkers felt that they had to reconcile the Revolution with God's providential order, and the dilemma was similar to that in which apologists of God's omniscience and of man's freedom have often felt locked. Ballanche, a Catholic mystic, in 1818 gave the lead. Religion must change, like all else. "The human spirit is constantly marching on. . . . It never is allowed to remain in place." And again, in apocalyptical parables in *Le Vieillard et le jeune homme* (1819):

Moral nature feeds on destruction and death, exactly like physical nature. . . . There is a law of Providence, according to which evil comes out of good; . . . the greatness of the good is measured by the extent and the intensity of the suffering.

Lamennais, the truest progenitor of social Catholicism and the prophet of the sort of reformation of the Church which the workmen priests have attempted a century later, pondered with more intellectual vigor on the Revolution, and more ardently still after July, 1830, had brought the prospect of a new upheaval close to the French, disgruntled with the inertia of their royalist Restoration since 1815. In his newspaper, *L'Avenir*, on October 16, 1830, he distributed his anathemas: "Woe to him who fails to recognize the hand of God in those enormous catastrophes which fill with dread the thought of man." And in the *Revue des Deux Mondes*, then three years old and a magnet for brilliant talents, he did not hesitate to assert, on August 1, 1834, after he had been condemned by the Vatican as a rebellious priest: "Revolutions are, as it were, God present to our eyes in the world." Lamartine, who had started his poetic career as a monarchist and a Catholic, also perturbed by the events of 1830 which were to direct him toward a political career, delighted in announcing and advocating changes, even in the dogmas of the Church. "The world has reached one of those crucial eras in which everything is being renovated so as to become better." In December, 1831, after a workmen's riot in Lyon, he repeated that God's watch over humanity allowed of no pause: thrones, nations, sooner or later had to give way. Mankind every night puts out the idea whose beacon guided it that day. God's message had to be incessantly reinterpreted as man became more enlightened.

> Vos siècles pas à pas épellent L'Evangile;
> Vous n'y lisiez qu'un mot, et vous en lirez mille;
> Vos enfants plus hardis y liront plus avant . . .

In his epic poem, *Jocelyn* (1835), the young priest fleeing the Revolution in a grotto of the Alps meditates on the theological and moral issue raised by revolutions. They stem from virtue, even if they are performed through crimes; the workman is divine, if the tool is mortal. It is an implacable law that revolutions profit not those who accomplish them, but their successors. The long speech has a grave philosophical beauty and ends in the oft-quoted line "Malheur à qui les fait, heureux qui les hérite!" Traveling in the East in 1835, realizing that the world was crumbling around him everywhere, his thought then closer to Voltaire than to his early Catholic teaching, Lamartine branded the royalists as the paragons of stupidity and wondered which man would not today gladly exclaim: "I am a revolutionary."

Not only did the massacres which seemed inseparable from the Revolution require a metaphysical or theological explanation, but another enigma tantalized the puzzled meditations of the French, whose nation had traditionally been considered as the most attached to its kings. Why had it happened in France of all countries? Was the French Revolution a unique and surprising phenomenon, or just one of several such upheavals which had reached its full impact in France and floundered elsewhere?

The question is one which has vexed historians of France in our time. It is the central theme of the important two-volume work by Robert Palmer, *The Age of Democratic Revolution* (Princeton University Press, 1961–1965), and of several studies in France by Jacques Godechot. It was already the question posed by Barnave, a French Protestant orator who joined the Revolution in 1789 and died under the guillotine in November, 1793. In a short but pregnant volume which the great socialist historian Jaurès had wisely praised, *Introduction à la Révolution française*, Barnave sketched the first social and economic interpretation of the great movement then raging, saw in it the working of some historical necessity, and added: "There is not, properly speaking, a French Revolution; there is a European Revolution which has its apex in France."

Materialistic explanations have long ago had to be rejected. Jaurès, whose eight-volume history of the Revolution, both remarkably documented and teeming with life, is entitled *A Socialist History*, was one of the first to submit that 1789 had not been caused by misery or starvation. Hard as it is to generalize about a country then far from uniform, with a standard of living which varied according to provinces as well as to social classes, it does indeed seem fair to conclude that, while the financial condition of the French kingdom was precarious in 1787–1789, the country itself was the most prosperous in Europe. There had been a poor crop in 1788, but there had been many far worse years throughout the century. The income of the French kingdom was then clearly higher than that of Britain, double that of

Austria, three times or more that of Prussia, Russia, or Spain. The population had increased to at least twenty-six million inhabitants, as compared to eleven or twelve million in Britain. C. E. Labrousse, the most competent economic historian today specializing in that period of history, sums up the results of his patient survey with the words: "The eighteenth century remains on the whole a great century of economic expansion, of increase of capitalist income, of progress for power and wealth of the middle class. . . . It thus prepares the Revolution, a Revolution of prosperity" (*La Crise de l'économie française à la fin de l'ancien Régime*, Presses Universitaires de France, 1944, I, xlviii).

Deeper causes which partly account for the emergence and the success of the Revolution in France and not in border lands (which, in any case, lacked the ferment of a large metropolis, a mass consciousness in the middle and lower classes) are clearly demographic, social, and, primarily, intellectual. The lessons they provide may well be pondered today, when the very same forces are operating in several continents, and have probably not even ceased to operate in parts of Europe. Under the impact of the usual factors (prosperity, better health and hygiene), the population had grown markedly in France and the increase had taken place chiefly among the young, who were impatient to find employment according to their merits and to displace their elders. Only 24 per cent of the French population in 1789 was over forty years of age; 40 per cent was between twenty and forty, and the rest (36 per cent) under twenty. Those young generations were restless; they included a fair proportion of educated young men who had read, or heard about, the ideas of the "philosophes." The number of former priests among the revolutionaries (Fouché, Grégoire, Sieyès, Talleyrand are only the better known) and their intellectual eminence and leadership are a singular phenomenon, only paralleled by the number of former theological students and pastors' sons among German philosophers. The men at the top under Louis XVI— aristocrats, archbishops, bankers of scant imagination like Necker— did not and would not understand that a dissatisfied and unemployed intellectual elite, trained in law and history, is the ideal human material to engage in revolutions. Léon Blum, the successor to Jaurès as the leader of the French socialists and a historian and critic himself, uttered a warning of some appositeness today in Africa, South America, Asia, and in the score or scores of countries in which revolutions are likely to take place before the twentieth century is over:

> Any ruling class which can maintain its own cohesiveness on the sole condition that it fails to act, which can survive on the sole condition that it refuses to change, which is incapable of adapting itself to the course of events or of putting to use the fresh strength of ascending generations, is doomed to disappear from history.[5]

Most of those thoughtful young men, remarkably observant of social and economic conditions, not at all doctrinaire in their thinking, contrary to Taine's gratuitous assertion, belonged to the middle classes. The phrase "middle class" is vague and has become a password with historians and journalists. One of the English historians of the French Revolution who have retained their sanity and eschewed paradoxes on a subject which causes many a head to reel, Alfred Cobban, remarked that ever since Adam and Eve were expelled from Eden, all of history has been the rise of the middle class (*The Social Interpretation of the French Revolution*, Cambridge University Press, 1964). The Marxists, who have popularized the concept, ill disguise their jealous admiration for the intelligence, the adaptability, the initiative, and the stubborn capacity for survival of the bourgeoisie. Karl Marx, as early as 1848, even interpreted the "sans-culottisme" of the proletarians who, after the first few years, joined the Revolution and acted in it and the Terror as "a plebeian manner of finishing off the foes of the bourgeoisie: absolutism, feudalism and petit-bourgeois mentality." The new orthodoxy among historians is to see in the Revolution a victory of the bourgeoisie, perfidiously stolen from the masses. This is not the place to challenge that doctrine, anachronistic as its use of terms often is. But it is true that the middle class, rich in brains and skill, was courted alternately by the king and by the nobility. However, the army as a career was open to only a very few commoners; only a handful of them were allowed to join the ranks of

[5] Léon Blum, in *A l'Echelle humaine* (1945). The book, in a certain way the author's testament, was composed in 1941, while he was held in prison by the Germans during World War II.

the nobility and enjoy its privileges and tax immunity. The others, aware of their talent and promise, were to become the Hoche and Marceau and Bonaparte, the Carnot, Marat, Robespierre of the great upheaval—leaders of soldiers and leaders of men. One of them, Camille Desmoulins, jotted down at thirty-three, in 1793: "I am thirty-three, an age fatal to revolutionaries, the age of the sans-culotte Jesus Christ when he died." Saint-Just, born in 1767, was even younger when, in 1791, he wrote his admirable *Esprit de la Révolution*; he died with Robespierre, "the Archangel of the Revolution" as Michelet called him, with Mozart, Keats, and Rimbaud (bourgeois all of them) one of the most prodigious young men to have made history.

The main difference between the French in 1787–1789 and the other nations of Europe, less prosperous than they and at least as oppressed, is that the power of ideas, disseminated through literature and encyclopedic or philosophical dictionaries, was immeasurably greater in France. Those thinkers and writers had convinced the people that conditions, having steadily improved for several decades, should improve still further. Revolt, to the readers of Voltaire and Rousseau, did not appear as a crisis of desperation, an aimless uprising certain to be crushed. The systems of the "philosophes" had offered positive reforms to be accomplished, remedies which could be applied. A preferable future was no longer just a utopia; it could be achieved here and fairly soon. Even if none of the political thinkers of the eighteenth century had consciously wanted a revolution, still less foreseen the course it would eventually take, they had profoundly altered the mood of the French through taking the affection or the attachment of the elites away from a regime which had been proved sluggish at reforming itself.

The Harvard historian Crane Brinton, in a book first published in 1938 and again in 1952 (by Prentice-Hall), *The Anatomy of Revolution*, attempted to establish the features common to four modern revolutions: the English of 1688, the American, the French, and the Russian. None of them occurred after or during a crisis of economic depression; all of them in societies economically progressive, hence resenting inequality more bitterly; all of them in cultures in which the intellectual elites had become disaffected from prevailing conditions.

The lesson is an ominous one for a country like the United States where most of the literature since 1919, a large part of the academic community since 1930, and those who now proudly call themselves "the intellectuals" have, in an instinctive and unorganized way, felt estranged from the regime or opposed to it. Even the folklore and the jests directed at Madison Avenue, at the organization men and the Establishment, point to a serious cleavage between the business life of the country and the writers, journalists, and scientists, most of whom are recruited from the ranks of half a million college teachers and some five or six million college and professional school students. Crane Brinton, an impartial historian with no ax to grind and with too acute a sense of humor to pose as a prophet of revolutions, smiles with benevolence at much of that literature in which authors (often in the academic profession and supported by the Establishment) vituperate "against bank vice-presidents and wish to drown them in the blood of advertizing men." The intellectuals play their traditional role, as their earliest predecessors, Plato, Xenophon, Aristophanes, Aristotle, had done, disgruntled with a political order in which they were merely the equals of any loafers on the agora.

> By nature, the intellectuals take a critical attitude toward the daily routine of human affairs. Lacking experience of action under the burden of responsibility, they do not learn how little new action is usually possible or effective. An intellectual as satisfied with the world as with himself would simply not be an intellectual.

The fact remains nevertheless that we are today, in the most advanced countries, faced with a disaffection of the thinking, and perhaps thoughtful, part of the nation which is fraught with perils. It could, if a grave depression were to occur again, and if scandals of corruption and venality were to tarnish the image of businessmen and politicians, turn the best-educated elements of the nation's youth, already unenthusiastic about business careers, resolutely against their elders and the established order. There are insidious new shapes which, in the democratic and highly technological countries, could be assumed by a revolution.

The dangers at home are made much worse by a more blatant failure of the United States, the most generous country ever to have risen to the summit of power and the one most pathetically eager to be liked and imitated abroad—the failure of the American Revolution, and even of "America's permanent Revolution," as *Fortune* magazine called it after World War II (the phrase was first coined by Proudhon), to serve as a model, or even to be invoked as a useful precedent, for the revolutions abroad which are occurring, or are likely to occur for another half-century. Hannah Arendt, one of the most favorably disposed toward American civilization among the intellectuals who have adopted this country since 1933, in a volume published in 1963 (New York: Viking Press), *On Revolution*, starts from a premise which few would challenge and which recalls a prophecy of Nietzsche: "Even if we should succeed in changing the physiognomy of this century to the point where it would no longer be a century of wars, it most certainly will remain a century of revolutions." She then stresses the point, among others, that, in this age of revolutions, the countries of Europe, of Asia, of Africa, even those of the Western Hemisphere from Cuba to Chile, all talk glowingly of the French Revolution, but act as if they had never heard of the American Revolution. Such was clearly the case for Lenin's 1917 revolution. Such is the case for Mao's China and the later Commune upsurge which has puzzled those who undervalue the power of historical myths over the revolutionists of today.[6] Many complex factors may explain the enormous obstacles which Americans encounter when they attempt to communicate to the rest of the world elements of their achievement other than the scientific and technological ones. But an essential one may well lie in the inability of their historians to endow their history with the appeal of a myth, as the historians of the French Revolution, even those who deplored the consequences of that Revolution, have done. Hannah Arendt surmises that the world-wide success of the French Revolution is due in part to the amount of thought and talented writing lavished

[6] Well-informed articles, for example in *Newsweek*, February 27, 1967, and in the *Economist* (London) of January 14 and February 11, 1967, have analyzed the strange fascination which the French Revolution and its aftermath, the Commune of 1871, has had for the Chinese. In the first of the two articles in the *Economist* here mentioned, the commentator wrote, perhaps with too hasty an inference that the Chinese upheaval is a death pang: "It is not just China that is stretched out under Chairman Mao's knife. So are two centuries of modern history. What has been happening in China . . . is the end of the road that started in Paris in 1789."

upon it by the French.[7] In contrast, "the American failure to remember can be traced back to this fateful failure of post-revolutionary thought." Much earlier, in an essay on "The Function of Criticism," which opens the first series of his *Essays in Criticism* (1865), Matthew Arnold, a wise Victorian who advocated cultural reforms rather than a revolution in his native land, had declared with no little courage:

> The French Revolution . . . found undoubtedly its motive-power in the intelligence of men, and not in their practical sense; this is what distinguishes it from the English Revolution of Charles the First's time. This is what makes it a more spiritual event than our Revolution, an event of much more powerful and world-wide interest, though practically less successful. . . . In spite of the extravagant direction given to this enthusiasm, in spite of the crimes and follies in which it lost itself, the French Revolution derives from the force, truth and universality of the ideas which it took for its law, and from the passion with which it could inspire a multitude for these ideas, a unique and still living power: it is— and will probably long remain—the greatest, the most animating event in history. And . . . France has reaped [from her Revolution] one fruit —the natural and legitimate fruit, though not precisely the grand fruit she expected: she is the country of Europe where *the people* is most alive.

[7] The English have recently had at least as remarkable a host of historians of the French Revolution whom that event has fascinated: Richard Cobb, Alfred Cobban, Godfrey Elton, Norman Hampson, George Rudé, J. L. Talmon, J. M. Thompson, M. J. Sydenham, and others. Carlyle himself, in his passionate rhetorician's style, could not help expressing his admiration for "this Thing, called La Révolution, which, like an angel of Death, hangs over France." He remarks, in his chapter "Grilled Herrings," that the guillotined of the Terror are certainly deplorable, but "some ten times as many shot rightly on a field of battle, and one might have had his glorious victory with *Te Deum*. . . . But what if History somewhere on this planet were to hear of a nation, the third soul of whom had not, for thirty weeks each year, as many third-rate potatoes as would sustain him? History, in that case, feels bound to consider that starvation is starvation."

THE INFLUENCE OF EIGHTEENTH-CENTURY IDEAS ON THE FRENCH REVOLUTION

No QUESTION is likely to divide students of the past more sharply than that of the action of philosophical ideas and literary works upon political and social events. Our age has been powerfully impressed by the economic interpretation of history proposed by Marxists; but it has also witnessed the important role played by men of letters and men of thought in the Spanish Civil War and in the Resistance movement of World War II. The conscience of many writers is more obsessed today than it has ever been by the temptation—some call it the duty—of "engaged literature." The affinities of many of the leading authors in France and other countries link them with the men of the eighteenth century. Sartre, Camus, Giono, Breton are not unworthy descendants or reincarnations of Voltaire, Diderot, Rousseau.

It may thus be useful to attempt a restatement of an old, and ever present, problem, without any presumptuous claim to renovate its data or its solutions, but with an honest attempt to observe a few conditions which are obvious but all too seldom met. A summation of such an immense and thorny question should be clear, while respecting the complex nature of reality. It should be provocative, in the sense that it should suggest that much remains to be said on these matters by young scholars determined to launch upon the study of ideas in relation to the Revolution. Above all, it should be impartial, if that is humanly possible, concerning questions on which it is difficult not to take sides, and it should attempt to retain in these questions the life with which they are instinct, without on the other hand sacrificing objectivity or solidity.

I

The problem of the effect of the philosophy of Enlightenment on the French Revolution is one of the most important problems that confront the pure historian as well as the historian of thought and of literature. It is without doubt the most complex of the thousand aspects involved in the study of the Revolution, that is to say the origins of the modern world. Together with investigation of the origins of Christianity and the end of the ancient world, this study concerns one of the two most important upheavals that the philosophically minded historian can conceive: Taine and Renan, as well as Michelet and Tocqueville, the four most important French historians of the past century, quite rightly realized its magnitude. This problem is inevitable for every teacher of literature who lectures on Voltaire and Rousseau to his students, for every historian of the years 1789–1799 in France, and likewise for every historian of those same years and of the beginning of the nineteenth century in Germany, England, the United States, and Latin America. It presents itself to every voter who reflects even a little about the things in his country's past that he would like to maintain and those that he desires to reform.

But because it presents itself so insistently to everyone, this problem has often been met with solutions that are crude or at the very least lacking in necessary overtones; because it closely parallels our present-day preoccupations, it has aroused the partisan spirit; because it concerns not only facts but ideas, it has favored excessively dogmatic generalizations on the one hand and, on the other, the voluntary blind timidity of chroniclers who have chosen to see in the events of the Revolution nothing but a series of improvisations and haphazard movements.

There is for one thing a long and devious current of ideas which, first springing forth as a swift and turgid torrent in the sixteenth century, becoming a more or less tenuous water course in the great period of the reign of Louis XIV, and finally like a river encircling the most obdurate islets of resistance within its multiple arms, seems to have engulfed the eighteenth century in the years 1750–1765. More and more clearly, those who set forth and develop these ideas take it upon themselves to influence the existing facts, to change man by education, to free him from outmoded superstitions, to increase his political liberty and his well-being. In no way do they dream of a general cataclysm, and several of them are not insensitive to the refined amenity of the life that surrounds them or to the exquisite blend of intellectual boldness and voluptuous refinement that characterizes their era.

Suddenly, this pleasant eighteenth-century security, "table d'un long festin qu'un échafaud termine," as Hugo's beautiful image calls it, crumbles. The Revolution breaks out, and within a few years, rushes through peaceful reforms, produces a profusion of constitutions, sweeps aside the old regime, devours men, and causes heads to fall. This great movement is certainly confused, turbulent, and irrational like everything that men accomplish by collective action. However, lawyers, officers, priests, and journalists play a part in it that is often important. These men had grown up in an intellectual climate that had been established by Montesquieu, Voltaire, Rousseau, Raynal, and Mably. May we accurately reach a conclusion of "post hoc, ergo propter hoc"?

It would not have been so difficult to answer such a question if partisan quarrels had not needlessly clouded the issue. Frenchmen are incapable of viewing their nation's past dispassionately or of accepting it as a whole. For a hundred and fifty years they have not ceased to be of different minds on their Revolution, which is doubtless a proof that it is still a live question among them; while in other countries the Revolution of 1688 or the Revolution of 1776 is calmly invested with the veneration accorded to a buried past. It is a curious fact that the great majority of their political writers from Joseph de Maistre, Louis de Bonald, and Auguste Comte himself, to Le Play, Tocqueville, Taine, at times Renan, Barrès, Bourget, Maurras, and many others, has pronounced itself hostile to the "great principles of '89" or at least to that which was drawn from those principles. Three fundamental assertions are the basis of most of the anti-revolutionary arguments: (a) The Revolution was harmful and anti-French; it could only be attributed to foreign influences that perverted the French genius of moderation, restrained devotion, and obedience to the hereditary monarch. It was caused by foreign influences that contaminated eighteenth-century thought: Locke, the English deists, the Protestants in general, the Swiss Rousseau, etc. . . . (b) These corrupting ideas were introduced among the French people, who had been sound and upright until then, by clubs called "Sociétés de Pensée" and by secret groups of conspiring intellectuals, the Freemasons for example and the "philosophes" themselves, who formed an authentic subversive faction (Augustin Cochin, *Les Sociétés de Pensée*, Plon, 1921). (c) The revolutionary spirit is the logical outcome of the classical spirit strengthened by the scientific spirit. This spirit delights in abstraction, generalizes profusely, and considers man as a creature apart from his environment, isolated from his past; it lacks the subtle empiricism which characterizes the English reformists; it is ignorant of everything touching reality. Accordingly it sets out to make laws for universal man, without regard for France's age-old traditions or the local conditions of the provinces. This contention advanced with talent and a semblance of thorough documentation by Taine has beguiled a great number of excellent minds because of its specious clarity.[1]

These contentions have not stood the test of serious scrutiny by literary historians trained in more rigid methods since the dawn of the twentieth century. The penetration with which Gustave Lanson has laid bare many of our prejudices concerning the eighteenth century forms one of his best-established claims upon our gratitude. Numerous investigators, Frenchmen and Americans especially, have since followed upon the path that he pointed out. Lanson's ideas in their turn have become accepted opinion, and doubtless it will be necessary

---

[1] It is well known that the documentation used by Taine has been checked by Aulard, with disastrous results for the philosopher, who is revealed as a mediocre analyst of documentary evidence and a hasty statistician (*Taine historien de la Révolution française*, Colin, 1907). Aug. Cochin, in the work mentioned above, has tried with little success to defend Taine against Aulard. Paul Lacombe, in *Taine historien et sociologue* (Giard, 1909), has shown that the sociologist in Taine often causes Taine the historian to advance ready-made or stock theses. A. Mathiez in the *Revue d'Histoire moderne et contemporaine*, VIII (1906–1907), 257–284, and H. Sée in *Science et Philosophie de l'Histoire* (Alcan, 1928), 383–398, have also exposed Taine's weaknesses as a historian.

to modify and complete them in the future by adopting new points of view. It is none the less true that it is thanks to him and to Daniel Mornet after him that we can state today that the three assertions summed up earlier are contradicted by the facts. The French Revolution is truly of French origin. If certain foreigners, in particular Locke, whose name may be found at almost all the century's crossroads of ideas, did exert a real influence in France, his influence was assimilated and naturalized there.[2] It had moreover implanted itself in a group of ideas going back to Bayle, Saint-Evremond, La Mothe Le Vayer, Naudé, and Montaigne, which were quite as indigenous and "French" as the absolutism of Bossuet. The philosophical clubs and similar groups that made themselves felt in France around 1750 and played an active part after 1789 are not all revolutionary—far from it! Furthermore, the part that they played in preparing the Revolution is nowhere clearly ascertained. The role of a gigantic conspiracy attributed by some to Freemasonry is a myth.

Finally and above all, nothing justifies the assertion made with assurance by Taine that the writers of the eighteenth century were men of reason alone with no experience of the realities of life. In their time there was some use of empty rhetoric, as there is in every time; the revolutionaries for their part will cherish a type of eloquence reminiscent of the ancients, and be occasionally intoxicated with words; they will also have an ambition to proclaim universal truths and formulate principles for all men. It is not certain that this ambition is not one of the finest qualities of the French Revolution. But it would be a mistake to forget that the eighteenth century is a great

[2] Tocqueville's work, *L'Ancien Régime et la Révolution* (M. Lévy, 1856), supports a thesis which is in some respects similar to Taine's on the spirit of abstraction of the "philosophes" and the influence of their views as theorizing and dogmatic men of letters on their century; but Tocqueville's statements show more subtlety than those of Taine, even if their style is less colorful and sometimes stiffer in its dignified oratorical seriousness. The bulk of Tocqueville's work, which rests on sound documentary research, tends to prove that almost everything attributed to the Revolution (often in order to condemn it) already existed in old France. He puts especially vigorous emphasis on the ownership of land, which came more and more into peasant hands well before '89, and on the general prosperity of the country, which along with discontent increased under Louis XVI.

century in science, as much or more so in experimental science as in deductive and abstract disciplines. The works of D. Mornet have proved that eighteenth-century thinkers were on the contrary suspicious of scholastic generalizations and of systems in general: they made observations and conducted experiments. They introduced into education the taste for very detailed empiricism and for actual practice in the arts and trades. They praised techniques and described them with care. They traveled, like Montesquieu, in order to see at close hand constitutions and the way people lived by them. They cultivated the soil, in the case of the physiocrats; lived on their lands, as did Helvetius; or administered provinces, like Turgot. The most thoroughgoing revolutionaries had not, like Marx or Lenin, spent years in reading rooms; they were petty lawyers in contact with the people, like Robespierre at Arras; veterinarians like Marat; in short, provincial men who knew the lives of the peasant, the artisan, and the humble country priest of France. Taine's abstraction existed chiefly in his mind, and perhaps in that of Descartes and in a few works of Rousseau. But the Revolution was hardly Cartesian and never put into practice as a complete doctrine the ideas of the *Contrat Social*, which are moreover as contradictory as they are logical.

II

So let us differ with those who claim a priori that the Revolution sprang from the teachings of the "philosophes" only in order to justify their condemnation of both the Revolution and the teaching. But in opposition to this group, the admirers of the "philosophes" and even more the admirers of Rousseau, who was not exactly one of the "philosophes," have taken up the cudgels in an attempt to deny the responsibility or even the guilt of the eighteenth-century political writers in the upheaval that ensued. Particularly notable among these efforts is Edme Champion's abstruse but well-informed book, *Rousseau et la Révolution française* (Colin, 1909). Bringing the concept of retroactive responsibility into these matters is a questionable method. "My God!" Karl Marx is said to have exclaimed on one of the rare occasions when he seems to have called upon heaven, "preserve me from the Marxists!" Rousseau has accused himself of enough sins without our taxing his memory with the errors of his followers. Without inquiring whether the Revolution was good or bad, which would be entirely too naïve in this day, may we not be able to show how and in what way it absorbed, reflected, or brought to fruition the ideas of thinkers who had prepared it without wishing for it?

Professional historians generally tend to limit the part played by ideas in world events: the best of them devote, apparently for the sake of form, one or two chapters to the literature, painting, and music of the periods studied by their manuals. But the history of civilization and culture is still very clumsily related to general history. Historians prefer to emphasize the purely historical causes of the Revolution: financial disorder, ministerial blunders, or the hostility of parliaments that had been alienated by encroachments upon their prerogatives, etc. Perhaps in doing so they are choosing the easiest way. Their history does grasp the events, the things that change, that is, the things that would be presented in today's newspapers as facts or news—a tax measure, a famine, the dismissal of a minister, a change in the price of bread, or a treaty. But it often fails to apprehend the slow subterranean movements which minds inclined to be too matter-of-fact find intangible, until they one day make their appearance as acts that make news or usher in a historical era. Now there are cases in which they never appear as acts; and orthodox history gives scant consideration to abortive movements or history's side roads into which the past has ventured briefly only to turn back.

The history of ideas has the advantage of being able to give leisurely consideration to elements of history that changed only slowly and did not necessarily express themselves in events which demand attention by virtue of their suddenness. It would gladly declare that ideas rule the world. This would doubtless be an over-optimistic creed, if one did not add immediately that these ideas often turn into those truths wrapped in the gilt paper of falsehood that our contemporaries call in France "mystiques," or that they crystallize into a few fetish-words which imprison or falsify them. The history of the idea of progress has been sketched, although insufficiently in our opinion, by J. Delvaille and the English writer J. M. Bury. History itself would owe much to the man who would attempt to write the story of the idea of evolution, or the idea of revolution, the idea of comfort, or the idea of efficiency and the myth of success in the United States, among many others. On occasion he would have to go beyond the texts or interpret them, but this should not be forbidden provided that it is done with intellectual honesty. One must also remember the fact that the history of ideas is not simply the exposition of theoretical views expressed in philosophical writings, but at the same time the history of the deformations undergone by those ideas when other men adopt them, and also the history of the half-conscious beliefs into which ideas first clearly conceived by the few promptly transform themselves. In his lectures published in Buenos Aires in 1940 under the title *Ideas y creencias* the Spanish philosopher Ortega y Gasset has rightly claimed for these half-formulated "beliefs" a position in historical works on a par with that of ideas.

The difficulties presented by such a history of ideas when they become beliefs, articles of faith, or emotional drives and impel men to action are enormous: they should, by this very fact, challenge research men. Up to now, sociology has failed to make over the study of literature to any considerable degree because histories of the prevailing taste and the environment in which a writer lived and of the social and economic conditions in which he was placed while conceiving his work have little bearing on the creation and even the content of the original work. But a knowledge of the public that greeted a literary work or of the work's subsequent career might on the contrary prove extremely fruitful. Such knowledge requires painstaking inquiry into the work's success, based on a great number of facts; it also demands a qualitative interpretation of history and statistics and the occasional intervention of that much feared "queen of the world" called imagination. For the most read book is not the one that exerts the greatest influence. A hundred thousand passive or half-attentive readers who bought and even leafed through the *Encyclopédie*, for example, count for less than five hundred passionate admirers of the *Contrat Social* if among the latter may be counted Robespierre, Saint-Just or Babeuf. A schoolmaster or a lecturer heard with interest may pass on Marx or Nietzsche to generations of barely literate people who will never guess the source of a thought that has modified their whole lives. It is not even necessary to have understood a book or even to have read it through in order to be profoundly influenced by it. An isolated phrase quoted in some article or a page reproduced at some time in an anthology may have done more to spread some of the opinions of Montesquieu, Proudhon, or Gobineau that thirty re-editions of their writings bought by private libraries and commented upon by ten provincial academies.

In 1933 Daniel Mornet published on the subject sketched here his work entitled *Les Origines intellectuelles de la Révolution française* (Colin), which is a study of the spread of ideas justly termed a model of intellectual probity and discretion. Henceforth no one can consider this historical and philosophical problem without owing much to this solid book. The author has avoided the error of so many other writers who make the Revolution inexplicable by drawing a rough contrast between 1789 and 1670 or even 1715. He has followed the slow progress of the spread of new ideas from 1715 to 1747, then from 1748 to 1770, the date when the philosophic spirit had won the day. He has made very searching inquiries into the degree of penetration of the reformist spirit among the more or less learned societies and academies, in the letters of private individuals, in provincial libraries, and even in educational curricula. His conclusions are new in many respects because of the exact information they offer and because they show those who are misled by the perspective of a later day into the error of limiting the group of "philosophes" to five or six names, that writers half-unknown to us (Toussaint, Delisle de Sales, Morellet, Mably) were among those most widely read in the eighteenth century. With fitting reserve they tend to show that the thought of the century, by itself, would never have caused the Revolution if there had not been misery among the people as well; and that misery, which was not a new thing at the time, would not have brought about the Revolution if it had not had the support of opinion that had long been discontented and desirous of reform. It is clear that the Revolution had various causes including historical causes, meaning economic, political, and financial causes, as well as intellectual ones. However it would seem that Mornet has limited the role of the latter causes to an excessive degree and further work still needs to be done after his admirable effort.

The most obvious justification for further research lies in the fact that his investigation leaves off at 1787 because of the very purpose of his work. Now if a revolution was ready to break out at the time of the preparation of the "Cahiers de doléances" for the States-General it was not the Revolution that actually developed. Neither the days of June 20 and August 10, 1792, nor the death of Louis XVI, nor the Terror, nor the constructive work of the Convention was contained in germ in the convocation of the States-General. In fact we know very little about the influence of Montesquieu, Voltaire, and Rousseau himself on the different phases of the Revolution or the way in which they influenced certain actors in the great drama.

The special quality of the French Revolution, compared with other revolutionary movements in France or other countries, obviously lies not only in the titanic proportions of this upheaval but also in an ardent passion for thought, for embodying ideas in deeds, and for proposing universal laws. This accounts for the unparalleled world-wide influence of the work of destruction and construction which was accomplished between 1789 and 1795. An abstract passion for justice and liberty, the latter being sometimes conceived in strange fashion, inspired the men who made the Revolution and those who prepared it. The original tone that characterizes the Revolution and the verve that enlivens it, which are fundamental things although they elude the grasp of facts and figures, are due in part to the movement of thought and sensibility which goes from Montesquieu to Rousseau and from Bayle to the abbé Raynal.

III

If there is really one almost undisputed conclusion on the origins of the Revolution reached by historical studies coming from radically opposite factions, it is that pure historical materialism does not explain the Revolution. Certainly riots due to hunger were numerous in the eighteenth century and Mornet draws up the list of them; there was discontent and agitation among the masses. But such had also been the case under Louis XIV, such was the case under Louis-Philippe, and deep discontent existed in France in 1920 and 1927 and 1934 without ending in revolution. No great event in history has been due to causes chiefly economic in nature and certainly not the French Revolution. France was not happy in 1788, but she was happier than the other countries of Europe and enjoyed veritable economic prosperity. Her population had increased from nineteen to twenty-six or twenty-eight million since the beginning of the century and was the most numerous in Europe. French roads and bridges were a source of admiration to foreigners. Her industries such as ship-fitting at Bordeaux, the silk industry at Lyons, and the textile industry at Rouen, Sedan, and Amiens were active, while Dietrich's blast furnaces and the Creusot were beginning to develop modern techniques in metallurgy. The peasants were little by little coming to be owners of the land. Foreign trade reached the sum of 1,153 million francs in 1787, a figure not to be attained again until 1825. The traffic in colonial spices and San Domingo sugar was a source of wealth. Banks were being founded and France owned half the specie existing in Europe. So misery in France was no more than relative. But truly wretched peoples such as the Egyptian fellah, the pariah of India, or even the Balkan or Polish peasant or Bolivian miners, for example, rarely bring about revolutions. In order to revolt against one's lot, one must be aware of his wretched condition, which presupposes a certain intellectual and cultural level; one must have a clear conception of certain reforms that one would like to adopt; in short, one must be convinced (and it was on this point that the books of the eighteenth century produced their effect) that things are not going well, that they might be better, and that they will be better if the measures proposed by the reformist thinkers are put into practice.

Eighteenth-century philosophy taught the Frenchman to find his condition wretched, or in any case, unjust and illogical, and made him disinclined to the patient resignation to his troubles that had long characterized his ancestors. It had never called for a revolution or desired a change of regime; it had never been republican, and Camille Desmouslins was not wrong in stating: "In all France there were not ten of us who were republicans before 1789." Furthermore he himself was not one of those ten. But only an oversimplified conception of influence would indulge in the notion that political upheaval completely embodies in reality the theoretical design drawn up by some thinker. Even the Russian revolution, imbued as it was with Marxian dialectic, did not make a coherent application of Marxism, or quickly found it inapplicable when tried. The reforms of limited scope advocated by *L'Esprit des Lois, L'Homme aux quarante écus,*

L'Encyclopédie, and the more moderate writings of Rousseau struck none the less deeply at the foundations of the ancien régime, for they accustomed the Frenchman of the Third Estate to declaring privileges unjust, to finding the crying differences between the provinces illogical and finding famines outrageous. The propaganda of the "philosophes" perhaps more than any other factor accounted for the fulfillment of the preliminary condition of the French Revolution, namely, discontent with the existing state of things.

In short, without enlarging upon what is already rather well known, we may say that eighteenth-century writers prepared the way for the Revolution, without wishing for it, because:

(a) They weakened the traditional religion, winning over to their side a great number of clerics, and taught disrespect for an institution which had been the ally of the monarchy for hundreds of years. At the same time they had increased the impatience of the non-privileged groups by uprooting from many minds the faith in a future life which had formerly made bearable the sojourn in this vale of tears that constituted life for many people of low estate. They wished to enjoy real advantages here on earth and without delay. The concept of well-being and then that of comfort slowly penetrated among them.

(b) They taught a secular code of ethics, divorced from religious belief, independent of dogma, and made the ideal of conduct consist of observation of this system of ethics, which was presented as varying in accordance with climate and environment. Furthermore they gave first importance in this ethical code to the love of humanity, altruism, and service due society or our fellow men. The ideas of humanity, already present in the teaching of Christ, in Seneca and Montaigne, but often dormant, suddenly exerted fresh influence over people's minds.

(c) They developed the critical spirit and the spirit of analysis and taught many men not to believe, or to suspend judgment rather than accept routine traditions. In D'Argenson, Chamfort, Morelly, Diderot, Voltaire of course, D'Holbach, Condillac, and many others, and even in Laclos and Sade, we will find the effort to think courageously without regard for convention or tradition that will henceforth characterize the French intellectual attitude. From this time on, inequality with respect to taxation, the tithe paid to the Church, and banishment or persecution for subversive opinions will shock profoundly the sense of logic and critical spirit of the readers of the "philosophes."

(d) Lastly, these very thinkers who have often been depicted as builders of utopias are the creators of history or the historical sense, or almost so. Montesquieu studiously examined the origins of law and constitutions and saw men "conditioned" by soil and climate in contrast to the absolute rationalists, who were foreign jurists and not Frenchmen. Boulainvilliers and many others of lesser fame studied France's past. Voltaire's masterpiece is probably his work on general history. The result of this curiosity about history was twofold: it encouraged faith in progress and convinced numbers of Frenchmen that it was their task to fulfill humanity's law, to endeavor to increase the sum of liberty, relative equality, "enlightenment," and happiness in the world; it also proved to many men of the law who examined old documents and the titles of nobility and property that the privileges of nobility were based on a flimsy foundation. The respect that these bourgeois or sons of the people might have felt for the aristocrats was accordingly diminished, at the very moment when the bourgeois saw the nobles not only accept with admiration but take under their protection destructive writings produced by the pens of commoners: sons of tailors (Marmontel), vine growers (Restif), cutlers (Diderot) and watchmakers (Rousseau). And the history of the origins of royal sovereignty itself seemed to them scarcely more edifying than that of the feudal privileges.

As for the means of dissemination of those ideas or new beliefs that the "philosophes" were spreading between the years 1715 and 1770 or 1789, it will suffice to enumerate them rapidly, for numerous studies have examined them: they were the salons, although very few of the future revolutionaries frequented society gatherings; the clubs that more and more called for tolerance, preached deism, demanded the abolition of slavery (Société des Amis des Noirs) and dreamed of imitating the American Revolution (Club Américain); books or tracts which made their appearance as works of small format, easily carried or hidden, lively and sharp in style and prone to surprise and arouse the reader; periodicals; the theatre, especially after the coming of the "drame bourgeois" and the "comédie larmoyante," and then with

Beaumarchais; and the education given in the secondary schools. Mornet's book sums up the essential material on the subject that can be found in documents. The other means of spreading new ideas, such as conversation, which is doubtless the most effective means man has always used to borrow and pass on new views, elude documentary research.

It is among the actors in the great revolutionary drama that investigations of broader scope might show us which of the ideas of the eighteenth century exerted influence and how and why they did so. Siéyès, among others, has been the subject of an exhaustive intellectual biography which has established with precision what the young abbé coming to Paris from Fréjus to devise constitutions owed to Descartes, Locke, and Voltaire in particular (for the negative side of his ideas), to Rousseau (for his impassioned logic), and to Mably (Paul Bastid, *Siéyès et sa pensée*, Hachette, 1939). Another good book, by Gérard Walter, is a study of Babeuf (Payot, 1937). It would be instructive to know how the minds of many of the revolutionaries were developed and by what books and meditations they were influenced; such men range from Mirabeau and Danton to Marat, from Rabaut de Saint-Etienne to Hérault de Séchelles, and from Desmoulins or Brissot to generals of the Convention who may have read Raynal and Rousseau with passionate interest, as Bonaparte did later. Only when many monographs have been written devoting at least as much if not more attention to the history of ideas and the psychology of the pro-tagonists in the Revolution than to the facts of their lives of action will we be able to make sure generalizations about the influence of Montesquieu or Rousseau on the France of '89 or '93.

IV

Montesquieu and Rousseau are certainly the two great names worthy of consideration in some detail. The presiding judge of the High Court of Bordeaux obviously did not want the Revolution; had he lived to see it, he would not have approved of its reorganization of the judiciary, or its audacity in reform, or the Declaration of the Rights of Man, or even the interpretation of certain principles he himself had enunciated. Still he is one of the spiritual fathers of the first two revolutionary assemblies. Like so many other men who have made history, he influenced the fateful years of 1789–1792 by what he did say almost involuntarily, by the thoughts other men read into his sentences and by the tone even more than by the content of his writings. His great work breathes a veritable hatred of despotism founded on fear; it shows no moral respect for monarchy, and so helped to alienate the most reasonable minds from it. The great principle of the separation of powers presumes the right to seize from the king the united powers that he believed he held as a whole by divine right. Finally, Montesquieu, however elevated his position as a citizen or as a magistrate may have been, uttered words which will assume a mystic authority in later times on the subject of the people's inherent good qualities and their ability to select their leaders: "The common people are admirable in choosing those to whom they must delegate some part of their authority" (II, ii), or "When the common people once have sound principles, they adhere to them longer than those we are wont to call respectable people. Rarely does corruption have its beginning among the people" (V, ii).

Finally, in his admirable XIth book, Montesquieu had defined liberty in terms that were to remain etched in people's memories: this liberty required stable laws, which alone could establish and protect it. Those laws were also to correct economic inequality. Certainly its historical examples adduced in great profusion, highly technical juridical considerations, certain generalizations that had been too cleverly made symmetrical, and its lack of order made this voluminous treatise hard to read. But Montesquieu's influence was not one of those that can be gauged by the number of readers: it expressed itself in action thanks to a few thoughtful minds who found in it a sufficiently coherent over-all plan capable of replacing the old order, which obviously was crumbling. Montesquieu's influence inspired a more important group of revolutionaries who were familiar with only a few chapters of his work, but these chapters were filled with the love of freedom and the great feeling for humanity that condemned slavery and the iniquitous exploitation of some men by others.

Montesquieu's influence on the French Revolution began to decline at the time when Rousseau's was coming to the fore. Many studies have been devoted to the subject of Rousseau and the French Revolution; and the subject deserves still further study, for perhaps no more notable case of the effect of thought on life exists in the whole history of ideas and of dynamic ideas in particular. But this broad subject has too often been narrowed down by the most well-meaning historians. So many dogmatic and partisan statements had portrayed Rousseau as the great malefactor who was guilty of the excesses committed by the Terrorists and as the father of collectivism that, as a reaction, the best-disposed scholars set about proving by facts and texts that the author of the *Contrat Social* was guiltless of so many misdeeds. As a result they have belittled his influence. But there is some narrowness and naïveté in these scholarly arguments.

According to some, everything that Rousseau wrote already existed, before his coming, in the works of a number of writers and thinkers both at home and abroad and Jean-Jacques brought forth very little that was new. That is quite possible, and scholars have been able to make fruitful inquiries into the sources of the *Discours sur l'Inégalité* and the *Contrat*. But the fact remains that whatever Rousseau borrowed from others he made his own; he rethought it and above all felt it with a new intensity and set it off to advantage by his own passion and his own talent. What he owes to Plato or Locke suddenly shook the men of 1792 only because Rousseau had charged it with a new electric current.

Furthermore Rousseau is rife with contradictions, and the most ingenious men of learning (Lanson, Höffding, Schinz, and E. H. Wright) have not yet succeeded in convincing us of the unity of his thought. For Corsica and Poland he proposes finely adapted and moderate constitutions that do not seem to have sprung from the same brain as the *Contrat Social*. He writes a very conservative article on *L'Economie politique* for the fifth volume of the *Encyclopédie*, while in his second *Discours* he had propounded anarchical theses burning with revolutionary ardor. "To expect one to be always consistent is beyond human possibility, I fear!" he himself had admitted in the second preface of the *Nouvelle Héloïse*. We will not go so far as to pày homage to Rousseau for his contradictions, and may choose to reserve our unalloyed admiration for other systems of thought more dispassionate and logical than his. But an author's influence does not have much to do with the rigor and coherence of his philosophical system. In fact, it would not be hard to show that the thinkers who have contributed the most toward changing the face of the world exerted influence because of their contradictions, since very different periods and highly diverse individuals drew from them various messages of equal validity. Let us add with no ironic intention that because of this the ingenuity of the learned will never tire of seeking the impossible golden key to these disconcerting enigmas, and that the hunger for systems, among those lacking the necessary imagination to construct new ones, will always exert itself to bring about a happy synthesis of the successive assertions of a Plato, a Montaigne, a Locke, Rousseau, Comte, or Nietzsche.[3]

After all, as the historians tell us quite correctly, the *Contrat Social* is only a part of Rousseau's political thought, and not the most important part in the eyes of his contemporaries; the author himself attributed only a rather limited importance to this logical utopian book. Rousseau never seriously contemplated a revolution in France; he did not think that a republic was viable, or perhaps even desirable for France. One might even make the assertion supported by texts that Jean-Jacques, that bête noire of the anti-revolutionaries from Burke to Maurras, Lasserre, and Seillière, was a timid conservative.[4]

[3] "Inconsistencies are the characteristic quality of men who have thought much, created abundantly and destroyed on a broad scale. They have necessarily said many things and among those things there are a great many that are at variance or even directly contrary to one another." This is the comment on Rousseau made in an article pertinent to the present subject by the solid founder of the School of Political Science, Emile Boutmy, in "La Déclaration des Droits de l'Homme et du citoyen et M. Jellineck," *Annales des Sciences politiques*, 1902, pp. 415–443.

[4] Rousseau has depicted himself in the third of his *Dialogues* as "the man who is more averse to revolution than any one else in the world, . . . who has always insisted upon the maintenance of the existing institutions, contending that their destruction would only take away the palliative while leaving their faults and substitute brigandage for corruption." It is true that here he is making an effort to present himself in the most favorable light! In his *Jugement sur la Polysynodie de l'abbé de Saint-Pierre* (Vaughan, *The Political Writings of Rousseau* [Cambridge, 1915], I, 416), he gave the following warning in 1756: "Think of the danger of once displacing the enormous masses that make up the French monarchy! Who will be able to check the shock once it is given or foresee the effects it may produce?" In the eighth of his *Lettres de la Montagne*, he again exclaims: "Eh! How could I approve of any one's disturbing the peace of the State for any interest whatsoever . . . ?"

It is quite true (D. Mornet has proved this once again) that the influence of the *Contrat Social* was very weak between the years 1762 and 1789; the book caused so little disturbance that Rousseau was not even molested; and it is probable that Rousseau would have been frightened by certain inferences that were later drawn from his ideas. What he wrote in 1765 in no way justifies an assertion on our part that he would still have written the same thing in 1793, and so it is quite as conceivable that Rousseau might have violently changed his point of view and espoused the cause of the revolutionaries, had he lived long enough to receive their acclaim. And above all, without having consciously wanted the Revolution, Rousseau did a great deal, if not to cause it, at least to give it direction when it had broken out. The success of Rousseau's works and the reception accorded them in his lifetime have been investigated in sufficient detail. From now on, groups of research men might well give their attention to the enormous influence Rousseau exerted on the men of the Convention and on those of the Empire or the Restoration or on the romantics. Granted that Rousseau was neither a republican nor a revolutionary, he was in revolt, and that is no less important. A. Aulard, who was not inclined to overestimate the influence of the intellectuals on the French Revolution, nevertheless accurately described the paradoxical result of any fairly broad study of this subject: "All these men in revolt want to keep the monarchy and all of them blindly deal it mortal blows. The French, monarchists to a man, take on republicanism without their knowledge."[5]

Not one of the men of the Revolution adopted Rousseau's philosophical system outright in order to put it into practice; that is only too plain. Not one of them understood Rousseau's thought in its subtleties, its contradictions, and its alterations as the scholar of the present day can understand it with the aid of much posthumous documentation: this is scarcely less obvious. Whatever chagrin it may cause minds devoted to strict methods, the unparalleled effect produced on the imagination of posterity by Montaigne, Rousseau, or Nietzsche can be credited to quotations drawn from their contexts and probably perverted from their original sense. This influence is not

[5] A. Aulard, "L'Idée républicaine et démocratique avant 1789," in the *Révolution française*, July–December 1898, tome 35, pp. 5–45.

so much an influence of ideas as it is an influence of "idées-forces," to use Fouillée's expression, and exerts its power more by setting men's sensibilities aflame than by convincing their minds.

"Man is born free, and everywhere he is in chains." This peremptory formula from the first chapter of the *Contrat Social*, in conjunction with a few others which declared the sovereignty of the people inalienable and affirmed the right to revolt in the event of the usurpation of powers by the government, contributed immeasurably toward crystallizing in the general mind from 1789 on the resolve to make the king subject to the only true rights which were inherent in the people. On October 5, 1789, Robespierre and Barère contended that the sovereign could not oppose the constituent power which was superior to him. The passion for equality which wildly inspires the revolutionaries and the modern world after them owes no less to Rousseau's fundamental idea that law should rectify natural inequality (which he was not foolish enough to overlook) by means of civic equality. The XIth chapter of the second book of the *Contrat Social* stated in striking terms: "For the very reason that the force of things always tends to destroy equality, the force of legislation must always tend to maintain it." The third book of the same work castigated the vices to which kings are prone, for if they are not narrow or evil on attaining the throne, "the throne will make them so." That does not make Rousseau a partisan of republicanism or a democrat; but had it not been for such aphorisms, Saint-Just never would have proclaimed in his fine *Discours concernant le jugement de Louis XVI* of November 13, 1792: "Royalty is an eternal crime against which every man has the right to rise up and take arms. . . . One can not reign in innocence."

The *Discours sur l'Inégalité* contained pages of impassioned rhetoric that were even more effective. The English writer C. E. Vaughan, who is a scrupulous commentator on the political writings of Rousseau, did not hesitate to state, after years of reflection of this subject: "Wherever, during the last century and a half, man has revolted against injustice and oppression, there we may be sure that the leaven of the second *Discours* has been working" (*The Political Writings of Rousseau*, I, 5). Doubtless Rousseau had never dreamed of the application of his declamations against property; but he had set forth the idea that inheritances ought to be whittled down by fiscal measures and that those who owned no lands ought to receive some, without necessarily advocating collectivism. He had also uttered against wealth words whose echoes will ring down the centuries: "It is the estate of the wealthy that steals from mine the bread of my children. . . . A bond-holder whom the State pays for doing nothing is scarcely different in my eyes from a highwayman who lives at the expense of the passers-by . . . , every idle citizen is a rogue."

The precautions with which Jean-Jacques had surrounded some of his bold affirmations quickly disappeared in the heat of action. The chapter called "Du Peuple," in the *Contrat Social* (Book ii, ch. 8), was most cautious; but its author had nevertheless hinted in it that sometimes, in the life of peoples, "the State, set aflame by civil wars, is so to speak reborn from its ashes, and regains the vigor of youth in leaving the arms of death." People retained phrases from the *Emile*, too—the prophetic phrases in which the educator had proclaimed to the people of his time that they were approaching the era of revolutions when men would be able to destroy what men had built. These few phrases, gaining added violence in tone from the fact that they were detached from contexts that often contradicted them, seemed charged with new meaning when the great upheaval had broken out. Such was also the case of the mystic system of happiness taught by the Genevan "philosophe's" entire work. Man is born good; he is made to be happy; he may become so if he reforms himself and if his governments are reformed. We know how the echo of these doctrines will resound in the noble formulas of Saint-Just, who was perhaps the revolutionary most deeply steeped in Rousseau's thought.[6]

[6] On March 3, 1794 (13 Ventose An II), "The Archangel of the Terror," as Michelet calls Saint-Just, declared before the Convention: "Let Europe learn that you no longer want either a single unhappy victim of oppression or an oppressor in French territory; let this example bear fruit upon the earth; let it spread abroad the love of virtue and of happiness! Happiness is a new idea in Europe." In his *Fragments sur les institutions républicaines*, published after his death, the young disciple of Rousseau and the Romans wrote: "The day that I am convinced that it is impossible to instill in the French people ways that are mild, energetic and responsive but merciless against tyranny and injustice, I will stab myself." It is regrettable that there is in existence only an inadequate Swiss dissertation by S. B. Kritschewsky, *Rousseau und Saint-Just* (Bern, 1859)

The aspect of Rousseau that Albert Schinz called "the Roman Rousseau" exerted no less influence on that other myth which prevailed or raged among the men of the Revolution (and among the women, too, as in the case of Madame Rolland)—the myth of the ancients and their passion for liberty and virtue. "The world has been empty since the day of the Romans," cried Saint-Just; and he stated to the Convention on February 24, 1793: "The Republic is not a Senate, it is virtue." The whole of Saint-Just's remarkable youthful work entitled *Esprit de la Révolution et de la Constitution de la France* is imbued with Rousseauist themes and ends on this cry of regret: "France has only now conferred a statue upon J.-J. Rousseau. Ah! Why is that great man dead?"

Robespierre, whom Michelet maliciously called a "weak and pale bastard of Rousseau" because of his cult of the Supreme Being, was indebted to Rousseau to no lesser degree than Saint-Just, although he does not show the mark of the born writer that stamps the formulas of the terrorist guillotined at the age of twenty-seven. It was by assiduous reading of Rousseau that he formed his style: and his style served him as a powerful weapon. It seems that the young student from Arras met Rousseau in 1778, the year of his death, and never forgot it. "I saw thee in thy last days, and this memory is a source of proud joy for me," he declared later in his *Mémoires*, placed under the aegis of Rousseau, and promised to "remain constantly faithful to the inspiration that I have drawn from thy writings." Dozens of sentences which reiterate formulas from the *Contrat Social* might be extracted from his speeches. It was Rousseau who had helped to turn Robespierre away from Catholicism, and of course he was the man from whom Robespierre borrowed his cult of the Supreme Being; his *Observations sur le projet d'Instruction publique* presented to the Convention in 1793 are based on the Rousseauist faith: "If nature created man good, it is back to nature that we must bring him." His speech made at the Jacobin Club on January 2, 1792, against the war at that time desired by the Girondins rendered homage to Rousseau in impassioned terms: "No one has given us a more exact idea of the

on the fine subject that the influence of Rousseau and other eighteenth-century thinkers on Saint-Just's noble thought would make.

common people than Rousseau because no one loved them more."[7] The secret of the enormous influence exerted by Rousseau lay less in the substance of his thought than in the burning tone of a man who had lived his ideas and had suffered (or thought he had) because he had sprung from the people and had known poverty. "According to the principles of your committee," declared Robespierre to the Constituent Assembly on August 11, 1791, "we ought to blush at having erected a statue to J.-J. Rousseau, because he did not pay the property-tax." The history of ideas and their influence on persons and things is full of elements that defy all possibility of quantitative or statistical measurement. How can one estimate all that the men of the Revolution owed Rousseau in the way of fervor, mystic hope, logic that was impassioned and even fierce on occasion, and—what is not less important, even for history, as Danton, Saint-Just, and Robespierre were aware—the imperious and incisive style that made their formulas resound in twenty countries and across one hundred and fifty years? "One does not make revolutions by halves," or "the French people are voting for liberty for the world"—these aphorisms or decrees of Saint-Just, like certain phrases of Mirabeau, or a multitude of orators of lesser stature,[8] and of Bonaparte himself,

[7] Here again this large subject deserves a lengthier and more recent monograph than the thesis of Richard Schass, *J. J. Rousseaus Einfluss auf Robespierre* (Leipzig, 1905).

[8] Among the speakers heard with interest at the time, one might mention D'Eymar, who had the honors of the Pantheon voted to Rousseau; Rabaut de Saint-Etienne, who often quoted Rousseau as one of the precursors of the revolution; the abbé Fauchet, who expounded the *Contrat* before a numerous audience, in 1790, at the "Universal confederation of the Friends of Truth." Mirabeau had long since (letter to Sophie of December 8, 1778) extolled "the sublime creative genius" of Rousseau, and had had homage paid to his widow on May 12, 1790. Marat had, so it is said, annotated the *Contrat* in 1788, and his sister Albertine testified how much he admired it. Let us hope that some historian with a knowledge of psychology will some day treat the great subject of "Napoleon I and Rousseau." Even the remarks of the Emperor in old age show that he was attracted by Rousseau: the *Nouvelle Héloïse* was one of the first books he read on Saint Helena. At the height of his glory, in 1806, he thought of organizing an official tribute to Rousseau, according to Stanislas Girardin. This same Girardin, in a curious passage in his *Mémoires* (Michaud, 1834, I, 190), reports

would not have been uttered, and would not have had the resonance that has kept them alive, if these men had not been imbued with the spirit and the style of the Citizen of Geneva.

The history of the cult of Rousseau during the French Revolution is easier to trace than that of his deep influence on the revolutionaries. The former has been studied in part, and the manifestations of this idolatry of Rousseau are often amusing. The setting up of the bust of Jean-Jacques in the Constituent Assembly on June 23, 1790; the consecration of a street of Paris named after him in the same year; the repeated editions of the *Contrat Social* (four editions in 1790, three in 1791, etc.); the constitutional articles put under his aegis; the decree ordering that Rousseau's ashes be brought to the Pantheon in 1794 and the pious emotion of the crowd; and lastly, the invocation to "his generous soul" by the Incorruptible One in his speech of May 7, 1794, on the religion of the Revolution, and the pompous application of his declamations on the Supreme Being—all these things have been mentioned more than once, and recently, too.[9] But the way in which Rousseau's influence profoundly modified the men and women of the revolutionary and imperial eras, and then the romantics great and small, and the continuators of the Revolution, in and out of France, in the nineteenth and twentieth centuries—these are the questions that intellectual history seems to have been reluctant to investigate.

Its timidity is regrettable and our knowledge of the past suffers twice over because of it: first, because history that devotes itself too exclusively to what we call material facts such as a military victory,

---

this reflection (did he understand it correctly?) of the First Consul at Ermonville: "The future will tell whether it would not have been better for the peace of the earth if Rousseau and I had not existed."

[9] See Gordon McNeil, "The Cult of Rousseau in the French Revolution," *Journal of the History of Ideas*, April 1945, pp. 196–212. Monglond's work *Le Préromantisme français* (Grenoble: Arthaud, 1930) contains, especially in the second volume, chapters i and vi, the most thought-provoking evidence on the effect produced by Rousseau on sensitive souls of the revolutionary era. Monglond quotes (II, 157) the curious sentence in which Bernardin de Saint-Pierre, in his *Etudes de la Nature*, had proclaimed some years before '89: "It seems to me that some favorable revolution is in store for us. If it comes, it will be letters that we will have to thank for it. . . . Oh men of letters! . . . You alone recall the rights of man and of Divinity."

the fall of a ministry or the opening up of a railroad track, seriously falsifies our perspective of what took place. The development of the Napoleonic legend, the quietly working influence of Rousseau or Voltaire, the growth of anti-clericalism, and the elaboration of socialist myths are phenomena which are partly literary or senti-mental in nature, but are second to no other order of phenomena in importance and in the effects they had on the course of human affairs. Our knowledge of the past suffers additionally because historians, by turning aside from the history of ideas and sentiments with their vigorous influence on the lives of men, abandon these research subjects to men less well trained than themselves in exact methods of study; the latter are disposed to write with the sole intent of finding in the past arguments to support their political views or their partisan claims. Meanwhile youth is tempted to reject history as it is officially presented—as an endless series of wars, diplomatic ruses, crimes, examples of intense selfishness and the impotent efforts of men to bring more reason into the world. It refuses to lend credence to those who advise it that man has remained a religious and ideological animal even more than an economic creature. Youth's awakening, when it is suddenly placed face to face with the terrible power of ideas, myths, and fanaticisms in the world, is sometimes a rude shock, as we have seen in our time.

The Frenchmen in particular who have thought fit in the past few years to deny their eighteenth-century thinkers as traitors to the classic and monarchical tradition of France have only to open their eyes in order to ascertain that no French tradition is more alive than that of the Century of Enlightenment. Pascal and Descartes are doubtless greater; Montaigne has more charm and Saint Thomas more logical power: but it is Voltaire and Rousseau, and sometimes Montesquieu and Condorcet, that one finds almost always behind the living influence of France on the masses and the ideologies of South America, of the United States itself, of Central and Eastern Europe, and that one will find tomorrow in Africa and Asia. The world of today expects from post-war France, and France herself expects from her political thinkers who lost the habit of expressing themselves in universal terms during the last fifty years, a renewal and a modernization of her liberal ideas of the eighteenth century, boldly adapted to the social and economic problems of today, but still inspired by the same faith in man and his possibilities.

Students from other countries remind the French of this fact, lest they forget it too readily. Their studies on the influence of Voltaire and Rousseau on the French Revolution and the revolutions that ensued elsewhere in the world are becoming more numerous and sometimes more objective than the French ones. A Slavic scholar, Milan Markovitch, in a large and exhaustive book on *Rousseau et Tolstoi* (Champion, 1928) set forth in detail the Rousseauism of the Russian novelist, who in his adolescence carried the portrait of Jean-Jacques around his neck like a scapular and wrote the following message to the newly founded Rousseau Club on March 7, 1905: "Rousseau has been my teacher since the age of fifteen. Rousseau and the Gospel have been the two great influences for good in my life." The German thinker Ernst Cassirer devoted a little book written in 1945 to commemoration of the admiration for Rousseau expressed by Goethe and Fichte as well as Kant, who declared: "Rousseau set me right. . . . I learned to respect human nature." [10] Thoreau and D. H. Lawrence are indebted to the Genevan for a good half of their thinking. George Eliot, on meeting the philosopher Emerson in Coventry in 1848, found herself being asked by him what her favorite book was; Rousseau's *Confessions*, she answered; at which the American transcendentalist cried: "It is mine too." Shortly afterwards, on February 9, 1849, she wrote Sara Hennel these extremely lucid sentences on the mechanism of intellectual influence:

I wish you thoroughly to understand that the writers who have most profoundly influenced me are not in the least oracles to me. . . . For instance, it would signify nothing to me if a very wise person were to stun me with proofs that Rousseau's views of life, religion, and government were miserably erroneous,—that he was guilty of some of the worst *bassesses* that have degraded civilized man. I might admit all this: and it would be not the less true that Rousseau's genius has sent that electric thrill through my intellectual and moral frame which has awakened me to new perceptions; . . . and this not by teaching me any new belief. . . .

[10] Ernst Cassirer, *Rousseau, Kant and Goethe* (Princeton University Press, 1945).

The fire of his genius has so fused together old thoughts and prejudices, that I have been ready to make new combinations.[11]

In the face of such proofs of a fruitful and life-giving though possibly dangerous influence, an important English historian who was moreover an admirer of Burke and usually more moderate in his statements, but was conscious of the importance of ideas in the events of this world, Lord Acton, was impelled to exclaim: "Rousseau produced more effect with his pen than Aristotle, or Cicero, or St. Augustine, or St. Thomas Aquinas, or any other man who ever lived."[12]

[11] For this reference and the one preceding, we are indebted to Professor Gordon Haight, who is thoroughly familiar with all that touches on George Eliot.

[12] This quotation from Lord Acton is given by Herbert Paul as uttered in his presence (Lord Acton, *Letters to Mary Gladstone* [New York: Macmillan, 1904], p. 10).

4 | NAPOLEON: DEVIL, POET, SAINT

THERE PROBABLY does not exist a single nation which has not, at some time or other, been diagnosed as suffering from a split personality. All the familiar antinomies of hostile forces magnified into gods or myths (Eros-Thanatos, inferiority-superiority, love as agape against love as a sado-masochist traumatism) wage fights inside every country as the twin souls do in Faust's breast. Individuals and nations could at one time deny such schizophrenia in themselves; they preferred to brand their foes with it in wartime, or that other foe in the war of sexes. Freud and C. J. Jung have now taught us proudly to claim, as the latter expresses it, "disagreement with oneself as the distinctive sign of the civilized man." The most tightly welded together and the most anciently unified of all modern nations, France, can also be the most divided politically and, at times, intellectually. It seldom can bear to gaze at its past placidly and to be reconciled to accepting it in its entirety. No children of any other land have the greatness of their history so insistently dinned into their ears; no other citizens have to rest, or to close, their eyes on so many statues of kings, queens, warriors, royal concubines, local worthies (Napoleon alone being conspicuous by his absence from these stone effigies). But none relish disagreement on their past more heartily. The Bonapartist myth has succeeded the Napoleonic legend and insidiously lurks behind many a corner of French political life to this very day. But Napoleon's detractors are also more relentless in their scorn of "lui partout, lui toujours" than are even the descendants of the

British, of the Germans, of the Spaniards whom that conqueror frightened or humiliated.

Rancor, spite, political dissent, the clear-sightedness of men of intellect long baffled by the denial given to all rational forecasts by an imaginative genius, aristocratic prejudices aroused against an upstart who had humiliated the European nobility while pampering it, all combined to inspire several of the sharpest denunciations of Napoleon by men of letters among his contemporaries: Chateaubriand; Benjamin Constant, whose *De l'Esprit de Conquête*, published early in 1814, must rank among the very greatest political writings ever to appear in the French language; and Lamartine. The last named, in 1822–1823, upon hearing of Napoleon's death at Saint Helena and after reading Manzoni's ode on that death, composed a long meditation, "Bonaparte," more felicitous, if longer, than either Blake's or Shelley's declamatory stanzas on the same theme. Lamartine wrongly imagined (as we know today from General Bertrand's *Cahiers de Sainte-Hélène*, published in 1959) that the dying conqueror had, *in extremis*, raised his eyes to heaven for a sign of the Redeemer. He concluded with a hesitant plea to divine charity, which might admit genius to be a form of virtue and pardon Bonaparte, the new Attila; but he later regretted that concession to the blasphemous cult of a greatness which was not tempered by holiness.

> Et vous, fléau de Dieu, qui sait si le génie
> N'est pas une de vos vertus?

Auguste Barbier's dashingly eloquent satire, "La Cavale," once learned by heart by most French children when their primary school teachers endeavored to instill true love for the lay, anti-militarist Republic into them, actually aroused in many of them a limitless admiration for the relentless horseman indicted in the poem. Such was the case with many another literary enemy of Napoleon in France, among conservative Catholics and leftist liberals alike. Those who on the contrary tried to serve the memory of the Emperor in their painstaking histories, like Adolphe Thiers, fell so far short of the mark that they belittled their hero. Indeed, it is to be wondered at that so few detractors of the tyrant ever sprang from the ranks of the republicans during the years, under the Second Empire, when the Republic loomed so beautiful in retrospect or in anticipation, or have arisen from among the socialists or the Communists in our own century. They must have respected in Napoleon the image of a crowned revolution, of a Robespierre on horseback, the successor, as he liked to call himself, of the Committee of Public Safety: the man who freed Europe of the litter of medieval feudalism and thus cleared the ground for the novel idea of equality—or of fraternity imposed with the threat of a pistol.

Tocqueville (even in his correspondence with Gobineau), Renan, who at the end of his life praised the French Revolution as perhaps the best deed ever performed by France and who had long envied the German universities their Fichtes, Hegels, Creutzers—all of them Napoleon's contemporaries—have remained surprisingly reticent about the man they might have branded as the foe of historical speculation and of philological research. The only truly outspoken adversaries of the Emperor among the historians of the last century were Michelet and Taine. The first reached the history of the Empire very late in his life (in 1872–1873; he died in 1874), long after having completed his masterpiece, *The French Revolution*, and after having been prevented by Napoleon III from pursuing his research in the Archives. His volume *Du Dix-huit Brumaire à Waterloo* has a vibrant preface on the vitality of Europe, challenged at the time by those who fostered the myth of decadence, and luminous pages on the czars (Paul, then Alexander) of a country which Michelet deemed especially fitted to be France's friend. The other chapters grudgingly admit Napoleon's military genius but exalt Masséna, Kléber, Desaix, and Bonaparte's early generals at the expense of the warrior bent on self-aggrandizement and more politically inclined than they. The First Consul is presented as the enemy of the republicans and the restorer of the privileges of the royalists. Michelet, who always spoke nobly of Lamarck, indicted the Emperor for having ignored or snubbed the great transformist biologist, and for having subscribed to Cuvier's reactionary scientific views. His volume on Napoleon bristles with rash assertions and gross inequities. His contemporary, Proudhon, was even more insulting and unfair. Edgar Quinet, Emile Littré, and Emile Zola stand among the few whose liberal convictions stood firm against acceptance of the man who had liquidated the Revolution while ratifying its social conquests.

Taine is not a sentimental liberal mourning the shackles imposed upon freedom by the Corsican general. He had undertaken to compose his monumental *History of the Origins of Contemporary France* after 1871, greatly under the impact of the Commune, which had caused him to fear for French political stability and laid bare man's fundamental savagery. He reached Napoleon in his ninth volume, in 1890, and painted a colorful and coldly dispassionate portrait of the Emperor. He branded him, in a strangely nationalistic spirit, as a foreigner, a Corsican and, in truth, an Italian, who never fully mastered the French language. Taine seems to have overlooked the fact that the statesmen or the sovereigns who evinced the keenest insight into the psychology of their adopted people and strove hardest for the interests of that people were just as alien to their land as the Corsican officer was to his: Alexander to Greece, Mazarin to France, Queen Victoria and Disraeli to Britain, Catherine II to Russia, recent German and Russian dictators to the core of the country from whose outlying provinces they came.

He then proceeds, in true Tainian analytical fashion, to taking to pieces the mechanics of the Napoleonic mind. The word "condottiere" holds most of the secrets of his make-up. He had no convictions, he obeyed no higher principles, but embodied energy and unscrupulous ruthlessness, like those men of the Italian Renaissance whom Taine, following his master, Stendhal, had much admired at one time. His flexibility and his ability to concentrate at will were far above the average. His brain could encompass a huge mass of heterogeneous facts and produce ideas inexhaustibly. But those ideas were never abstract phantasms or unpractical chimeras. His imagination was geographical and topographical as well as psychological; he knew how to anticipate the reactions of most of his fellow beings. The future was as vivid as the present to him. His answer to an aristocratic lady, as reported by Bourrienne, is characteristic: "I only live two years from now."

Taine as a determinist traced back all the features of an individual to one ruling passion. Napoleon's was self-love. Patriotic and generous motives are denied him. He could feign better than any comedian, fly into half-simulated and skillfully dramatized fits of anger during which he probably watched himself play a part. His selfishness did not hesitate to devour armies, steal the mistresses of his ministers, silence all contradiction, plunder vanquished nations and appropriate their works of art. The historian can see no spiritual greatness in Napoleon, only the implacable architect of a geometrically built France constrained to serve one man's ruthless ambition.

Taine's indictment was, for all his lavish footnotes and vast documentation, so partial that for the next thirty years historians of the Emperor reacted by adopting a much more favorable attitude. Henri Houssaye, Frédéric Masson, Arthur Chuquet, Albert Vandal, Albert Sorel, Octave-Aubry, and others undertook to exculpate Napoleon from many of the charges preferred against him. They actually assigned to Britain the main share of blame for the wars of 1804–1815 and took at their face value the exiled sovereign's sentimental declarations at Saint Helena. The *Memorial of St. Helena* of Las Cases, ever since its publication in eight volumes in 1823, had been one of the most widely read books in France. It is the most skillful piece of self-advertisement undertaken by any general since Caesar. None of our twentieth-century soldier-writers has yet approached it. De Gaulle and Churchill, both Napoleonic in several features of their personality, and the former the sole French leader in one hundred and fifty years to have repeated the miracle of the Consulate, are the closest runners-up to Napoleon in talent and success. None of the leaders of Russia since 1917, none of the other statesmen who guided their countries through World War II, have sedulously carved their statue for posterity as did Napoleon during his captivity. Wise was he not to have sought death on the Waterloo battlefield.

The freest minds in our century have continued to be fascinated by Napoleon's genius. Men of letters have upbraided him for sterilizing the literature and the art of his reign, for admiring Canova, *Werther*, Ossian, and above all else for his early worship of *La Nouvelle Héloïse*, which, he assured Roederer, he had read at the age of nine. Only contact with the Orient and "natural man" in his native state had, he averred, cured him of Rousseau. Was he, however, truly cured of him? The wistful remark made to M. de Girardin as he contemplated Rousseau's grave at Ermenonville is famous: "Better would it have been for mankind if neither Rousseau nor I had ever existed!" Rousseau had impregnated his thought with the all-important idea of equality as "the passion of the century, and I am, I want to remain the child of the century," he wrote in a letter. But writers seldom object strongly to a man of action's contempt for their own kind; each of them is convinced that he alone is immune from the faults thus stigmatized. They cannot but be impressed by the gift which Napoleon, alone with Balzac among the Frenchmen of the last two hundred years, possessed to such a superlative degree—imagination. "It is not enough to be a man; one must be a system," asserted Balzac, who carried an inordinate gift of imagination into his business speculations as he did in his fiction. Napoleon was more fortunate in being able to live many of his imaginative dreams. A curious polygrapher, a nobleman from Auvergne, who emigrated, became one of Napoleon's barons, and later Archbishop of Malines, and his sovereign's unsuccessful negotiator at Warsaw in 1812, Dominique de Pradt, has left us a revealing analysis of Napoleon's character.

> The Emperor is all system, all illusion, as a man needs must be when he is all imagination. He "ossianizes" in affairs. Whoever followed his career saw him create for himself an imaginary Spain, an imaginary Catholicism, an imaginary England, nay, even an imaginary France. . . . He intoxicates himself with his dreams. . . . Although he deceived much, he was deveived more often than he deceived others.[1]

The most contemptuous of those who in our own time set out to strip Napoleon of myth is doubtless the impetuous and peremptory André Suarès, in his *Vues sur Napoléon* (1933). He accuses him of cowardice in the Russian war, of meanness, of greed, of having fathered Lenin and all the modern bureaucrats and high priests of conformity. He underlines his hatred of all spiritual greatness, his blindness to all that is religious. Still, he admires him even while he hates him. "He is the most enormous spectacle of action. Evil or not, within twenty years, that human cyclone condensed ten centuries of

[1] In his *Histoire de l'ambassade dans le Duché de Varsovie en 1812* (2d edition, 1815, pp. 94 and 96). The passage is quoted in one of the two most intelligent books recently published in French on Napoleon, that of Maximilien Vox (Seuil, 1960); the other is Emile Tersen's volume (Club français du livre, 1959).

history." Paul Valéry himself, hardly prone to uncritical admiration of men other than those whom he could reshape in his own mold—Leonardo, Poe, Mallarmé—marveled at the accomplishments which can be achieved only by men blind to men's powerlessness. "Such an insensitiveness is precious. But it must be confessed that criminals are not, in that respect, very different from our heroes" (*La France veut la Liberté*, Plon, 1938). In a little-known essay on Daumier, reprinted at Geneva in 1945 in the volume *Daumier raconté par lui-même et par ses amis*, Paul Valéry digressed brilliantly on the bourgeois, that "monstrous" creature of the post-Napoleonic era, and ascribed his emergence to Napoleon, the most daring of all warriors, the adventurer who courted all possible risks, but who made sure that Frenchmen would incur no risks after him. That same man provided his country with a rigid Civil Code, the hierarchy of a pyramidal administration, laws on dowry, inheritance, and equal division of the land among all children, with mortgages, fixed-interest bonds, and the sacrosanct diploma. Security, planned parenthood, thrift, the enjoyment of choice dishes and of fine wines, and aversion to war were to characterize the French middle class that sprang from Napoleonic institutions.

The fascination that the man of the eighteenth Brumaire inspired in the historians, the thinkers, and even the politicians of the French left offers a puzzling paradox to the observers of that deeply illogical land in love with logic. For the last century and a half, writes Maximilien Vox, "France has been dreaming of a bonapartism without Bonaparte, or of a Bonaparte without bonapartism—and above all without Bonapartists." Georges Lefebvre, assessing the economic and agrarian measures taken by the Emperor, found much to praise in them and resigned himself to successive generations of young Frenchmen, whatever the political hue they painted themselves, "haunted by romantic dreams of power, in the fleeting and murky ardor of their youth, visiting, like the heroes of Barrès, Napoleon's tomb as a source of exaltation." The volume of the *Histoire Socialiste* (inspired by Jaurès) on "Le Consulat et l'Empire," by Paul Brousse and Henri Turot, is strikingly fair to Napoleon's achievements in the economic and social realm: its documentation (on prices, wages, artisans, factories, on public opinion as manifested in songs and prints of the First Empire) is rich and rare. It may be deplored that Napoleon expended on foreign wars so much of the energy which France drew, between 1795 and 1815, from the new layers of population suddenly aroused from their slumber by the Revolution, and did so little to effect a drastic industrial revolution at home. It is true that he failed to understand the genius of Lamarck, to divine the potentialities of Fulton's submarine and of his steam engine; that he regimented scientists instead of giving their inventive powers free rein; that he allowed his country to lag behind Britain's industrial renaissance and failed to encourage dissidence and heresy among French scientists. Still industry leaped forward more boldly in 1801–1802, aided by industrial exhibitions, by national societies founded to encourage it, and by research in agriculture, than it was to do for another forty years in France. Education was reorganized, even if too rigidly; and it was the Emperor who wrote: "Of all our institutions, public instruction is the most important. All depends upon it, our present and our future." And it was the young General Bonaparte who wrote to Camus, one of the members of the Académie des Sciences: "The true power of the Republic lies henceforth in not permitting one single new idea to exist which does not belong to it." It was the First Consul who, a little later, magnificently defined his purpose as "to hasten the maturity of the century." Even in strategy, French generals (and non-French ones, from Ludendorff to Rommel, from Wavell to Patton) have, in our own age, marveled at the inimitable models of speed, of unpredictability, of masterly violation of all the rules offered by the general who has been called "the Picasso of strategy." He owed much to Carnot's ideas and to the army forged by Carnot; he owed much, as we may surmise, to the prophetic volume *Essai général sur la stratégie*, published anonymously in London, in 1773, by the Court de Guibert (otherwise famous as Mlle de Lespinasse's lover). But his genius, coveted in vain by Weygand and Gamelin and others among his French epigoni, lay in the application of the most imaginative flights to which the art of war ever soared.

Indeed, the secret of the well-nigh universal fascination exercised by Napoleon on ourselves can best be expressed by the words "artist" or "poet." André Suarès, after venting his bile against the misdeeds and the lack of nobleness of the Emperor, belittling him as one would-be condottiere (Suarès called himself thus) can perceive the failings of another, bowed before the myth of Napoleon. "Nothing enhances Napoleon more than the fact that he was France's idol. The passion he inspired in so many Frenchmen . . . is one of the noblest poems ever to have emanated from the valiant heart of man. . . . Is anything more beautiful than such a religion? Napoleon is thereby justified and supremely honored." Rapturous eloquence unleashing torrents of "non sequiturs" is indeed even more native to the French than logical reasonableness.

The most extraordinary French book on Napoleon is probably, in the twentieth century, the even more apocalyptic but also more penetrating volume of another man of the left (a Protestant, while Suarès was Jewish), a doctor of medicine, an art critic, one of the most comprehensive minds France has produced in our age, Elie Faure (*Napoléon*, Crès, 1921). Faure worshiped two men: the saint and the hero. He identified most great creators and those whom he called, in an admirable volume thus entitled, "The Constructors," with either of those two groups. To him, the great warrior was a saint in his own way and Christ, like St. Francis of Assisi, was a warrior too. The famous verse of St. Matthew, "I come not to send peace but a sword," haunted this bold reinterpreter of Christianity.

His early chapters on Napoleon baldly state that the two-faced monster can sustain comparison with one person alone, Christ. In the name of ethics, which to Elie Faure meant the hideousness of stability, the attempt to force conformity and equilibrium upon man's creative powers, Napoleon, like Christ, has been condemned. Yet "in depth, he [Napoleon] is closer to Christ than any of His disciples ever was; no two men ever appeared on earth who are further remote from St. Paul than Jesus and Napoleon." Two chapters develop the parallel between them. Both were Mediterranean, hence (for Elie Faure) Orientals; both were heroes, that is, daring conquerors, "marching with their whole being, to meet God." Both shared one passion, which the French Emperor defined as "the most powerful of all, the ambition to control minds." Both attempted to remold man: "Men are what you want them to be" was the Corsican's aphorism.

Both appealed to the impossible as the only goal worthy of mankind. "Imagination governs the world." Faure does not quite color his portrayal of Christ to the point of turning him into a sublime magician or a refined and condescending thaumaturge, as Renan had insinuated; but he hails in the French Emperor a superior actor, of the same race as Alexander, Caesar, Isaiah, Jeremiah, Calvin, and Cromwell. For "the bad actor is the one who lies. The good actor is a prey to his own illusion. The greatest artist is a sublime liar; he sees as in conformity with reality the images which he draws of it. Like Shakespeare or Rembrandt, Napoleon believes what he says." Elsewhere, the poet of action is compared to Masaccio and to J. S. Bach, to Rembrandt, even to Buddha himself!

The word "poet" sets the tone of the whole volume, which is a most curious blend of rapt delirium, of prophecy and lucid insight. Even with women, with whom Bonaparte displayed his most romantic side, until Napoleon, a brutal male, chose to deny them his time and tenderness, the hero's conduct is justified by his admirer. If he did not love women very much, that is to say, enough, "he loved love, which is far more dangerous." "The powerful man is a prey to the torments inflicted by women for two reasons: because his outward power attracts them, because his inner power is but a deviation of the formidable sexual instinct." He was brutal, diagnoses the doctor, because he was shy. He demanded inordinate sacrifices from the French people, because the intensity of love can only be measured by the sacrifice which it requires. The titles of Elie Faure's chapters are eloquent: "The Mission," "The Apostolate," "Prometheus." Napoleon is declared by his French admirer, as he was by Goethe, to be "the perfect hero." He had to conquer heroism, because only an entire domination could order his passionate chaos. "The perfect hero is he who, loving war, keeps slaughter down, loving love masters women, loving power disdains its caprices, loving glory scorns praise, loving life risks death." But Napoleon erred in one thing: he could not, as Jesus had done, grind down in himself affection for his clan, and his family brought about his ruin.

Few French intellectuals would unashamedly admit it: Napoleon is not only the most prodigious sovereign in their history, far eclipsing

St. Louis, that paltry, bigoted king deprived of all imaginative vision of the future; Louis XIV, markedly inferior to Napoleon in intellectual power; and even Henry IV. France, for so long a time the nation of Europe which cherished its glamorous rulers most ardently and was most deeply molded by their characters, never had one who could match Napoleon I in sheer intelligence—the quality it held most dear. Elie Faure is not alone among French writers in hailing Napoleon, not only as the man most aptly to be compared to the Son of Man, but also as the French Shakespeare or the French Goethe—the supreme poet of his race, if primarily a poet of action. Lenin alone has changed the face of his nation as completely as Napoleon had done it; but Lenin's revolution did not extend to the rest of Europe or of the world as Napoleon's had. After 1815, France remained permanently dazzled by the blaze of glory which separated her forever from her past and from her monarchy. The legal and administrative framework of the country, its education, its economy, were to retain the Napoleonic imprint for over a hundred years. Foch; Weygand; De Lattre de Tassigny; Lyautey himself; the Free French officers in Africa, Italy, and in the thrusts across Rhine and Danube during World War II; Clemenceau the radical socialist; and André Malraux the former leftist seeking in politics "the tragedy of our age" have all had, in their subconscious if not in their overt behavior, many a feature of Bonaparte. De Gaulle, that Machiavellian mystic, that practical dreamer who hopes to lead a new continental system in Western Europe and who has proclaimed in imperious aphorisms that "France must espouse her time" ("Il faut que la France épouse son temps") and "We are made to be a great people. We want to be one and we are one," is still living the Napoleonic myth—and proving it true.

History would be a tedious record of men's attempts and failures if we were not allowed to speculate on what might have been: it abounds in missed opportunities, and no amount of determinism after the event will ever deter some of us from fancying that things could easily have gone otherwise. Reducing the unpredictable surge of events to rationality is perhaps, when all is said, lazier than admitting that reality is fundamentally irrational and that chance is not just a disguise assumed by some goddess of Necessity. Robert

Aron indulged, in a small volume in 1937, *Victoire à Waterloo*, the speculation which every student of history must have entertained: "Soudain, joyeux, il dit: 'Grouchy.' C'était Grouchy."[2] Waterloo might indeed easily have been a victory for Napoleon, as Marengo had been. Would a modified form of the Napoleonic empire have then persisted or was Napoleon's fatality driving him to ever more conquests? It is easier to answer prosaically that nothing could really sway the course dictated by a warrior who had to feed on ever more conquests. And yet, doubts linger in imaginative natures. It had been so easy for the French General and Emperor to knock down slumbering Egypt and the Venetian Republic and Austro-Hungarian rule in Italy, and Prussia and Holland, and to create new states and new nations. The history of Central and of South America, that of Scandinavia, of Belgium, that of Africa under our very eyes, of Pakistan, Indonesia, Vietnam yesterday proves that, by carving a territory, endowing it with an administration and a government, a state can be artificially created which, soon after, produces a nationality and feeds on nationalism. A Napoleonic Europe might indeed not have been an impossibility. One is never through with the creator of a myth.

[2] Victor Hugo's well-known line ended, of course, "C'était Blücher." In an article, curious since it comes from a compatriot of Pitt and of Wellington, Arnold Toynbee wonders "whether it would not have been better for the West, and for the world as a whole, if Napoleon had succeeded in uniting Western and Central Europe under his ascendancy.... Should we not be sleeping more soundly today than we find ourselves able to sleep now?" (*Saturday Review*, April 29, 1967, p. 18).

5 | WHAT GREECE MEANS TO MODERN FRANCE

THE PROPHECY which Goethe, in the evening of his life, made to Eckermann, of a nascent world literature in which Germany would play her legitimate and conspicuous part, has been fulfilled. The evolution of several Western literatures has, since romanticism and even more since the advent of realism, naturalism, and symbolism, taken place along parallel lines; yet each of them has remained profoundly national while being universal, or has become universal through being national: Joyce, Faulkner, Valéry, Proust, Kafka have certainly not been prevented from winning a world-wide audience by the close ties which bound them to Dublin, Oxford (Mississippi), Paris, or Prague. The interpenetration of several literatures through mutual influences has done little to alleviate the evils of nationalism, but it has brought the reading publics of some twenty countries far closer in their tastes and outlooks without inflicting upon them intellectual monotony and spiritual conformity.

A strange and comforting fact is that the place of antiquity in modern literatures, if not in modern education, has decreased but little, in spite of the discovery of many new literary and artistic realms, extending all the way from Russia, the Far East, Polynesian and Negro art, to South and North American fiction. In France in particular, never, even during the Renaissance, was there such an obsession with the themes of Hellenic mythology or of Platonic imaginative thought, such a sincere and enriching admiration for Greek drama, such an enlightened appreciation of Greek architecture and sculpture, as have

100

been witnessed in the last fifty years. Compared to our own era, the French seventeenth century, which in other senses deserves its epithet "classical," was marked by hostility to ancient writers or blissful unconcern with Greek art, Greek history, Greek speculation, and even Greek poetry. Pascal very probably never read Plato or Aristotle; Descartes advocated a "tabula rasa" and discreet contempt for the past, though he was not wholly unaffected by medieval thought. Corneille, Mme de Sévigné, Saint-Simon, Molière, Retz, even Bossuet were certainly not haunted by the glory that was Greece. No drama is at heart more un-Greek than the tragedy of passion, of inner disorder, of immoderate and insolent rebellion against the gods and Fate which Racine enshrined in an outwardly orderly form. Only La Fontaine, Fénelon, and Poussin may be said to have recaptured in some of their works the true essence of Greek antiquity.

Today, on the contrary, very few are the important writers who have remained unmoved by Greece or who have not resorted to Hellenic myths, if only as convenient symbols for their own bold fancies or as props to support their flagging imagination. Claudel translated Aeschylus and admired Euripides, "the Baudelaire of Greece," as he called him somewhere, and nothing flatters him more than to be compared to the Greeks—not even a comparison to the biblical prophets or to Shakespeare. He disclaimed all affinity with Northern, and especially with German poetry, and was lenient only to Heine, "who, at least, was witty." For the rest, said he, "Those people believe that imagination should lead into the unreal, the mists! Never any clear images! . . . A perpetual inability to define, eternally wild stammerings."

Gide and Valéry have chosen Greek subjects for some of their plays. The former, who had praised the lasting beauty of Hellenic myths, wove one of his last, if not of his most inspired, stories around one of those myths, that of Theseus: Valéry's Socratic dialogues are famous, and the most "Greek" among them is perhaps the least well known, *L'Idée fixe ou deux hommes à la mer*. Giraudoux, Cocteau, Anouilh, Sartre, Thierry Maulnier, and many other dramatists have gone to Greece for their subjects. Long before the problems of conscience were raised in occupied France during World War II and expressed through Antigone's defiant assertion of unwritten laws,

Péguy had been in love with the Greek virgin and repeatedly affirmed that "out of a pagan soul, the best Christian soul is often made." Even a philosopher like Bergson, who tried to think forward and not backward, never forgot that he had been steeped in antiquity. In his youth he wrote a commentary on Lucretius and gave a speech on "Common Sense and Classical Studies" (1895), read Plotinus in his last years, celebrated the miracle through which the Greeks invented precision, a quality probably hardly native in man, and thereby channeled the whole course of thinking away from psychical research (in *L'Energie spirituelle*, p. 88); and he confessed, apropos of Ravaisson, who had given up philosophical speculation for the study of Greek sculpture, that "out of the contemplation of an ancient marble there may spring forth more concentrated truth than may be discovered in a whole treatise of philosophy."

Thibaudet, perhaps Bergson's truest disciple along with Péguy, likewise became the interpreter of the most advanced literature of his time after having admired Greek sculpture, prayed at the Erechtheum, "the Sainte-Chapelle of Athens," followed Barrès and Maurras in their Attic and Spartan pilgrimages and, during World War I, campaigned, as he called it, with Thucydides, having been sent to the Salonika front.

Mauriac also fought in Greece in 1915, and revisited her later (see *Journal II*), triumphing over the repugnance which, as a Christian, he thought he should have felt. In Olympia, he found comfort in the realization that Greece was not the land of reason as opposed to the supernatural, but embodied "one of the great religious, even mystical, eras of human history." Atys and Cybele are the myths which inspired his volume of verse, and his novels are full of shudders at the presence of Pan lurking behind the Gascon countryside. To him, pagan Greece is ever imminent around us, and Catholicism must never relent in denouncing its pitfalls. Lacretelle, Mauriac's contemporary and colleague at the Academy, first nurtured on Proust and Gide, but too cool and detached in his novels, wrote his most ardent work in praise of Greece, *Le Demi-dieu*. Montherlant, who outbids any other Frenchman in his freedom from humility, asserted in *Earinus*: "I believe no other writer of my age-group is impregnated with antiquity to the same degree as I am." One of his earliest literary attempts was

entitled "Notes on the Feeling for Beauty Among the Greeks."
Earlier still, at the age of ten, he had written to one of his schoolmates:
"My dear fellow, I languish at the thought that we are going to leave
Rome in our history course and pass on to the Middle Ages. Luckily,
at the beginning the teacher will treat Roman civilization in Gaul."
If he did not attain the so-called moderation and wisdom of Greece,
he is not unworthy of Alcibiades, and he found a brother in
Peregrinos, whose conversion and deconversion, and passion for
other forms of ambidextrous "alternance" have been described by
Lucian. Greece and Hellenized Asia Minor have meant at least as
much to him as Spain.

Nor is the passion for Greek antiquity limited to the sons of the
bourgeoisie, who might cherish their knowledge of ancient letters as
their private legacy and the badge of their class culture. What is
characteristic of this renewed ancient influence in our times is that it
works mostly through translations, through reproductions of Greek
masterpieces, and through myths dreamed about and pondered over;
it extends to many children of poor families who hail the robustness
of antiquity. Such is Giono, who discovered Homer, then the Greek
dramatists, while reading alongside peasants threshing wheat. His
Naissance de l'Odyssée, his *Serpent d'Etoiles* have recaptured much of
the violence of ancient Greece. His vocation as a writer sprang from
the dazzling light with which Homer and Sophocles, read in some
cheap French version, captured his gaze. "From that day on," he
confessed, "I knew where my path lay: toward a renovation of the
great tragedies of Greece."

Michel Leiris, a strange surrealist subsequently won over to anthropology and the author of one of the most revealing of all autobiog-
raphies, *L'Age d'Homme*, is haunted by the myths of Greece; and it
was in Greece, while visiting the Acropolis, that Raymond Queneau,
hardly an academic writer, conceived the idea of his first book,
entitled *Le Chiendent*, and started creating a popular language as
distinct from literary French as spoken Greek is from official Greek.
Camus, an Algerian boy who grew up in poverty (his father having
been killed in World War I, his mother working as a charwoman), felt
the pulse of antiquity beating in him. His early and most sincere
volume, *Les Noces*, shows him akin to the Greeks, and in an essay on

"Helen's Exile" in a volume devoted by the *Cahiers du Sud* to the "Permanence of Greece," he contrasted the sordid surroundings of our cities with Greek life, everywhere steeped in nature. "We have exiled beauty, the Greeks took up arms for it." "Helen" is also the title of a poem by one of the finest French poets of our age, Pierre-Jean Jouve, who worshiped Greece through Hölderlin and through much mystical and psychoanalytical torment. Jouve followed it in *Mesures* in 1937 with a poem on Orpheus. Pierre Emmanuel likewise composed an eloquent and rather biblical *Tombeau d'Orphée*. Many are the contemporary poets thus lured back to Greek themes, and the strange thing is that very few of them fail to renew them. Indeed, it would be difficult to discover important writers since the end of the romantic movement who have resisted the spell of Greece: Baudelaire (three or four poems excepted) professed a preference for Latin poetry, the Goncourt brothers scoffed at antiquity as "le pain des professeurs," Paul Bourget claimed to be cold to the splendor of Greece. They weigh lightly when compared to the cohorts of those who, from Renan and Anatole France down to Malraux, have celebrated the uniqueness of the Greek miracle.

This survival of Hellenism among the moderns is astonishing to many who are wont to lament the passing of the humanities and the disappearance of Greek as a language studied by the younger generation. It must be confessed that the perfume of Greek art and letters has intoxicated more people since Greek ceased to be a subject required of schoolboys and to appear as the monopoly of teachers who were paid for their enthusiasm. It was doubtless badly taught when it was widely taught. Enjoyment and study are not easily combined, and the passion of the nineteenth century for philology, too often dryly conceived as a jugglery of interpolations, restitutions of hypothetical earlier words and letters, mastery of the mechanism of Greek particles, killed the enthusiasm of many potential readers of the *Oresteia* and of Plato. "He who is content with breathing the perfume of a flower does not know that flower, and he who plucks it only to study it does not know it either," said Hölderlin at the beginning of his passionate novel of adoration for Greece, *Hyperion*. Ignorance is not bliss, but any knowledge that is not creative is vain, too. Raphael, Mantegna, and Poussin felt Greece more intensely through a few broken columns than if they had consciously explored the treasures of her art. Keats probably never read any Greek in the original and saw only a little Greek art in London; yet his "Fragment of an Ode to Maïa" is probably more splendidly Hellenic than anything ever written on Greece by poets who knew Greek like Landor, Swinburne, Chénier, and Goethe himself. The latter, when he gave up his attempt at writing an epic upon a Greek subject, the *Achilleis*, sadly acknowledged that "only faulty knowledge is creative."

No tribute to the perennial beauty of Greek literature could indeed be more eloquent: the influence of ancient philosophers, epic and dramatic poets, is second to none today, and yet their works are for the most part accessible only in fragments, and read in translation. Translations of ancient works have thus become one of the most precious factors in our culture, and it is regrettable that more care is not expended upon multiplying them and enhancing their quality. A few crabbed scholars may grumble and contend that a poet can be felt only in the original. The stubborn fact is that very few are those who can read more than two ancient or living languages with perceptiveness; and that many of us have been enraptured by whatever we could divine of Lermontov, Dante, the Greek lyricists, or Catullus in translation. The fact that Greece is remote and that we read her authors in a borrowed and dulled linguistic garb probably encourages many moderns to appreciate their subjects and their heroes. We should feel self-conscious if we acted similarly with *Le Cid* or *Othello*. Only Don Juan and Faust can rival Oedipus, Orestes, and Prometheus in their appeal to our contemporaries.

If the extraordinary spell cast by Hellenic writings is thus independent of a precise knowledge of the language or of the country, the land has been visited by many literary travelers since Chateaubriand and Lamartine. Through a rare privilege, shared only with Japan to some extent, Greece is the one country which has inspired a uniformly good literature of travel. A few lapses into superficiality or bad taste can be pointed out, such as Maurice Bedel's *Le Laurier d'Apollon*; but, compared with the uniformly superficial volumes emitted by the French presses every year on America, even on Scandinavia, India, or Italy, they remain unfortunate exceptions. Even in Sicily, Tuscany, or Castile, French writers seldom have found that stimulant to feel powerfully, to think nobly, to write brilliantly, which Greece gave to them.

The danger was great nevertheless. For they might have been tempted to echo Renan's too famous prayer and palinode to Athena, or to redo Chateaubriand's Greek sunsets and moonlight landscapes. Most French travelers in Greece revolted against their predecessors, closed their books, opened their eyes. They resisted idealization. Maurras rejoiced upon landing in Greece on a dull day, when statues and columns had little of the much vaunted marble-like brightness dear to the Parnassians. Barrès refused to be moved by Athens, lest he become uprooted from his native Lorraine, which he left on repeated voyages in order to love it the better from afar. But he wrote with emotion of the Byzantine church of Daphne and on Sparta: his *Voyage de Sparte*, although it strains after some affectations of originality, contains perhaps his best prose. Louis Bertrand purposely neglected the ancient ruins in what is also his best book or his only good one: *La Grèce du soleil et des paysages*. He stressed the landscape, the Oriental character of the people crowded in smelly streets and tiny shops, and distrusted the idealization of Greece first begun by Sophocles, Isocrates, and a few other ancient writers of the people who surpassed even the sons of Provence in tale-telling. Islam is to him the nearest approach we have to what the country of Aristophanes must have been like—with the difference, we should add, that Islam never did for science, for sculpture, for drama and philosophy what Greece did. Bertrand recalled how horrifying to modern Philhellenes would be the sight of statues daubed with polychrome varnish, of goats and other animals butchered at the very door of the Parthenon or of the Theseion, "a temple one would take to have been built, like the King's palace, by some Bavarian architect," and of the heavy Greek jewels fit for savage women. But the grumpy traveler cannot conceal his affection for the Greece thus debunked. It is apparently impossible to remain bad-tempered very long about Greece, as Duhamel was about America, Evelyn Waugh about Mexico, Henri Michaux about Asia.

Three brothers, Henri, Jean, and André Bremond, one of whom achieved fame as a historian of religious feeling, had also tried to object to the traditional raptures of the traveler reaching the Acropolis.

As Christians, they felt they should distrust enthusiasm for pagan beauty. Yet they were won over, and they rationalized their admiration for Greece by confessing that Greece had had many premonitions of Christianity, and that some true prayers uttered by Socrates or Plato may after all have ascended to God (*Le Charme d'Athènes* and, by André Bremond alone, *La Piété grecque*). André Beaunier in *Le Sourire d'Athéna* rebelled against the notion of Greece as the land of reason. No country ever was reasonable, or truly tolerant, or wise. But he was conquered by the mystery of Aegina and Epidaurus, the pediments of Olympia, and the enigmatic statues of the Korai in the Acropolis museum. Maurras vituperated the same statues: "Won't someone take away these Chinese girls?" he grumbled, but he came back from Greece a firm believer in reason and a contemptuous foe of democracy. Long before his *Anthinea*, he asserted rashly in *Les Vergers sur la mer* (1937) that Greece had been the land of unity in the realms of science, of art, and of the spirit. Herriot, in politics at the opposite pole from Maurras, was seldom more inspired than when he celebrated Greece, with eloquence but also with a precise knowledge of ancient writers and with the modesty of a former student of Greek to whom his teachers at the Ecole Normale had repeated that a man's intelligence can be measured by what he is satisfied not to understand (*Sous l'Olivier*, 1930). It is to the credit of Greece that not two of the thirty or forty volumes devoted by so many literary travelers to that country in the last half-century have ever agreed on any one of its features, and have yet all concluded with the same admiration. "Greek, sir, is like lace," said Dr. Johnson. "Every man gets as much of it as he can."

The survival and the growth of this well-nigh universal admiration for ancient Greece among us cannot altogether be explained by clear reasons: they belong, when all is said, to what Pascal would have termed "l'ordre du cœur" and are irrational like passion. A country will think its literature slighted if it is compared in excellence to Latin letters; writers and artists will often rise in revolt against the Old Testament and gladly deny any link with Christianity. But Germany, England, France will vie with one another in their desire for recognition as the genuine follower or rival of Greece in the modern world. Spain alone seems to have been reticent in advancing such a claim.

If, however, some aspects of Greek culture may be selected as those eliciting the warmest admiration from contemporary France, art should obviously come first as the most universal language of Hellas. Is it too much to suggest that the age of the greatest enthusiasm for Gothic architecture and sculpture is perhaps over, and that many of our contemporaries are more sincerely moved either by baroque art or, more frequently still, by Romanesque churches? Scholars, surprisingly enough, have not yet written much on "Greek baroque"; but qualities akin to those of early Romanesque sculpture have been discovered in archaic Greece. Several writers have lately taken up the once famous and subsequently disproved assertions of Renan, who saw in Gothic cathedrals "fanciful creations of barbarians," defying reason and solidity; Julien Green in his *Journal* (II, 138, 194) prefers the temples of Greece to the nervous unbalance of Gothic architecture; Lacretelle, diffident of emotion, praises Greek art in the very acute and sensitive pages of his *Demi-dieu* as the only one which blended reason and nature, which could express the suggestion or the potentiality of motion and serene gracefulness. He admires the functionalism of an art where, according to Stendhal's phrase, beauty is only "la saillie de l'utile" and where luxury or overpowering effects of bigness are never mistaken for beauty. Malraux's *Psychology of Art*, one of the most pregnant books of our age, vibrates with passionate insight into Greek beauty. The author, after exploring the art of Asia, taking part in revolutions and wars, and confronting the West with the mirage of the East, ends with a redefinition of humanism in terms reminiscent of the Greeks: "I have refused what was wished by the brute in me, and have become a man without the help of the gods."

The French, whom naïve followers of T. S. Eliot sometimes consider an extremely classical nation, seem to feel a periodic need to resort to Greece in order to learn anew the supreme value of measure, "to metron," of wise and artistic as well as ethical temperance, "sophrosyné," of an order which is never frozen or purely geometric but instinct with life. No one has praised the value of economy of means more fervently than Claudel, and no one, probably, has practiced it more commendably in our century than Valéry. France invented art for art's sake but has never had a very peaceful conscience about it;

she knows that the vice of her writers is frequently to worship art as the supreme or the sole end of life and to indulge in aestheticism or, worse still, in sterile aesthetic discussion. Many of her authors, stubborn and unrepentant moralists that they are, are fond of looking back toward Greece as the land in which literature and art did not have to be divorced from morality, and the artist, as we fondly imagine, could feel at one with his audience. Many French admirers of Aeschylus and Sophocles consider it to be the superiority of these dramatists over their beloved Racine that their drama is not divorced from a moral and religious view of life. Santayana and several English critics have brought the same charge against Shakespeare, with even more cogent reasons, preferring to him the ancient drama in which "the human everywhere merges with the divine."

The other danger to French letters comes from the very long cultural past of a nation which cannot forget or assimilate its rich heritage easily. The consciousness of an overwhelming history has certainly not condemned French literature and art to passive imitation; most of the artistic revolutions originated in Paris. But to revolt against one's past is another manner of being obsessed by it. French literature prides itself upon many works of very astute intelligence and of high technical skill; but one occasionally feels that they were not written from an inner necessity, and that freshness of imagination is lacking. Giraudoux and Cocteau are very fine artists of the second rank, if one may insist upon establishing degrees in greatness; they have seldom invented their subjects, or recreated with violence what they borrowed. They cannot or will not escape a charming self-consciousness and a desire to shine or to shock. Gide himself confessed that imagination with him rarely preceded the idea. The charm of such writers, urbane, gently perverse, lucid, and always impeccable as craftsmen, is beyond question.

But one occasionally misses the simplicity and the naïveté of those artists who could hold the mirror up to nature without effort. Part of the seduction exercised by the Greeks comes from their naturalness. Alone perhaps among the great literatures of the world, theirs had no ancestors. If they borrowed from predecessors in art, the Greeks at once forgot about their loans, and turned into gold whatever came into their hands. They had no critical spirit in the sense that they were incapable of conceiving anterior ages as they had been, and as different from themselves. They indulged in subtlety; Platonic dialogues, Greek lyrics, the Erechtheum, and even some choruses in tragedies certainly go rather far in the cultivation of graceful intricacy and verge on preciosity, sophistry, or jargon. It remains true nevertheless that many moderns yearn for more freshness, more brevity, a greater closeness to nature, a greater freedom from introspection and from the passion for the intimate journal and nude confession which is today devouring much of French literature. The Greeks provide the most telling lessons in brevity (none of their works appears too long), in direct contact with life, and in total absence of didactic preaching as well as of complacent engrossment with oneself—two of our amiable sins.

But even more than a dispenser of classical models, Greece is to many of us today the land of what, for lack of a more adequate term, may be called romantic, or Dionysian. A unique feature of the influence of ancient Greece is that it has seldom or never proved a sterilizing influence; except with a few Renaissance humanists, it has not led to passive imitation or to awe-struck intimidation. It has aroused fervor and passion in those who dreamed of Arcadia and of Delos, who recited Pindar or Plato's *Ion*, who loved Sappho or Praxiteles' Aphrodite. Of ancient Greece it may be said, as of the Christian Kingdom of Heaven according to St. Matthew, that only the violent seize it, and that it has to be seized by force. Claudel and Suarès have especially stressed that aspect of Greek culture; the latter pictured the Greeks as he wished them to be and in his own image, in several of his anti-Nietzschean aphorisms, contending that they were admirable because they lacked taste and preferred greatness, and for their denial of *amor fati*. Father Festugière, a Hellenic scholar of high repute, wrote a whole volume to show that the Greeks were steeped in anguish and sorrow because they could not accept the omnipotence of Fate and were waiting unconsciously for the Christian revelation which was to free them from their obsession. It may be generally asserted that the pessimism of the Greeks, first emphasized in Nietzsche's famous volume on tragedy, is what endears them most to our contemporaries.

Next to it is probably their spirit of revolt against the gods, which, unconsciously but skillfully distorted by modern interpreters, makes Xenophanes, Parmenides, and Euripides appear as elder brothers of the Existential heroes. Greek mysticism fascinates others, again prone to reading overmuch in Hellenic mysteries or in Plotinus. But the word "myth," which is one of the fetishes of contemporary youth, has proved the most potent of all in sending admirers back to Greek texts. Anthropology and psychoanalysis are the two goddesses worshiped by many who refuse to see nothing but literature in literature and must fill it with problems that they promptly proceed to solve with ingenuous ingeniousness. Mythology indeed provides the key to the understanding of Greek sensibility and of much of Greek lyricism. Our contemporaries have rejoiced in their discovery that the Greeks evolved from a primal stupidity or "Urdummheit" (the Germans have been the most joyful at this discovery), to harmony and humanity. They have been reassured on finding that fear of the dead, superstitious omens, magic rites of fertility, a profusion of phallic associations and cults, survived underground, and often above the ground, in Greek civilization. The Greeks have for some reason seemed more human for this occasional propinquity to animal existence. Their myths seem to have taken on richer layers of meaning since symbolists, surrealists, Existentialists alike, and five or six other "ists," resorted to them as the only vessels into which they could pour their wine, or their dishwater. The debility of our mythopoeic imagination coincides with the intoxication of our scholars with myths and symbols.

When all is said, we quote the Greeks, we read and reread the Greeks, we travel in their land, we reproduce casts of their statues in our galleries, we build our post offices and our libraries according to their architectural models because we feel a growing kinship with them in our modern age. They feed our secret distrust of our own civilization, bent on technique and comfort: the Greeks were hardly concerned with applied science, they disdained material wealth, they lived on the poorest of lands and probably in sordid dirt and in a woeful absence of sanitation. Their history is a glorious challenge to any economic explanation of history. Yet to them we owe the main lineaments of our science, of our art, of our ethics and metaphysics, of our criticism, of our view of man and the world. We obviously interpret Greek literature in many a distorted fashion, as Virginia Woolf reminded us in a subtle and brilliant essay "On Not Knowing Greek." But we dimly realize that, as the language of Greece is less and less studied, modern writers, thinkers, and artists must step in and embody the best of Greece in their own works. The French have done it in the last century more conspicuously than ever before in their history. They know, at a time when the West is trying to acquire a fuller consciousness of its unity, that the distinctive feature of Western man in world history has been, as Ernst Troelsch put it, "his uninterrupted assimilation of the ancient world."

6 | ENGLISH LITERATURE SEEN THROUGH FRENCH EYES

ONE OF THE minor vices of the French nation is its charming and exasperating intellectual arrogance. The French may undergo calamitous defeats on the battlefield; be overrun by invaders; be outdistanced as engineers, as bankers, as statesmen; feel venomous spite at no longer ranking among the very great powers. Secretly, however, they will continue nursing one ineradicable faith: that of being superior to all other peoples in the "arts de la bouche," as they call cooking and the enjoyment of its savory products, and expressing tender and enticing thoughts and desires through words and other motions of their lips. They are equally convinced that their culture stands supreme and that the outside world, whatever its other advantages, bows to the literary and artistic fashions started by Paris, and deems it a supreme honor to have its plays performed in Parisian theatres, its books translated into choice French and elucidated by French critics.

Strangely enough, however, and notwithstanding occasional campaigns started by nationalists against the contamination of French classical purity by foreign works, the French have been remarkably receptive to a variety of influences from other literatures. Goethe, Schiller, Heine, more recently Hölderlin and Rilke, have enjoyed far more than a passing vogue in France. Russian literature was discovered by the French as early as the eighteenth century, and subsequently by Mérimée, Voguë; nowhere has Dostoevsky's influence permeated the novel so deeply as in France between 1910 and 1930.

113

More recently, Kafka has been naturalized by the French and profusely imitated. The success of Faulkner, Dos Passos, and Steinbeck in France since 1935 has amazed and dismayed Americans, who lately tried to sweeten the bitter impression made by those apostles of violence through some doses of Truman Capote, Gore Vidal, and of Coca-Cola. But the literature which has most vividly fascinated the French over several centuries and which has been, alternately or simultaneously, most cherished and most misrepresented by them, is that of England, "the great mysterious island" as Proust called it.

It took no small stretch of imagination for the average Frenchman to convince himself that there could exist an English literature approximating French literature in quality. He would board the Channel packet, roam around the London taverns, sleep at the wayside inns, and notice that books were being published in Great Britain. But the question in his mind was a candid, and perhaps a valid, one: "How can a people have any literary inspiration, when it drinks no wine? How can books of any quality be written on life and the . . . *unum necessarium* in literature if not in life, in a land where the food is so little conducive to eroticism or to impassioned conversation?" If the traveler from France was curious enough to visit the sister universities, he soon learned that when it is said of a young man that "he did well at college," it meant he had made the rowing team, or played cricket with the required patience and skill, or received a gentleman's grades and carried his liquor like a gentleman if not like a lord. He attempted in his broken English to elicit some information about English letters and art at the dinner table, and soon discovered that talking on literature was a typically foreign breach of good manners. He crossed the Channel back home, comforted intellectually by the Cartesian reasoning that a literature of any value could obviously not flourish in a country wrapped in fog for the better part of the year.

A monumental study by the late Georges Ascoli has collected all the evidence of Franco-British intellectual contacts from the Middle Ages to the seventeenth century. Froissart, Charles d'Orléans, Ronsard went to England or to Scotland, but apparently never heard the name of one English writer. Rabelais, whose knowledge was omnivorous, records speeches in seven or eight ancient, modern, or imaginary languages delivered by his hero Panurge, but none in English—too forlorn a tongue apparently to provoke a shock of recognition or even of laughter. Saint-Evremond could spend most of his life as an exile in England and speak no language but his own. The main conclusions reached by French observers of the English presented the compatriots of Hobbes, Mandeville, and Locke as a nation of thinkers: "the English think profoundly" and are born philosophers, was the consensus of opinion. But, and possibly as a consequence, they are addicted to sadness. Saint-Amant and others repeated it: "Life to them is a burden; they hang themselves on the slightest pretext." A little later, the means used to meet death halfway ceased to be hanging, according to the Swiss Muralt, and they cut their throats instead. Destouches, who lived in England for several years, rhymed an epitaph for a typical Englishman, in one of his comedies:

> Ci-gît Jean Rosbif, écuyer,
> Qui se pendit pour se désennuyer.

This fondness for suicide was looked upon as a mark of courage as well as a result of a wretched climate. But the opinion prevailed in France for many decades that the British were an unruly and violent nation, ready to behead their sovereigns in a fit of revolt. Cromwell filled Bossuet and other subjects of the Sun King with feelings akin to those which might have been aroused in timid souls in 1935 by Hitler and Stalin combined into one.

As to the literary attempts of that northern and turbulent nation, they were blissfully ignored by the French. As late as 1719, Dubos notes as a matter of evidence that "there have only appeared in that remote northern land savage poets, crude versifiers and cold colorists." The few continental Europeans who, before Voltaire, made bold to open English works agreed that it was regrettable that their authors should have written them in their native language. French, naturally, would have proved a more refined vehicle. Jusserand has discovered the famous comment (perhaps authentic) made in France on Shakespeare's works by Nicolas Clément, who, around 1680, established the first catalogue of the library of Louis XIV: "That English poet has a fair enough imagination, he thinks with naturalness, expresses himself skillfully; but those beautiful qualities are spoilt by the filth he introduces into his plays." Fouquet, the wealthy superintendent of finances, had also owned a copy of Shakespeare, kept, however, along with his other English books, not in his luxurious library but in the garret, and valued at one franc in the inventory drawn after Fouquet's fall: it was probably the first folio!

The story of the discovery of English literature by the French Huguenots, then by Voltaire, who added little but wit and style to the patient efforts of those émigrés, is too well known to bear repeating. Neither the French emigration of 1792–1815, nor the Russian emigration of 1917, nor perhaps the German and Jewish emigration of the years 1933 and following have equalled the intelligent labors and the cultural influence of the French Protestants expelled by France after 1685. They compiled grammars of the English language, Anglo-French dictionaries; they translated English works, analyzed their content; they created the first international periodicals in Europe. To them can be traced the Anglomania which was to seize the eighteenth century. English books became the rage in France, and spread from France to the rest of continental Europe. Locke and Newton, the English deists, but also Pope and Richardson, then Milton, Gibbon, Hume, Horace Walpole became all the rage in France. And Shakespeare was at least translated, after a fashion.

Of course the very close intellectual rapprochement between France and Great Britain did not take place without many of those misunderstandings which give such zest to comparative literature studies. "Minuet" is the name given by F. C. Green to the elegant and shifting give and take which then took place between the two countries. The originality of each remained under the veneer of French culture in England and of enthusiasm for British letters in France. Occasionally a traveler who had observed his idol too closely gave vent to those spiteful remarks which help cure the "acedia viatoris" in his fits of despondency at being misunderstood and lonely. Even the abbé Prévost, a sincere Anglophile who trusted the credit of England to the point of forging the signature of an English friend on a check and risking being hanged for it, remarked: "The English are commonly regarded as a hard and proud race, fit only for war and navigation, cultivating the arts less from taste than from utility." Later in the century Mirabeau, another admirer of England and an advocate of a Franco-British alliance, noted that there was nothing polished among the English but steel.

On the whole the picture of the English formed by the average cultured Frenchman in the eighteenth century, mostly through literature, can be briefly sketched as that of a thoughtful nation. They are so addicted to reverie, a lady observer noticed, that they must have blood and daggers in their drama to arouse them from their profound and sad listlessness; hence the contrast between their violent theatre and that of the French. They are also a nation endowed with a virtue which puzzled the envious French: a rare capacity for silence. Tea parties "à l'anglaise," such as Ollivier painted in a picture in the Louvre Museum, became the vogue in Paris; but the French had no mean difficulty in trying to hold their tongues while sipping tea and eating cakes, and even while listening to the music being played, and yet silence was the prerequisite to appearing British. George Moore, who had lived long in France and had learned there, or in his native Ireland, the gift of loquaciousness, once distinguished the two kinds of lovers: the French couple who will talk to each other even in moments of deep sentiment and even in scenes of vivid estrangement, and the English couple. The first are the babbling kind, the second the silent kind. The London boy and girl will meet on the Thames, spend most of their Sunday in some backwater of the river, looking at each other's eyes and at their tea basket occasionally, then part at five P.M. saying ritually: "Well, dear, next Sunday at the same time." The traditional view of the British as phlegmatic originated in the eighteenth century and won admiration among the French. Baudelaire, who dreamed of being a phlegmatic dandy, admired an English painting in which a typical gentleman from across the Channel, looking at the water in which his wife is accidentally drowning, remarks casually from the shore, "Oh! the deep, deep sea!"

The English also appeared as a nation of melancholy and sentimental people, but more restrained in expressing their sentiments than the vivacious extroverts from Latin lands. The bourgeois drama of Lillo and Moore enjoyed an inordinate vogue on the Continent: tears were shed profusely over *The Gamester* and *The London Merchant*. Diderot went into a fit of anger when it was hinted that

Richardson's novels could be too long, and wrote a warm eulogy of the father of English fiction. But spleen was taken to be the favorite disease of a once merry England. Voltaire related, with his tongue in his cheek, how on a foggy day he had seen Londoners queuing up at the entrance of London Bridge, awaiting their turn to jump into the Thames and thus relieve themselves of the fog, the spleen, and of their lives. The graveyard poetry of Harvey, Gray, especially of Young's *Night Thoughts* and of Ossian strengthened the conviction of the French that meditating on tombs and about death was a sign of distinction and of profundity "à l'anglaise."

The Revolutionary and Napoleonic wars did little to estrange the French from the English on the intellectual plane. British fashions, literary and other, reigned supreme after 1815. The terrifying novel thrilled the French and was at the source of a good deal of Balzac. Walter Scott set the European novel in motion. Byronism spread from Portugal to Russia. Dickens and George Eliot have drawn floods of tears from the eyes of French youth: Proust, Charles Du Bos cried at the adventures of the youthful heroes of *The Mill on the Floss*. Kipling took the French by storm in the early years of the present century. Meredith then came into fashion, and Gide once declared that he would rather have written *The Shaving of Shagpat* than any other novel. Hardy, Conrad were adopted in due course as the greatest of British masters, then Joyce, Lawrence, Graham Greene. Obviously the choice made by a foreign nation reflects the tastes and needs of that nation; it differs sharply from the values put on the same writers in their native country. Wordsworth has never moved the French as Byron, Poe, Whitman have. The social novel bears transplanting abroad with difficulty, due in part to the time lag which makes nothing appear so dead as a social problem (in H. G. Wells, Shaw, or Galsworthy) after it has been solved. Charles Morgan and lately Graham Greene have been acclaimed in France as men of much greater stature than theirs is in truth or than it is at home. Mary Webb, Katherine Mansfield, even Emily Brontë have similarly been overrated, perhaps because women novelists were something of a rarity in modern France.

But, when all is said, the distortion of English literature as seen by the French has been relatively slight and it is informing more than ludicrous. The scholars and serious critics of France, ranging from Forgues and Montégut to Jaloux, Du Bos, and lately Astre, have devoted penetrating volumes to sympathetic appreciation of British letters. The most difficult English poets, Donne, Blake, Keats, Browning, have come into their own in France some decades after they did so in England; T. S. Eliot has been very ably translated by Leiris. Shakespeare has been translated in the last hundred years (and lately and in toto by Messiaen, then by Lalou) far more often than Molière or Racine have been into English. His plays have been performed on the Parisian stage more often, since 1910, than on the New York and on the London stages put together. *Henri VI* itself has been adapted by Barrault; *Antony and Cleopatra, Twelfth Night* have had very long runs; *Coriolanus* almost created a revolution in 1934 when an authoritarian meaning was read into it by an over-sensitive public. Not content with the plays actually written by Shakespeare, French authors turned *The Rape of Lucrece* into a play. The *Sonnets* alone have not yet been staged. The idea of British foreign policy held by the French owes not a little to their conviction that Hamlet, vacillating, trying for compromise, fearful of "engage-ment" and sympathetic to the Germans since he was trained at Wittenberg, is the typical Englishman. The admiration of many Frenchmen for English women may well be due also to their reading of Shakespeare. They readily see a Juliet in an English girl, as Berlioz vowed he would marry Harriet Smithson, who had played Juliet in Paris, or commit suicide. His suicide attempt proved abortive; he succeeded in persuading the English actress to accept him as a hus-band—and they were unhappy ever after. Both Vigny and Lamartine married English wives, as did the historian Tocqueville and, later, Jules Laforgue. The Panurge complex, deeply rooted in Frenchmen, who fear infidelity in their spouses when they embark upon the adventure of marriage, drives them to look to Great Britain for marital security. The reading of Shakespeare may have encouraged them in the fond belief that, for one tempestuous Lady Macbeth, England offers many Ophelias, Cordelias, Desdemonas, and Imogens, submissive, re-signed, tenderly willing to go to a nunnery when so instructed, to forsake their inheritance, or even to lie down and let themselves be stifled if their honor and their master's voice demand "the pity of it."

There appear to be some constant features behind the taste which have drawn the French to many works of English literature in the last two or three centuries. First, the French, who have often been lauded as a nation of critics (undeserved as the compliment, in our opinion, may be) and who have evolved and formulated most of the literary and artistic doctrines from classicism to Existentialism, relish the literature of their northern neighbors because it is refreshingly free from theories, manifestoes, and eloquent dissertations on what a novel, a play, or a movement should be. Literature plays a very modest part in the daily life of Englishmen, and yet they write masterpieces occasionally, and good works in as large a number as any other nation. Seldom does an English writer entertain a body of opinions on literature as a whole and on his own art in particular; when he does, like Coleridge, Arnold, or Pater, it is likely to prove detrimental to his talent as a creative writer. Literary magazines are scarce and, in the present century at least, short-lived. There are no academies, except in painting, or if there are, they remain blissfully uninfluential on production. They do not therefore drive the young men to rebellion as they do in France; but they do not tame them too soon with the prospect of honors, decorations, comfortable slumber in an official armchair while venerable and equally slumbering colleagues propose their edicts as to which words shall be authorized. If a poet is, every ten or twenty years, knighted by the King or appointed poet laureate, the magnificent piece of news is relegated to the tenth or fifteenth page of the newspapers, after the sport and financial reports and the accounts of dog and flower shows.

French preference goes in consequence to English books which do not show too much self-consciousness, too much refinement in technique, and too much style. Sir Thomas Browne, Dr. Johnson, De Quincey, Landor, Newman, Pater, Stevenson have never been the favorites of the French. Meredith, Samuel Butler, Lytton Strachey, Aldous Huxley have equally failed to capture their admiration, for they were too "Frenchy" already. Fielding, Defoe in *Moll Flanders* and even in *Robinson Crusoe* (though the French wonder why the author failed to improve his story through giving Friday the female sex), Dickens, Carlyle for a while, D. H. Lawrence have been more warmly appreciated by the French, for they did not polish their prose to an excess. They enjoyed the solid advantages that the French envy the English, and now find in the Americans, since the English after World War I seemed to neglect them for more sophisticated intellectuality. Gide, writing on his tastes for the more vigorous writers of England in the review *Verve*, once defined the quality which he valued most highly in the English novel as that of "raw meat," in contrast to the subtle flavoring and over-elaborate preparations which French cooking imposes on meat and (only the sturdiest fanatic of British tastes will deplore it) vegetables. There is an earthy, empirical quality to Dickens and Trollope, a stolid vigor to Kipling and even to Arnold Bennett, "muffins and not the promise of muffins," as Emerson said in his *English Traits*, which appeal to the French. That same robust vitality, "a rude strength newly applied to thought, as of sailors and soldiers who had lately learned to read" (Emerson), has been relished by the French in the American novel and been hailed as an antidote to their own over-conscious psychological fiction.

The English novel has often appeared to the French superior to their own. "Au pays du Roman" is the title of a critical work by Edmond Jaloux, and the land thus designated was understood by everyone to be Great Britain. The compliment has often been paid the French in reverse by British critics and novelists who consider Balzac, Flaubert, Proust (even, alas! Maupassant) as giants dwarfing their own writers of fiction. The English novel is taken by the French to be longer than their own, slower in pace, and therefore more apt to suggest and create atmosphere and to induce the collaboration of time. Like the players of golf or the builders of the British Empire, the British writers of fiction are more leisurely and enjoy the conviction that time is theirs. Giraudoux defined the French novel as a short story which got out of hand or as a shower, alternately hot and cold, but vehement in its effect; while the English novel would be closer to the epic, or to a long bath in tepid water in some country house.

The French long preferred the English novelists to their own for other merits. As long as novel-reading was not accepted as a worthy occupation, as it is in our time when few books of philosophy or science are as strenuous reading as modern novels, English fiction offered the advantage of presenting problems: sex-problems occasionally (since the hyphenated phrase seems the natural one among Anglo-Saxons) but carefully disguised, and such other problems as Janet's repentance or Silas Marner's avarice, inhuman treatment of children, the loss and subsequent recovery of his faith by a clergyman after Darwin and the higher criticism had dealt it a few blows, how to marry the four or five daughters of a vicar to the local squire or squires, and generally speaking how to reach some stable happiness and to maintain it through the minor ordeals of fox-hunting, week-end festivities, foreign travel, and occasional imports of dangerous ideas from France and Germany. "Man does not aspire after happiness," Nietzsche could write in his *Twilight of the Idols*. "Only the Englishman does that."

French admirers of English books relish in them another virtue which might be defined as youthfulness. Latin literature was deficient in one feature among others that it had no children's books, no fairy stories, no *Don Quixote* or *Gulliver's Travels*. France has produced many fairy stories and pleasant tales of childhood, at least in the age of Anatole France, Proust, and Gide. But those works are seldom endowed with the quality of innocence which is found in many of the nursery rhymes, tales, and novels of England. The very words "candid" and "innocent" which, in other tongues, have retained a complimentary flavor, imply some mockery in the French language. Innocence, for the Gallic mind, is mostly valued as the one thing which it gives one pleasure to lose. A child is in France a creature with whom something is decidedly wrong: he has not yet grown up. If some women can be found whose charm lies in their having preserved the little girl in them, few men in France would be praised for having remained boyish. Education aims at maturing the children as quickly as possible, so that they reach the "age of reason," pass their exams, embark upon their sentimental education, and settle down to a rational enjoyment of life.

For several centuries, the child was virtually absent from French literature. In their insular neighbors, the French found a worship of the child, raised in the nursery, then in public or in country schools, away from the contaminating influence of grown-ups, that amused them as a touching foreign peculiarity. They have never adopted the English system of education. But their anglomania actually drove a few compatriots of Descartes to admiration for *Alice in Wonderland* and for *Peter Pan*. The success of some women novelists like Rosamond Lehmann, Katherine Mansfield, Margaret Kennedy was great in France and due in part to a girlish quality in them which endeared them to French males. It is not uncommon among French students of English letters, after they have steeped themselves in *Alice in Wonderland* and Gilbert and Sullivan's operas—probably the hardest of all English creations, next to cooking, to naturalize abroad—to develop an interest in ghosts as the evidence that nothing British remains a sealed book to them. Such suspension of disbelief, however, usually remains momentary. Most Frenchmen, after their early flurry of hard-won naïveté "à l'anglaise," would probably make the same comment that a friend of Yeats ventured when the poet of the *Vision* was trying to conjure up ghosts: "If there must be spirits, I prefer mine out of a bottle."

A similar youthful freshness in English poetry offers a strong appeal to the French, whose own poetry is characterized by its insistence upon general views on life, nature, love, and death clothed in solemn "meditations" and "contemplations." It would not be unworthy of the attention of comparative scholars to contrast the themes which have been favored by each of the romantic poetries of Europe. Flowers, at least the least dangerous of flowers, the humble celandine or the daisy, devoid of intoxicating fragrance, have received more tributes in England than in France, unless making liqueurs and seasoning herbs with them be the most genuine of all loving tributes. Birds have likewise been more popular with French gourmets than with French poets. Celebrating the skylark, "pilgrim of the sky," or the February thrush as Meredith does, and, of all birds, the cuckoo, brings smiles to the lips of French readers. Coleridge and Edward Thomas have written enthusiastically on the charms of rain, and many poets from Sidney to Coleridge on the loveliness of solitary sleep, two themes apparently inappropriate for the poets of Gaul. Even after they have had their symbolists and other apostles of unreason and of irrationality who have not been scarce in this century, the French must stretch their imaginations to enter into the fresh wonder at life which seems to be the gift of their British neighbors. The German Keyserling once remarked that only in England could a great general be honored publicly as having possessed the typical English virtues: "his instinct, and his faith in his instinct." Elsewhere the compliment would only be deemed worthy of a good pointer.

Yet, of all the features of literature and of life in Great Britain which have attracted Frenchmen for over a century, none has won truer affection than English poetry. Young Valéry once declared gravely to Mallarmé that, in every provincial city of France, there was a fervent youth who would fain give his life for the master of esoteric symbolism. In every French *lycée* and wherever English is studied, there are adolescents who discover English poetry with passionate raptures and decide forthwith to sacrifice all other plans to a visit to Great Britain and to further loving study of Shakespeare or Donne, or Blake or Shelley or Keats or Yeats. This admiration for English romanticism in France came at the very time when the intelligentsia of England was outgrowing its former belief that the French were an unpoetical race, and were celebrating Baudelaire, Rimbaud, Laforgue as far above their own modern poets. Literary relations between two peoples with close affinities are often marked by such fecund misunderstandings. "Felix culpa!" could be said of many intellectual as well as of moral mistakes.

The music of the language and of British versification have often proved a strong attraction to the French, even when they only half-understood its subtleties. But the word "imagination" is probably the one which best expresses the set of qualities which the French admire in English poetry as contrasted to their own. No elucidation of English critics, from Coleridge to I. A. Richards and C. M. Bowra, has succeeded in defining clearly that imaginative supremacy of English poets. But the French reader, aroused from his early super-stition which presented the British as a nation of shopkeepers, steeped in an over-intellectual education in his school and in a hard, realistic environment in his home, discovers with an exaltation akin to a liberation that another literature has depicted the world as a "phantasmal scene" (Shelley), "an unsubstantial faery place" (Wordsworth) where, as Macbeth proclaims on his first appearance in the tragedy bearing his name, "nothing is but what is not."

Frenchmen, secretly dissatisfied with their own romanticism, which had remained too reasonable in its challenge to reason and too prone to eloquent preaching, relish the more direct and more intimate tone of the English romantics. The cosmic sorrow expressed by some of Shelley's Dirges and Laments, by Keats in his "Ode to a Nightingale," even by Yeats, frustrated in his love for Maud Gonne, seems to strike a deeper note than Lamartine and Musset. The pantheistic communion with the cataract which haunted Wordsworth like a passion, with the West Wind or the Cloud, with the bright star "in lone splendor hung aloft the night" envied by love-torn Keats reveals to adolescents secrets other than those they had learned to decipher in the French moralists. The French, as a nation probably little inclined to the silence of the mystics, usually unhappy when they cannot understand themselves clearly, blessed with the happy gift of extroversion, obtain through English poets (or very exceptionally through some German poets or some Spanish mystics) the revelation that "wise passiveness" is no less valid than intellectual lucidity and enables man "to see into the life of things" no less keenly. Love for the country and the sea and the mountains is probably as ardent among the French as it is among any other nation, in spite of some oft-expressed prejudice to the contrary among foreign observers of the urban and talkative French people. But it is in not a few cases an acquired passion, fostered in them by the reading of poets who, in English in particular, have curbed the questionings of impatient minds to submit passively to a still interchange with nature. Shelley in "Mont-Blanc" had concisely defined such a pantheistic communion:

> My own, my human mind, which passively
> Now renders and receives fast influencings,
> Holding an unremitting interchange
> With the clear universe of things around.

There is more than a mere paradox in the assertion that life imitates literature. In an era which, in our press and elsewhere, has reduced relations among nations to economic exchanges of coal, steel, oil, and cotton, it is a comforting thought and a legitimate one to entertain that Great Britain and France are spiritually and intellectually closer to each other than they ever have been; and such mutual understanding has been due in no mean measure to a keener appreciation of their respective poetry by the cultural groups in each nation.

7 | SHAKESPEARE'S WOMEN— A FRENCH VIEW

FOR A CENTURY and a half Shakespeare's fame has been firmly established in France. More translations and adaptations of his plays have been attempted in French than in any other language, perhaps because none ever matched the unchallenged quality of the versions made in German by Tieck and Schlegel, and in Russian by Pasternak. There is hardly a French producer of talent who has not staged several of his plays, from Gémier, Copeau, and Dullin, to Vilar and the provincial companies of Marseille, Saint-Etienne, and Lyon. In 1948, at the Edinburgh festival, Jean-Louis Barrault declared: "The fact is here which needs no elaboration: Shakespeare is a positive need for the Frenchman. Shakespeare is almost as much acted in France as Molière and more often than Racine." All of Shakespeare's plays have been staged in the present century, including the most demanding ones for a company and an audience (*King Lear*, *Antony and Cleopatra*), the most bewildering to the French (*Measure for Measure* and, in 1963–1964, *Troilus and Cressida*). *Coriolanus* provoked a near-revolution in Paris in 1934. Even a very undramatic poem like *The Rape of Lucrece* was turned into a play between the two World Wars. We have been told that the *Sonnets* in which Shakespeare is drawn alternately to the bewitching and treacherous Dark Lady and the enticing young man with "a woman's face with nature's own hand painted," "the master-mistress" of the poet's passions, have been acted as a play in several dramatic studios in Paris.

Still it would be indeed disappointing to find the French understanding Shakespeare exactly in the same way as English critics.

126

They approach him through translations which inevitably transfigure his poetry as much as Racine or Baudelaire are distorted when turned into English. They are conditioned by a taste, acquired early, for dramatic structure and for psychological analysis. They are surprised, if enchanted at times, by a poetry which breaks the dramatic continuity and relieves the tragic anguish. Some of them—why not confess it?—do not disagree totally with Voltaire's slurs on "the drunken, coarse barbarian" when they read *Pericles*, or the hair-raising scene in which Titus Andronicus violates and mutilates his daughter Lavinia, or Lady Anne's sudden agreement to marriage with the same Richard III who has just murdered her beloved husband.

The French underwent the contagion of Shakespeare idolatry first from Letourneur, and then even more from their romantics during the period ending about 1875. Some of the best and most laudatory writing on Shakespeare was done by Hugo, Montégut, Mezières, Taine, and Stapfer. The present French adulation for the Bard would seem to be cooler, and more discerning. The same can probably be said of the United States, where the 1964 centenary has been marked by coolness, to say the least, and even of Britain, where the celebration has assumed an official character to which the challenge of sharp dissent would have been preferable. Not many are the critics who would today readily endorse the raving praise which, one hundred and twenty years ago, flowing from the pens of Hazlitt, Lamb, and Coleridge, deified Shakespeare. Coleridge postulated in his lectures on Shakespeare that "in all points from the most important to the most minute, the judgment of Shakespeare is commensurate with his genius." When he encountered, in *Coriolanus*, what appeared to be an imperfection, he felt certain that he would eventually realize that it was in fact a profound excellence. His criticism of Shakespeare, and his esthetics generally—including the absurdly overrated and hardly meaningful opposition between imagination and fancy—have in our century provoked an idolatry of Coleridge in academic circles which borders on lunacy. Hazlitt's taste was far surer and his psychological insight immeasurably sharper. Shakespeare may be too colossally great to "abide our question." But surely there are and will be oscillations of the pendulum of taste where even he is concerned. Tolstoy and G. B. Shaw may have proved paradoxical, opinionated, or petty in their misguided assaults on him. Reasonable doubts raised in good faith by French and other admirers of Shakespeare may, however, be more enlightening than one more over-sophisticated analysis of Shakespearean imagery or one more banal tribute to his universality.

We have pointed elsewhere[1] to three areas of evaluation in which modern French criticism of Shakespeare has voiced its strongest reservations. The first, naturally enough for a country in which Racine, and even Corneille, have in the present century again become models of dramatic perfection, is that of the structure of Shakespeare's plays and of their lack of fitness for the stage. Charles Lamb himself once pointed to that lack of fitness in a striking *Essay of Elia* which dealt with *Lear*. The second lack, again scathingly denounced by George Santayana and by scholars such as Herbert Grierson, eloquently and independently deplored by Catholic poets like Claudel and even by agnostic but spiritual Frenchmen, is the absence of religious concern in Shakespeare: he writes as if sin, redemption, the Bible, and Christ had never had meaning or reality for him. He has been said to have understood well-nigh everything except the religious experience.

Our purpose here is to stress what is doubtless a third and even more potent stumbling block to a genuine admiration of the Bard by many continental readers. For many people across the Channel, literature is the vehicle through which they have, early in their lives, acquired some knowledge of love and some insight into women. For the French, even love is matter for analysis, and gains through adequate imaginative and intellectual preparation. Now Shakespeare's women are, for the most part, adorable creatures of sweetness and grace, eerie phantoms of delight, angels of purity and of spontaneous abandon to the man *they* have chosen—for the choice more often is theirs rather than their partner's. But are they true, credible, convincing women? Or, as Hazlitt puts it in his *Characters of Shakespeare's Plays*, is " their peculiar excellence that they seem to exist only in their attachment to others? " They are, he adds, " pure abstrac-

---

[1] In an essay published in 1964 in a collective volume on Shakespeare (in honor of Professor Robert W. Babcock) published by the Wayne State University Press, Detroit: *The Persistence of Shakespeare Idolatry.*

tions of the affections." Has not Shakespeare failed to probe searchingly into those unconscious, erotic, or even intellectual secrets of love which soon after his time were to become the most enthralling of literary subjects in the works of Donne, Racine, Richardson, Prévost, Marivaux, Rousseau, Goethe, Stendhal, and Tolstoy? The modern reader of Proust and Rilke, or even of Mann and Moravia, must feel carried into a fairy tale or nursery rhyme world of unreal fancy when he compares the women he knows from life and from today's novels with the charming Rosalind, Juliet, Imogen, and Miranda; with girls disguised as young men (Rosaline, Viola, Celia, Sylvia, even the dignified but pedantic Portia), or monsters like Goneril, Regan, and that amoral eldest sister of Lolita and of Queneau's Zazie, Cressida.

The Victorians naturally judged otherwise. A Mrs. Jameson and other women writers, contemporaries of Tennyson, were multiplying volumes and keepsakes in which Shakespeare's brainless angels of purity and paragons of fidelity were set up as models for the virgins of Her Majesty's empire. Ruskin, whose private life failed to display any mature insight into the other sex, in the second of his *Sesame and Lilies* lectures summarily decreed that Shakespeare had no heroes, only heroines. Most of these heroines are faultless, "steadfast in grave hope and errorless purpose." The men in Shakespeare cause catastrophes through their faults or their folly; but "the redemption, if there be any, is the wisdom and virtue of a woman, and failing that, there is none." Even the harsh and, to many, repulsive Isabella in *Measure for Measure* stands in Ruskin's eyes for "the victorious truth and adamantine purity of a woman." Only one of those women is declared weak: Ophelia. Only three (Lear's eldest daughters and Macbeth's wife) are wicked—"frightful exceptions."

Ruskin's preference went clearly to what Verlaine called, following E. A. Poe, a "child wife." For a few months, or a few days, in each man's existence, such a preference for a baby doll may be indulged. Nora, in the opening scene of *A Doll's House*, thus amuses her condescending husband by her affected childishness. Anna Karenina does likewise, under even heavier constraint; so does the loveliest of all fictional heroines, Natasha, in *War and Peace*. But they soon weary of that role, and any man wearies even sooner of having married an inconsequential prattling little girl with the head of a bird and the immutable fidelity of a dog. Taine, in the sixth section of the chapter on Shakespeare in his *History of English Literature*, after portraying the males in his theatre as coarse barbarians, "lumps of flesh made heavy with wine and fat," contrasts the women to them: "They are charming children, who feel to an excess and love to the point of madness." Compared with them, the heroines of the French stage almost look like men. Taine's nephew, Chevrillon, who was fond of seeing a Celt in Shakespeare (whose birthplace lay not too far from Wales), wrote even more rapturously of the entrancing femininity of those heroines; he saw them as sisters of the Gaelic fairies who had none of the practicality of the Anglo-Saxons typified by the prosaic and empirical Robinson Crusoe.

With utter naïveté, Shakespeare's women throw themselves at the necks of the men they have decided to love—with utter abandon and not much understatement. Juliet, whom Shakespeare made four years younger than she was in the Italian story by Luigi da Porto, during her first interview with Romeo, proffers her love to the ardent young man with as little guile as Candy Christian in the recent American satire:

> My bounty is as boundless as the sea,
> My love as deep; the more I give to thee,
> The more I have, for both are infinite.

The gentle Miranda catches sight of Ferdinand, the third man she has ever seen and the first for whom she has sighed: she naturally falls in love with him at once. At their second encounter, she offers to carry in his place the logs which her father enjoined him to remove and pile up. She disobeys her father, who watches her amusedly. Desdemona renounces hers to follow the Moor; with no less candor and with utter disregard of all feminine diplomacy, she awkwardly and insistently pleads the cause of Cassio, wholly unaware of her husband's character. Jessica flouts her father, Shylock, with no qualms and, seated near Lorenzo, oblivious of "the Jew" who is being taught lessons of mercy, she prefers to admire "how the floor of heaven/ Is thick inlaid with patines of bright gold." Almost any piece of flattery can win these unsophisticated girls, whom no mother has ever warned against the deceit of golden tongues. Indeed Shakespeare's women

(Ophelia, Desdemona, Cordelia, Imogen, and a host of others) have no mothers and never seem to have undergone a mother's restraining influence. Sir Valentine, one of the two *Gentlemen of Verona*, sums up the practice and conviction of honey-tongued Shakespearean males when he declares to the Duke:

> Though ne'er so black, say they have angels' faces.
> That man that hath a tongue, I say, is no man,
> If with his tongue he cannot win a woman.

The suitors do not even have to strain their wit and dip long into their store of poetical compliments to win these girls. Cressida, the only genuine coquette—along with Cleopatra—among these "ladies," did offer the semblance of some resistance; but she promptly reassures a clumsy Troilus who was going to imagine her hard to win:

> Hard to seem won: but I was won, my lord,
> With the first glance. . . .

The others seldom hesitate to take the first step in love. As Hazlitt (the author of that lamentable *Liber Amoris* which shows how much more expert he was in bookish love than in dealing with women in real life) explains discreetly, Shakespeare's heroines "are taught by the force of feeling when to forego the form of propriety for the essence of it." Even the wittiest and most playfully restrained of these heroines, Beatrice in *Much Ado About Nothing* (another orphan), forsakes her pride and her contempt after she realizes, like one of Marivaux's more analytical *jeunes filles*, that she has fought against her inclinations long enough and is attracted to Benedick. She does not hesitate, in a brief monologue, to lay down the weapon of her self-control and of her sharp tongue:

> And, Benedick, love on: I will requite thee,
> Taming my wild heart to thy loving hand.

Would to God, many a continental man would exclaim, women were indeed so easy to conquer, or rather so prompt to surrender and to remain steadfastly constant ever after! Chateaubriand, the first French critic to comment upon the monotony of these angelic Shakespearean creatures, whose language (at least to a foreign ear) is hardly distinguishable from one to the other, probably was swayed by that idyllic picture of the English girl when he fell in love with an English pastor's daughter, Charlotte Ives. Many a Frenchman did the same, Berlioz being the most notorious example of a Frenchman's infatuation with Shakespeare's heroines. But while Chateaubriand had left a constant wife at home and had to withdraw before the prospect of bigamy, poor Berlioz married the actress whom he had applauded as Juliet and Ophelia (not understanding a word of what she recited) and suffered the consequences. Lamartine, Vigny, Tocqueville (most inconstant husbands, all) likewise elected for their brides gentle and patient compatriots of Cordelia and Imogen: what poor forlorn wives they became!

With second thoughts, however, a typical Frenchman wonders what merit there may be in winning a lady so entirely devoid of complexity, so prompt to reward hyperbolic poetical compliments, so inexpert at understanding the deployment of wit, of imaginative lies, of tender self-analysis, of intellectual mastery to which a male resorts when he enjoys the pursuit even more than the catch. We may envy the married life which Rodrigue will lead with Chimène, with a monthly visit in their children's company to the grave of Chimène's father; the existence which Xipharès could have had with the modest, simple, and regally proud Monime, the ideal woman for many a male dream; even that which Alceste, if he had been a little less irascible and a little more charitable, might have enjoyed with Célimène. Those ladies would delight men with their changing moods, their evening reminiscences by the fireside ("Rodrigue, qui l'eût cru?"— "Chimène, qui l'eût dit?"), their intellectual debates with their "gloire" and their lucid self-control, their moral qualms. Husbands would even prefer that their mates be exposed to occasional temptations and even yield to them, so that the males would have the advantage of forgiving them or of savoring the sophisticated delight of a reconciliation.

Coleridge insisted upon lauding the lily-white guilelessness of Shakespearean heroines. "Shakespeare has no innocent adulteries, no interesting incests, no virtuous vice," he averred. What earned his moral eulogy may appear as a lack of psychological depth to the modern reader who has fed on Stendhal, Flaubert, Chekhov, Strindberg, and Proust. He may regret that the poet of the *Sonnets* did not lend to enough of his angelic creatures some of the inner conflicts which had torn him when he penned numbers 142 and 144 of his sonnet sequence: *Love is my sin and thy dear virtue hate*, or, *Two loves I have of comfort and despair*. The debates which move our minds as well as our emotions in Corneille's Pauline or in Racine's Andromaque, and which few women in real life have escaped, are almost wholly absent from Shakespeare. Their struggles are with outside circumstances or with a destiny inscribed in the stars, seldom with inner motives which might have stood against their feelings, whether they be pride, dignity, filial devotion, religious scruples, conflicting sexual or sentimental attractions, political concerns. There is little soul-searching in the women's soliloquies in Shakespeare. It may appear seductive to a very young man, eager to assert his own ego by crushing a woman's, to dream of an obedient mistress like Desdemona who, at the male's bidding, would lie down and readily accept strangulation; or, like Imogen, meekly submit to her husband's order to have her murdered; or, like the clumsy Ophelia who is used as a decoy by her father, be incapable either of understanding or of curing Hamlet, of sharing a single one of his tortured thoughts, consenting meekly to get herself to a nunnery. Continental dramatists and novelists have accustomed us to more complex character-drawing than we find in these gentle heroines. Richard Feverel himself would not long have remained under the sway of the characterless and childish daughter of Prospero. Basil de Selincourt remarked that "the English mind has a native affinity for unanalyzed adjustments and reactions." We are less certain today than were the Victorians that such a refusal to look inward enhances the interest of literary heroines.

Elmer Edgar Stoll, the American critic who quoted the above sentence from Basil de Selincourt, was thoroughly conversant with French classical drama. His study of *Shakespeare's Young Lovers* (Oxford University Press, 1937) multiplies intelligent reservations on the lack of variety and of truthfulness in Shakespeare's women in love. He resists the charm of Imogen—by whom even G. B. Shaw had been enraptured—who indeed behaves like a gullible, foolish girl, altogether devoid of critical sense. He is less annoyed by Portia's "affectation and pedantry" (the terms are Hazlitt's), by her silly acceptance of her father's whims, which is followed by her deception of him and her ludicrous trick with the rings, than many other readers of *The Merchant of Venice* would be. But he impatiently brooks the traditional ravings of English critics over the many unreal girls who populate Shakespeare's pastoral comedies, from Hermia and Helena in *Midsummer Night's Dream* to Perdita, the flower-girl of *A Winter's Tale*. He does not balk at the characterization of Shakespeare's maidens as "those long-legged, loose-mouthed hoydens in rompers" offered by one of the most original literary critics of America in the first half of this century, Prosser Hall Frye. It is no wonder, then, that in order to preserve the fetishism which, since Garrick and Mrs. Montagu, has surrounded even the loosest and flimsiest of Shakespeare's comedies, some American symbol-hunters among the lately "new" critics have endeavored to discover religious and spiritual meanings concealed under *Cymbeline* and *A Winter's Tale*!

A Frenchman's disadvantage lies probably in his not having read, early in childhood, Lamb's *Tales from Shakespeare* or gentle poetical excerpts from Shakespeare's comedies. When he comes to them at a later age, having already admired the mature complexity of Euripides' and of Racine's women, shared the struggles between love and "amour-propre" of Corneille's heroines, read *Madame Bovary* and half fallen in love with La Sanseverina, he is liable to be only mildly amused by the inconsequential and desultory behavior of those open-hearted but light-brained English girls: Rosalind and Celia in *As You Like It*, Olivia in *Twelfth Night* (who quickly forgets about the brother whom she was mourning), and even the nun, Isabella, who discourses like a pedant and first tosses aside her brother's life with the words: "Die, perish . . . I'll pray a thousand prayers for thy death./ No word to save thee." Later she finds strangely lax excuses for the lewd hypocritical tyrant Angelo. Like *Alice in Wonderland*, Gilbert and Sullivan's operas, and, on another level, *The Pilgrim's Progress* and the sonorous cadences of the Authorized Version of the Bible, such works would have to be absorbed early in life in order to hold under their sway those who were born on the wrong side of the Channel or of the Atlantic.

In Shakespeare's tragedies (and *Measure for Measure* comes close to being one), the heroines' vocation seems to be to bring about errors, mistakes, crimes, and, through their very virtues, to rush headlong to their ruin. Never has the common saying of Latin men rung truer: women's manifest destiny, like that of philosophers, is to complicate in problems of ideas and of life what might otherwise have become too disgustingly easy. French Catholics in particular, among them an Academician, Jean Guitton, are fond of pondering over what to them is one of the greatest mysteries of faith: why did God create two sexes? Paul Claudel, than whom no dramatist in France was more Shakespearean and a great admirer of the Bard, deplored bitterly the frightening absence of God in Shakespeare's theatre, the utter lack of any vertical transcendence in *Macbeth* and *Lear*. As he read and reread Shakespeare, "that genius who never found God," he came also to miss a portrayal of women comparable to Agrippine, Phèdre, Roxane, Athalie. He suffered for poor Cordelia and her lamentable awkwardness, cried over the five times repeated "never" of the dying king who has recovered his daughter only to watch her die; but what a prosaic funeral epitaph Albany uses to conclude the most ghastly drama ever written: "The oldest hath borne most." The pagan Goethe at least allowed his Gretchen to be saved!

Claudel spoke and wrote repeatedly on Shakespeare, notably when he succeeded Louis Gillet, another admirer of the Bard, in the French Academy. In 1931, Gillet had written an elegant and very French popularization on Shakespeare. A pillar of the Catholic and conservative *Revue des Deux Mondes* and a warm admirer of Dante, about whom he wrote an even better book than his *Shakespeare*, he could but lament Shakespeare's total unawareness of the Holy Trinity, the absence of any repentance in the *Sonnets*, the virtual absence of any sense of sin in his plays, the exclusion of Christ from his dramas. More than any Greek, French, or Spanish tragedy, Shakespeare's (*Othello*, *Macbeth*, *Lear*, and, even more exultingly, *Antony and Cleopatra*) end in a universal triumph of death. Even as he has stabbed Iago before he himself welcomes the sting of death—which Cleopatra compares to a lover's kiss—the Moor bitterly rejoices that he has not quite killed his deceiver. "I'd have thee live;/ For, in my sense, 'tis happiness to die." Like many a French reader of Shakespeare (and of English poetry from Sidney through Coleridge to Auden's "Lay thy sleeping head, my love"), he wonders at the weird obsession with the theme of sleep—sleep in solitude, naturally, and in utter oblivion of all, even of dreams—among English writers. But his most cogent remarks on what he, and his compatriots, miss in Shakespeare revolve around our theme here. His women have little depth and hold scant attraction for a Latin.

Not one of his plays bears a woman's name for its title. The contrast with French classical drama, with Hugo, and with the authors of *Hedda Gabler* and *The Three Sisters* is indeed sharp. In many of the great tragedies, their role is perfunctory: Portia in *Julius Caesar*, or Virgilia in *Coriolanus* who says hardly forty lines in the course of the play. Cordelia utters about one hundred in all and disappears from the drama after the first scene and does not reappear until the end of Act IV. Her silence during that first scene in which Lear displays his inability to read into his daughters' characters, though praised strangely enough by the King of France as "a tardiness in nature," defies all verisimilitude: it enables the touching Cordelia to fulfill a role not unlike those of Desdemona and Ophelia: she wreaks havoc when she wants to serve. All these women who believe—Gillet hints at this—that they were born to save were in truth born to destroy. They lack all insight into the psychological and moral world, as does Gertrude in *Hamlet*: she remains unperceiving of the moral issue which tortures her son, even though she boastfully declares in Act III: "yet all that is, I see." Lady Macbeth, though she may forsake her sleep and her reason, does not even rise up to the spiritual and moral sense of guilt which torments her husband.

As to Cressida, the less said the better in the view of those Frenchmen who admire Homer, or even Giraudoux. They would call her "une petite peste." Even Heinrich Heine, who professed to hate the English, was surprised by her crudity. Commenting on Shakespeare's women in a volume published in 1838 to accompany engravings of those ladies "of the most odious nation which God in his anger created," he attempted to be more cynical than the French. "We err," he hinted, "in thinking that women cease to love when they betray us. They do but follow their nature." But Cressida's shameless deceit of Troilus under his very eyes is too much, even to a reader of *Manon Lescaut* and of *Les Liaisons dangereuses*. Coleridge, while quoting the lines in which Ulysses gives a physical description—a rare occurrence in Shakespeare—of that born courtesan who feigns innocence

> (Nay, her foot speaks; her wanton spirit looks out
> At every joint and motive of her body.)

resorted to clouds of circumlocutions to explain her lewdness. In her, he explained, "Shakespeare has drawn the portrait of a vehement passion that, having its true origin and proper cause in warmth of temperament, fastens on, rather than fixes to, some one object by liking and temporary preference" (*Notes and Lectures: Shakespeare*). The English art of understatement!

Neither the Frenchified Heine nor French critics (even if they belong to the Academy) can lay claim to prudishness when reading *Pericles* or *Troilus and Cressida* and pretend to be outraged by brute immorality. Rather, they are exasperated by the whimpering and inconsistency of that wily creature in whom Shakespeare seems to have sketched a weaker image of his Cleopatra. She is not even truly perfidious or cruel, as Racine's heroines can be. (The hideous Regan of *Lear* may be an exception.) Shakespeare's females do not seem even to realize what evil is. Mauriac and other modern descendants of Racine, and Claudel himself in his splendid creation of Ysé in *Partage de Midi*, have been more subtle in portraying the Baudelairian trait which makes criminal women truly profound—"la conscience dans le mal."

When much has been said (for all never will be said on Shakespeare), at the root of the feeling of embarrassment which lurks in many a continental European's (and apparently also in many an American's) rather lukewarm reaction to Shakespeare's women—once we have outgrown the rapturous tributes of the romantics—is another realization: Shakespeare's portrait of love is magnificently and luxuriantly poetical, idyllic, paradisiac. It is a summation of all the power over words and music which the English Renaissance achieved even better, perhaps, than had the Italian. The most enchanting of the lyrics with which the comedies are interspersed ("Take, O take those lips away") and many of the dramatic and passionate cries of baffled men, like the Moor's "Yet I do love thee, and when I love thee not/

Chaos is come again," rise above anything else in the whole range of literature and of music.

But in a century which has delighted in the Russian and French novels which, since Flaubert, Tolstoy, Joyce, Proust, have analyzed love after physical possession and eroticism, which considers Lawrence's *Women in Love* as a classic, hails *Lulu* on the operatic stage, buys *Nana* and *Fanny Hill* at every bookstand, it must be confessed that Shakespeare's timidity in delving into the harrowing mysteries of sensuality alienates him from many of us. We would not blame him for having come at the end of the Middle Ages and for being closer to medieval romances than to modern psychological fiction. Enough critics have nevertheless undertaken to prove that he anticipated Freud and Havelock Ellis. But we cannot help finding that an abyss, not of one hundred but of five hundred years, separates his Rosalind, Viola, Perdita, Imogen, and Portia from Roxane and Phèdre. His women, even the married ones like Imogen and Desdemona, even the sophisticated ones like Beatrice, seem never to have either experienced or imagined the realities of love, or its physical substratum. The French used to smile at the Victorian novel which took it for granted that lovers had no lips. Their lips, in Shakespeare's plays, serve for prattling and babbling, often in a charmingly pure friendship between two maidens: Hero and Beatrice, Celia and Roxane, Viola and Olivia. They are seldom used for kissing. Edmond Jaloux, a great admirer of Elizabethan drama, once remarked on the scarcity of the scenes in Shakespeare in which even an embrace is exchanged by a couple. Cressida, at her boldest in the fourth act, would be one of those rare exceptions, and Cleopatra the outstanding one in the unforgettable first scene in which she and Antony exchange a caress:

> *Cleo.:* If it be love indeed, tell me how much.
> *Ant.:* There's beggary in the love than can be reckon'd.

Antony, defining their kissing as "the nobleness of life," challenges the rest of the world to match such a peerless delight. Elsewhere we are left to wonder if Lady Macbeth ever entertained any love for her husband—a more pertinent question than that proposed by the now famous mock essay "How Many Children Had Lady Macbeth?"

What powers did Desdemona wield over Othello in the silence of the night, what appeal did the hunchback Richard III have for Lady Anne or the vile Edmund for Regan and Goneril? Men are seldom loved for their brains or for their mature firmness of purpose in Shakespeare; more usually it is for some exterior handsomeness. Neither admiration nor desire, neither respect for a male personality nor an impulse stemming from the senses plays much part in the love of these strangely unsexed women. It is hard to realize that the same poet who was so timid at facing the realities of passion in his plays has also conjured up the most burning ecstasies of sensual gluttony in the stanzas of *Venus and Adonis* which begin "Now quick desire hath caught the yielding prey. . . ."

The explanation was offered by Cibber, early in the eighteenth century, and by many others since, that any suggestive embrace or close caress would have been grossly incongruous on the Elizabethan stage where women's parts were played by young men. Nothing, however, indicates that audiences in Shakespeare's times were aware of anything ludicrous, or were in any way repelled, when the adolescent who took the part of Cleopatra thanked a messenger with the words: "There's gold, and here/ My bluest veins to kiss." Or when the man who impersonated Lady Macbeth alluded to "his" feminine and maternal bosom: "I have given suck, and know/ How tender 'tis to love the babe that milks me." Or: "Come to my woman's breasts,/ And take my milk for gall."

Others have, on the strength of the *Sonnets*, hinted that Shakespeare might have nurtured a preference for the kind of love favored by many Greeks and therefore lacked a genuine interest in the opposite sex. But Sophocles, though it is well known that he shared the inclination which was to be that of Oscar Wilde and Gide (each a married man like the Bard), of Proust and Tchaikovsky, nevertheless created Antigone; and Proustian women stand in no lack of convincing truth. Speculations about Shakespeare's private life and tastes have never yielded much fruit; they explain nothing. Facts simply point to Shakespeare as a man of his time, not of ours. Except for the creation of the coquettish, haughty, and capricious Cleopatra, whose love was satiated—even though she herself "makes hungry/ Where most she satisfies"—his women are not endowed with the fullness and the complexity of Racine's, of Webster's, or even of Shakespeare's younger contemporary, John Donne, the cynical poet of "The Flea" and of "Love's Constancy."

It may be a mark of French levity to contend that, since most literature has been composed by males, the supreme achievement in it is to succeed in creating women who are not only all that men may desire in their fondest dreams—lovely, changing, fickle, entertainingly varied, unpredictable, intuitive, in St. John Chrysostom's words, "a desirable calamity"; but also what they can actually be: intelligently analytical, sensible, practical, maddeningly logical, not unmindful of the senses and not loving themselves and their moods more ardently than their partner, as Cleopatra herself does. Shakespearean idolatry, and the admiration for his women instilled in most English people from their childhood on, may be responsible for the relatively small number of true women to be encountered in the sweep of English literature from Fielding to Hardy, passing through Wordsworth, Shelley, Keats, Tennyson, Swinburne, Wilde, and Hopkins. Of Christabels there are many, and of ladies appearing with a dulcimer in drug-provoked dreams, and of witches of Atlas, and of dreaming Madelines of the *Eve of St. Agnes*, and of Ladies of Shalott, and other Tennysonian maidens having "but fed on the roses and lain in the lilies of life." But if literature does play a considerable role in molding the feminine as well as the heroic ideals of a nation, a foreigner may ascribe to Shakespeare's portraits a certain fairy tale and Prince Charming notion of woman which perhaps accounts for some profound sexual dissatisfaction at the core of English and American culture. The notion, endorsed by Pope at the beginning of his "Epistle to a Lady," that "Most women have no characters at all" finds some reinforcement in the reading of the loveliest pastoral and romantic plays of the Bard.

8 | RELIGION AND LITERARY SCHOLARSHIP IN FRANCE*

IT IS DOUBTFUL whether there is any modern literature, even that of Spain or of Russia, to which the many questions concerning religion are so central as they are in France. The oft-quoted saying of Nietzsche, in *The Dawn of Day*, is not a paradoxical assertion put forward by a German admirer of French culture: "It cannot be denied that the French have been the most Christian nation in the world, not because the devotion of masses in France has been greater than elsewhere, but because those Christian ideals which are most difficult to realize have become incarnated there, instead of merely remaining fancies, intentions or imperfect beginnings." Nietzsche adduced as examples not only Pascal or Fénelon, and French Protestants, but freethinkers as well, and he praised the latter "because they had to fight against truly great men and not, like the freethinkers of other nations, merely against dogmas and sublime abortions." A student of French literature who had no familiarity with the religious background and traditions, no interest in the many controversies which have opposed one sect of Catholics to another, Catholics to Protestants, believers to unbelievers, clericals to anti-clericals, would be crippled at every stage.

Yet few fields of study are beset with greater difficulties. There are

* Essay presented in substance to the second Conference of the Frank L. Weil Institute (Cincinnati) for Studies in Religion and the Humanities. The purpose of the author was to survey recent work in that vast area and to suggest further research.

many diverse, if not conflicting, approaches to the consideration of religion in literature and no single set of methods can ever prove adequate. The obstacles are such that, in America in particular, scholars appear to have been singularly lacking in audacity in that field. The French Reformation; Jansenism; Bossuet; unorthodox purifiers of religion such as Rousseau, Lamennais, Renan; the extraordinarily rich group of twentieth-century religious writers (Péguy, Claudel, Mauriac, Bernanos) have aroused relatively mild interest among American scholars and been the subject of extremely few books. Indeed, even in the general reading public, it appears to have been harder to naturalize those French writers who were imbued with a Christian sensibility (which normally meant a Roman Catholic one) than any others. This Anglo-Saxon timidity in the presence of feelings—religious or other—which is perhaps a legacy of public school (or American private school) education,[1] has harmed the understanding of a foreign nation whose seriousness has been underestimated and whose levity has been turned into a comforting cliché by pseudo-innocents abroad in search of that very levity. Rabelais and Molière have attracted the interest of scholars far more than Pascal or Bossuet; the eighteenth-century masters of liberal thought far more than the many mystics, "illuminés," pantheists of the same era or of the romantic age; the present-day Existentialists more than those clerics or laymen who, in the last three decades, have totally transformed the face of, and the public for, religion in France.

The aim of this paper is to point out what are the most substantial results achieved by scholars who have, for the majority in France, studied the relations between literature and religion, to stress even more the areas in which fruitful research remains to be undertaken, and perhaps to stimulate new scholars, in the country today most active in scholarship, America, to attempt such research. Relevant and general questions of method in such a complex and delicate study will at the same time be raised. "'Tis an awkward thing to play with souls," Browning's character noted, after attempting to rid his friend

---

[1] E. M. Forster remarks in *Abinger Harvest*: "It is not that the Englishman can't feel—it is that he is afraid to feel. He has been taught at his public school that feeling is bad form. He must not express great joy or sorrow, or even open his mouth too wide when he talks—his pipe might fall out if he did."

from the toils of a "light woman" through attracting her to himself. Any careful consideration of religious ideas, feelings, dogmas, rites, and vague aspirations as they appear in the distorting mirror of literature requires some vocation for what the French call the role of "un amateur d'âmes," a sense of spiritual values, the broad outlook which embraces collective and social forces as well as the mysteries of conversion or of individual search for saintliness, critical spirit but also sensibility and respect for the irrational "reasons of the heart." It is clear that no easy recipe can be proposed, no convenient methodology—only a very prudent, tactful, and ever pliable approach could be appropriate.

The first requirement in a scholar who bends over the past is perspectivism, as the Germans like to call it: the ability to abstract oneself from the present and to share the moods, the beliefs, the implicit assumptions, and the aspirations of a bygone age. Such a plasticity is not uncommon among modern historians, who have inherited from the end of the eighteenth century and from the romantic revolution the relative spirit which had ruined the previous reign of an absolute (religious, philosophical, political). But the historian proper tends to be more engrossed in facts and in events, in concrete details, abrupt changes, conflicts of forces than concerned with the inner lives of the individuals who survived those changes and fretted as paltry actors in a dubious battle.

The historian of literature, on the other hand, deals with a few exceptional beings for whom the world of the imagination was truer than the concrete, real one and who expressed themselves not only with intensity, but also with the ambiguities inherent in the use of language. Anyone who endeavors to trace the intricacies of the workings of religious faith in the souls of men now defunct must unravel that semi-fallacy that literature often is, and analyze the self-delusions, the rationalizations of subconscious urges, the inconsistencies, the blend of hatred with love, of ruthlessness with charity which are often encountered among religious persons, as among others. A close attention to the collective, that is, to the links which bind people of the same faith and to the force of irradiation which emanates from great reformers, is required. But equally needed is that gift for drawing individual portraits which ancient historians, and modern ones such as Gibbon or Michelet, possessed and were not afraid to exercise. There may be such a thing as superhumanly objective history and the striving toward it is certainly laudable; but history of religious sensibility and even of religious ideas and dogmas, and history of literature, can hardly ever avoid being the past reborn and relived in the consciousness of the scholar.

At the same time, and while the historian tries to reconstruct the past "as it actually happened," in Ranke's formula, and therefore to mold himself according to the mood of the age into which he spiritually emigrates, he is forced also to envisage that past in its consequences. The passing of the Rubicon by Caesar, the flight of Louis XVI, the arrival of Lenin at the Finland Station in 1917 might have remained insignificant incidents and must have appeared as such to many contemporaries: only their aftermath has loaded them with far-reaching import. The historian cannot ignore the perspective of time which endows an event with significance and therefore with reality. The same is even truer of religious happenings which could have slipped altogether unnoticed by history—Luther's posting of his theses at Wittenberg, Pascal's night of religious illumination, Renan's loss of faith while at the seminary—had they not proved heavy with consequences which alone rendered them meaningful. The historian literally makes the past because he recreates it in the perspective of his privileged hindsight.

In the process he is liable to lend more unity to an age, to a country or a province, even to an individual mind, than there ever was in it in truth. We have to reason, even to rationalize, in order to understand and to descry unity behind contradictory variety. Our mind seems torn between the impulse to see or to put sense into baffling human affairs, and the insidious and discouraging realization that probably that rational explanation is only a need of our limited if unconquerable human mind. Simmel remarked more than once that "the works of the past are absurd. . . . Historical science is an effort to give meaning to what has none." The late Sir Lewis Namier likewise confessed that "possibly there is no more sense in human history than in the changes of the seasons or the movements of the stars." Yet we have to believe that its lesson may eventually be put to some use by our successors, or that at any rate we shall have gained something from a keener insight into the mistakes of others. We are personally convinced that few generalizations are as conveniently lazy and as unfounded as the one which, long after the events, disregarding many of the opposing features and escaping into the comfortable sophism that exceptions confirm the rule, asserts that there was a harmonious unity in an age like the thirteenth century in Paris, the Renaissance in Florence or in London, French classicism, or the age of positivistic realism. We then undertake to demonstrate that unity of a certain *Zeitgeist* through subtly deciphering parallels or correspondences between the philosophy and the religion of that era, its novel, its poetry, its painting, its music, its fashions. We conclude by lamenting the loss of that cultural unity among us (as the contemporary observers regularly have at all times) and advocate a return to scholasticism, to classicism, to the peace and harmony which supposedly prevailed among the men of the Enlightenment or the Victorians. Reality always was far more complex. One of the chief advantages of including the study of religious movements and of religious natures in the consideration of literature is that it teaches us to make room in history for irrational motives and feelings and not, like some imperious rationalists, to scorn as superstitions or to force within the purlieus of reason what gains nothing through being thus reduced.

The first specific illustration we shall mention here will be drawn from recent studies on the relations between religion and literature in the French sixteenth century. Those relations were then much closer in France than in England, where much of the Elizabethan drama and not a little of the lyrical poetry was strangely untouched by religion in a country which changed its faith four times at the bidding of its sovereigns; they were even closer than in the Italy of Machiavelli, Ariosto, and Tasso. Yet, outside the translators of the Bible and a few ecclesiastic writers, the great writers of that age took little part in the controversies which were raging in a country which might then have gone over to Protestantism altogether. In several respects the most intriguing problems for the literary or social historian are proposed by the French Reformation and particularly by Lefèvre d'Etaples: did he actually precede Luther (the relationship with Zwingli would be even more obscure) and is the French Reformation therefore original and autochthonous? Imbart de la Tour and Renaudet have in our time thrown much light, in an impartial spirit, on these questions. The late sixteenth-century Protestant poets, now too easily dubbed "baroque" (D'Aubigné, Du Bartas, De Sponde) have attracted attention in the last thirty years; but too little is known of an admirable school of exegetic interpreters of biblical texts who flourished under Henry IV and founded that branch of scholarship in Europe. The history of scholarship is unfairly sacrificed to the history of literature—to which it is often a valuable handmaiden; but it deserves being written in its own right.[2]

The most original reinterpretation of three of the storytellers of the French sixteenth century whose religious attitude is puzzling to many moderns has been offered in the years 1942–1944 by the vigorous historian Lucien Febvre, of the Collège de France. One of Febvre's lifelong concerns was to hunt out anachronisms in our approach to the past and to warn us against lending our own views of today to men of three centuries ago who could not possibly have entertained them. His ambition was to attempt the writing of a sort of history which would supplement that of institutions or of economic and political facts and might be called the history of sensibility. Literature, exceptional as it is, since it is felt and written by beings out of the ordinary, affords posterity the safest documents in which to explore the manner in which men of an earlier era experienced joy, fear, anguish, remorse, pleasure, or woe. Terms themselves are misleading, for they lacked precision until the eighteenth century, or later, where the description of psychological or affective states was concerned.

But literary scholars are trained to sharpen their subtlety to such a point that they can seldom resist proving more complex, thus perhaps more intelligent, than the very creators whom they interpret. They are fond of imagining that the great writers of former ages hid several

---

[2] Augustin Renaudet's finest books are *Préréforme et Humanisme à Paris* (1916, new edition, 1953) and *Humanisme et Renaissance* (1958). Father Walter Ong has given us the best study by far on Ramus (Harvard University Press, 1958). The names of those remarkable commentators of the Scriptures in France between 1600 and 1625 were Casaubon, Turnèbe, Saumaise, Louis Cappelle. They anticipated Richard Simon and Spinoza and modern exegesis.

layers of meaning in whatever they wrote and were far too shrewd to offer us their prose to be taken at its face value, as if beauty could never be simple and genius never naïve. They insist upon seeing fore-runners of our modern iconoclastic opinions in men of the Renais-sance who delighted in myths and tales. A case in point is that of Rabelais.

Predecessors of Lucien Febvre had gone so far as to view Rabelais as an atheist; others called him, at the very least, an unbeliever and compared him to Lucian, the universal mocker of late Greek culture; others still surmised, not unjustly, that he must have been favorable to the Reformation, at least early in his literary career, and had attacked the Church of Rome as an agnostic. Febvre replaces Rabelais in his age, which was close, in more ways than one, to the autumn of the Middle Ages; in the frame of mind which was his— that of a former Franciscan monk, as Etienne Gilson showed, but also that of a born and ebullient railer at the prejudices, conven-tionalities, and ridicules of his contemporaries. The question to be asked, and to be answered negatively, is this: was it possible to be an unbeliever in the sixteenth century, when all the intellectual, artistic, social life was directed by the Church or linked to it? The most independent and jocular of men were also credulous creatures, to whom the weirdest cock-and-bull stories were acceptable. Montaigne himself was strangely uncritical and superstitious some days. Science had not yet learned the price of a precise language or of exact measurements, philosophy was unsystematic; those very men who have done most to prepare our conception of the modern world— Kepler, Galileo, Descartes, and Newton—were all, as Renan once remarked, believers. A modern man may choose to reject or to accept Christianity; several substitutes for faith are available to him; schools other than religious schools for his children, festivities, communal rites, legal channels are open to him and his family. Such was not the case for a man in 1540 or even a century or two later. He could be irreverent, he could satirize monks and convents, rites and mysteries; but neither Rabelais nor the author of *La Celestina* was, or could be, or needed to be, an unbeliever. It is a naïve mistake we tend to make, to imagine that they were hypocrites concealing their active unbelief under a cloak or that the tyranny of the Church weighed as unbearably on them as it would on us if we had to go back four hundred years and live under it.

Precision in thinking, objectivity and method in observing, perspicuity in wielding the tool of an exact language were lacking until the next century, the seventeenth, began to accomplish its task of scientific modernization; so was consistency. Modern historians of ideas are fond of organizing the past along clear-cut lines; the renaissance of paganism opposing medieval asceticism, mysticism in some individuals, and moral austerity, lewdness, and delight in boisterous and farcical stories in others, and those diverse groups seldom meeting. Our favorite explanation for the past is thus to do away with its contradictoriness.

But things happen otherwise in our very midst; even coy maidens, brought up under the shadow of a church and trained to repress spontaneousness and the promptings of instinct in them, may listen to, or relate, anecdotes of candid frankness. A religious person is not equally religious every minute of the day; religion, moreover, may embrace more than stern morality. Lucien Febvre made a case study of Marguerite de Navarre, the sister of Francis I, who sheltered many Protestants, was steeped in the Platonic current of the first half of the sixteenth century, wrote mystical and deeply religious verse herself, and lived her faith with her heart as well as with her mind. While not quite a Protestant herself, she was imbued with the Scriptures and with the pages in which St. Paul claims that faith alone can lead to salvation; she turned away from the artificiality and the exterior rites and quibbles of the narrower kind of Catholicism against which many minds were then rebelling.

That same great lady and fervent Christian, shortly before she died in 1549 and while in her early fifties, composed the bawdy tales of the *Heptameron*. The stories are somewhat less libertine than Boccaccio's; their purpose is didactic, no doubt, as was the purpose of much literature until almost our very day; yet the modern reader cannot help being taken aback by the contradiction between the substance and the tone of these tales directed against monks and seeming to delight in sexual immorality and even in violence, and, on the other hand, the refined and profoundly religious personality of their author. Lucien

Febvre, devoting a volume to that mystery and giving it as a subtitle "Sacred Love, Profane Love," displayed prudence and insight. "A person of the sixteenth century must be intelligible, not relatively to us, but relatively to his contemporaries," he declares. The apparent incompatibilities in the Queen of Navarre's character are incompatibilities only for us, moderns, who will admit contradictions as the successive phases of an evolution but view them as evidence of hypocrisy, or of mental unbalance, if they occur simultaneously in the same complex soul. Our conception of religion would be less naïvely simple if we broadened it through familiarity with history and enriched it through the study of contradictory characters like Luther, John Knox, John Wesley, or even Pascal and Rousseau.[3]

Sainte-Beuve, in a famous chapter of his monumental *Port-Royal* (Book iii, ch. 3) portrayed Montaigne as a mocker of religion, pretending to obey the dicta of the Church but in truth playing a comedy and luring the reader into the recesses of a labyrinth in which he suddenly blew out the only light by which he had guided him there. The partly Jewish moralist of the *Essays* thus became an anticipator of the Dutch Jew Spinoza. A debate on Montaigne's religion has raged ever since Sainte-Beuve, with scholars taking up diverse positions and keeping Montaigne contradictory and alive through their debates. Once again the flaw in many of their interpretations was lack of perspectivism and a strange determination to view Montaigne differently from the reading which his contemporaries,

---

[3] Lucien Febvre's volumes alluded to here are: *Le Problème de l'incroyance au XVIᵉ siècle. La Religion de Rabelais* (Albin Michel, 1942); *Autour de l'Heptaméron. Amour sacré, amour profane* (Gallimard, 1944). To them must be added a challenging interpretation of the one genuine negator of religion in the first half of the same century, Bonaventure des Périers, whom Febvre explains through the influence of Celsus as preserved in Origen's refutation: *Origène et Des Périers ou l'Enigme du Cymbalum Mundi* (Droz, 1942), and a rich collection of essays, *Au Cœur religieux du XVIᵉ siècle* (Sevpen, 1957). See also "La Sensibilité et l'histoire," in *Annales d'Histoire Sociale*, III (1941), 1–20. The best studies in English on the religion of Rabelais are those of M. A. Screech, *The Rabelaisian Marriage* (1958); and on Montaigne, the wise and discerning chapter on a much debated subject (to what extent and in what manner was Montaigne religious?) is that of Donald M. Frame in *Montaigne's Discovery of Man* (Columbia University Press, 1955). See also Richard H. Popkin, *The History of Scepticism from Erasmus to Descartes* (Assen, The Netherlands: Van Gorcum, 1960).

including the Catholic hierarchy, made of his *Essays.* The most "ondoyant et divers" of thinkers has been forced by lovers of logic into a consistent reasoner, disguising his true meaning under the cloak of fanciful digressions. Montaigne was thus transfigured into the arch-skeptic, as Emerson was to depict him. Others, on the contrary, especially Catholic priests, several of whom have lovingly studied Montaigne (Joseph Coppin, in 1925 and 1927; A. Forest, 1929; Hermann Janssen, in 1930; Maturin Dréano, in 1936), have been reluctant to surrender Montaigne to the libertine current which had proclaimed him as its fountainhead, and have been guilty of the most common and forgivable fault of religiously minded scholars studying the past—partisanship.

The debate revolves around the meaning to be placed upon the central, although not the final or the most personal, chapter of the *Essays,* the lengthy *Apologie de Raimond Sebond.* The contradictions in that chapter are very probably involuntary; Montaigne poured into it passages composed at different times without integrating them or reconciling their assertions; he allowed himself, like many a writer, to be carried away by his verve and to indulge his paradoxical turn of mind. Like a novelist or a dramatist, he became temporarily the character whom he was imagining and experienced the role that he was acting. It is even probable that he failed to perceive many of these contradictions, for he lived them and they coexisted in him peacefully. Montaigne went to mass regularly, visited shrines like a good pilgrim during his travels, believed in miraculous cures, prayed dutifully, and he distrusted Protestantism even if he remained on good terms with Huguenots in his own family and was ready to serve a Protestant court, for to him the reformed faith in France was the novelty; and Montaigne, bold in many of his ideas, was a foe of innovations. He even admired an "apostate" and a persecutor of Christianity like Emperor Julian because, stubbornly if mistakenly, he stood for ancestral traditions and conservative stability. No one in his own time, and not even the Jansenist Pascal and the Oratorian Malebranche, who, in the following century, upbraided him bitterly, accused Montaigne of irreligion. In 1676 his *Essays* were placed on the Index, but not as an agnostic or anti-Catholic work. Among the Catholics, he distrusted human reason overmuch and too complacently proclaimed the powerlessness of man when deprived of human grace; he had been too ingenious in envying the gifts bestowed upon animals.[4] He probably did not share the delight in repentance in which more tormented souls have basked and his chapter on the subject (III, ii) is certainly devoid of masochistic exaltation. Even his earlier chapter on prayers (I, lvi), perhaps his most Christian one in the modern sense, may sound cool to ears attuned to the ardent strains of Péguy, Claudel, or of the Spanish mystics who were Montaigne's exact contemporaries. But there are many mansions in the house of Catholicism and, as one of the sanest scholars who wrote on the subject, Marcel Raymond, remarked, we are today, in France in particular, much too prone to see Christianity only in its Jansenist or Calvinistic forms. In a Catholicism less tinged with Jansenist hues, the realm of nature is not necessarily opposed to that of grace. Grace completes and sanctifies nature, without annihilating it. The many statements in praise of nature in the sixteenth century carried no anti-Christian implication with them. They marked the passing of the theocentricity of the Middle Ages to an era in which anthropocentrism was eventually to prevail. That was probably the only manner in which religion could be preserved at all: through compromising, as the Jesuits wished, with man's frailties, accepting good works along with pure and rigid faith as tools to one's salvation and even some consideration of cases or of circumstances, which casuistry was then to turn to less honest purposes. The triumph of Jansenism in 1650–1670 might well have spelled the ruin of Catholicism in France and accelerated the victory of unbelief and of a lay ethics.

Modern scholarship has done a valuable service in scanning the texts more meticulously than ever before. While earnest unbelievers like Sainte-Beuve, Lanson, Villey, and the philosopher Brunschvicg had inclined to see Montaigne in the mirror of what followed him, hence as a tepid believer whose book was one of unbelief, the

---

[4] Not necessarily an anti-religious attitude, and often a moral one! Walt Whitman, in his famous lines in the "Song of Myself," voiced his desire to turn and live with animals: "They do not lie awake in the dark and weep for their sins." The philosopher Max Scheler advised his disciples: "Learn to know animals, so as to see how difficult it is to be a man" (*Mensch und Geschichte*, Zurich, 1929).

Catholic admirers of the *Essays* rightly recalled to us that fideism was a frequent position in the sixteenth century: the Paduan school of Pomponazzi had spread it in France. Without necessarily deserting orthodoxy, which had many facets then as now, several thinkers contended that reason alone is incapable of reaching the truths of religion; they are mysterious and reserved to faith. A fideist could be a sincere believer, as Karl Barth's disciples are today, while immolating reason altogether to faith. So could he and so could a rationalist, who leans on reason as divorced from faith. Montaigne remained a contradictory, and perhaps an unclear, thinker, undisturbed as many of us are by his unreconciled positions; and in our opinion, once again, we are impoverishing his fanciful and poetical thought by constraining it to a conjectural unity.

Our double mistake is to contend that an essayist is also a logician and that to understand him, we have to reach the unity and consistency which he carried within him unbeknownst to himself, and to admit implicitly that the Pascalian, or mystical, conception of Christianity is the most sincere one. Montaigne did not feel God's presence as St. Paul or St. Augustine may have done; he did not live with Christ's presence close to him or in him; he was not obsessed by the fall and the stain of original sin in us; he distrusted mysticism, and even the "daemonic" or "ecstatic" side of his hero, Socrates; he preferred Epicureanism to any asceticism. The quality of his faith may thus not have been the highest, according to our romantic standards. But he did not attempt to dupe his readers. He was a sincere, if not an exalted, Catholic—and not an unchristian Catholic, as other conservative Catholics of the twentieth century, such as Barrès and Maurras, have deserved to be called.[5]

One is never through with Pascal, remarked Sainte-Beuve over a century ago. Pascal's fascination for the French has never been more potent than in the last twenty or thirty years. He is the intercessor to Christianity for a large number of French people, brought up as

[5] Besides the volumes by Hermann Janssen, *Montaigne fidéiste*, and by another cleric, Maturin Dréano, *La Pensée religieuse de Montaigne*, see Marc Citoleux, *Le Vrai Montaigne, théologien et soldat* (1937); Gustave Lanson, *Les Essais de Montaigne* (1930); Jean Plattard, *Etat présent des études sur Montaigne* (1935); Marcel Raymond, *Génies de France* (Neuchâtel, 1942); Jean Guiton, *Romanic Review* (April 1944), pp. 98–115.

nominal Christians until they discover the *Pensées*. He may well have disturbed the complacent orthodoxy of just as vast a number of French schoolboys and brought to them a tragic sense of existence and an unquiet unbelief which a partial reading of Pascal fostered in them: from Goethe to Nietzsche, indeed, passionate readers of Pascal had noted that, if the positive sections of his *Apology* are rejected (and few can avoid rejecting their argumentation, founded on miracles, prophecies, and the fulfillment of the Old Testament by the New), the whole fabric of his thought crumbles into debris. Books on Pascal appear, three or four a year in French and as many in the other European languages; only in American scholarship have Pascalian studies lagged, despite the two excellent biographies by Roger Soltau in 1927 and Morris Bishop in 1936. A whole volume would be necessary to sketch a survey of the recent Pascal scholarship.[6] It might be more opportune to trace the areas in which new or renewed research on the most influential of French Christian writers might still be undertaken.

The biography of Pascal has not yet yielded all its secrets. A number of legends have been exploded by recent scholarship: on Pascal's first conversion, which hardly deserves that name, and on his so-called mundane period, which has been grossly exaggerated. True it is, however, that Pascal may well have felt intellectually closer to the *libertins* than to the conventionally devout. The *libertin* seldom answers the impassioned apologist, in the imaginary dialogue which the *Pensées* constitute, but his silence is eloquent; and it may be questioned whether Pascal himself was fully convinced by the famous sophistry of his wager, meant to frighten the agnostic gambler into a posture of faith. Not a few theologians are averse to admitting that he might ever have included it in a completed apology of Christian religion. But the most valuable research on obscure sections of Pascal's life has explored his strange behavior to his sister Jacqueline when she entered the convent of Port-Royal and his dying words, which have been read by some as a denial of his Jansenism. On the

---

[6] I have attempted such a fragmentary survey twice, very imperfectly, in "Pascal et la critique contemporaine," *Romanic Review*, XXI (1930), 325–341; and "Friends and Foes of Pascal in France Today," *Yale French Studies*, No. 12 (*God and the Writer*, 1953), pp. 8–18.

first point, Jean Mesnard has shed new light and made incisive comments in his excellent and terse volume on Pascal (*Pascal, l'Homme et l'Œuvre*, 1951), and in articles in *XVIIe Siècle*, (Nos. 9–10, 15; 1951, 1952). Pascal did act imperiously and greedily to prevent his sister from entering the Jansenist cloister and tried to rob her of her share of the family patrimony. On Pascal's confessions, made almost on his deathbed to a Paris priest, who drew up his reminiscences thirty years after the event, at the age of eighty-three, and whose memoirs were only discovered in manuscript in 1911 by Ernest Jovy, animated controversies have raged. The priest, Father Beurrier, was a credulous soul, more than confused on Jansenism, who, two and a half years after Pascal's death, reported to the Archbishop of Paris that Pascal had disowned his former friends, the Jansenists, as he lay dying and, through his orthodox submissiveness, deserved the Sacrament of Extreme Unction which the aged priest had ministered to him. The ablest discussion of the confused, often unreliable evidence on this point is that of Morris Bishop, "Did Pascal Die a Jansenist?" (*Romanic Review*, xxx [1929], 352–360). It is impartial, coming as it does from a wise and detached American, while Jansenism is, to French scholars, still a live issue in which they cannot refrain from partisanship. It is clear, regret it as many Catholics such as Abbé Bremond will, that Pascal's whole adult life, more significant after all than the reported confession of a sick man, was that of a Jansenist, and that his writings and his theology were Jansenist, even when he disagreed with his friends, whom he judged too tepid. Archives and accounts from the Paris notaries have only been opened, for the seventeenth century, since 1948 or so, and curious discoveries are still to be made there.

The second field of research which scholars would find fertile is the exploration of the semantics of Pascal, and of his age. It is idle to discuss the philosophy of Pascal in terms which have, for us today, connotations which were not attached to them in the seventeenth century. And it is almost as idle to isolate Pascal (or, for that matter, Bossuet and Fénelon, both very complex personalities and today the most neglected and the least read of France's towering writers) from the theological movement around him. We know far too little about the education they received, the prayer books they learned by heart, the manuals of logic, of ethics, of piety in which they studied, the legacy of scholasticism, or of Augustinism, which was everywhere lingering in that century of nascent modernity, the connotations which they put behind the words to which they had to resort. The seventeenth-century background has been less ably elucidated for France than it has been for England by Basil Willey. Pascal had one of the most rigorous, most passionately geometrical, of intellects. Yet his vocabulary lacked precision, and the rigor of his peremptory aphorisms is often only apparent. A meticulous scrutiny into the several meanings of "reason," "imagination," "sentiment," "heart," "will," in Pascal's language, in the language of the Jansenists and of other religious moralists, in the language of the *libertins* and of Montaigne's posterity, should be undertaken. Even more urgent is an inquiry into the content which Pascal the geometrist and Pascal the fervent apologist put into the word "order." The distinction among the mineral, vegetable, and animal realms; the parallel order of bodies, minds, and souls; and of material power, intellectual greatness symbolized by Archimedes, and charity (according to Christ and to St. Paul) appears to have been fundamental in Pascal's thought. Only unsystematic approximations at clarifying it have been attempted thus far.[7]

A true revolution in our view of the French classical age, once petrified into a marble edifice of pure rationalism and of formal decorum, has been effected by the research of historians, theologians, and literary scholars of the last three decades. Its result has been to unearth very rich mystical strata under classicism, indeed, to present France after the Council of Trent as teeming with mystics of all varieties. The most considerable, in its bulk (eleven volumes) and in the originality of its material as well as of its ideas, of all the works devoted in our century to French religious literature is Abbé Henri

[7] See Ed. Benzécri, *L'Esprit humain selon Pascal* (Alcon, 1939); Jeanne Russier, *La Foi selon Pascal* (P.U.F., 1949); J. Prigent, "La Conception pascalienne de l'ordre," in *Ordre, Désordre, Lumière* (Vrin, 1952); Jacques Morel, "Réflexions sur le 'sentiment' pascalien," *Revue des Sciences humaines*, No. 97 (January–March 1960); and the excellent recent volume by an English critic, *Blaise Pascal*, by Ernest Mortimer (New York: Harper and Brothers, 1959). In 1962 appeared *Pascal et l'ordre du cœur* by Ch. Baudoin, in the collection "Recherche de l'absolu."

Bremond's *Histoire littéraire du Sentiment religieux* (11 vols., Bloud et Gay, 1916–1933). Bremond's history is not, and no history of religion can be, strictly impartial. A former Jesuit himself, and a subtle Provençal from Aix, closer through every fiber of his nature to Fénelon than to imperious Pascal, Abbé Bremond more or less consciously undertook to dethrone Port-Royal from the sovereign position traditionally granted it by French academic critics, since Sainte-Beuve's classic work. To him, Jansenism was, and still appears as, a heresy; its task of austere purification of French Catholicism was already being accomplished, less rigidly, by a number of other groups, during that age of Counter-Reformation, and religious life was richer, certainly more spontaneous and more joyful, more radiant in the tradition of St. Francis, or of St. François de Sales, in other Catholic groups than in Port-Royal. The whole fourth volume of Bremond's monumental history aims at surrounding the traditional French admiration for Pascal with reservations.

Pascal's theology, the Abbé contends, is indelibly Jansenist, hence open to suspicion, for it sacrifices God to Christ, in the sense that the believer addresses his prayers to Christ, with passionate and fervent familiarity, communicates with Him directly, through the heart, and because Christ has destined him, Pascal the sinner, to be saved, marking him with a sign when He revealed Himself to him in a night of ecstasy. Metaphysical evidence, on the other hand, is resorted to, to prove God. But Christ, sent by his Father as a mediator to redeem the world, has, in Bremond's insinuation, failed signally in that mission, since, for the Jansenist, the world is still plunged in error, evil, and misery, and only a mysterious few can be preserved from the wrathful condemnation which awaits all the others. Pascal may have entertained the belief that he was among those few set apart from the *massa damnata* of men, for he had enjoyed a visitation of Christ and heard the sublimely selfish verse of "Le Mystère de Jésus" (*Pensées*, Brunschvicg edition, No. 552): "I thought of thee in Mine agony, I have sweated such drops of blood for thee." He thus could be joyful, as indeed he was, in the midst of his physical torments. He was profoundly Jansenist if the Jansenists' implicit, or secret, conviction, insidiously summarized by Abbé Bremond, can be summed up as "Christ did not die for all men, but He died for us." But this theology, for Bremond as for the great Catholic layman Jacques Maritain,[8] was execrable.

Can Pascal, at least, rank among the genuine French mystics? Bremond is not certain of it, and prefers to him the many subtler, less tragic mystics whom he had unearthed in the seventeenth century between St. François de Sales and Fénelon. Pascal's mystical experience has been scanned by specialists in mystical psychology, theologians, philosophers; and their answers are not unanimous, for personal interpretation of those mysteries of a man's soul or of his visions must remain arbitrary, or imaginative. Protestants, especially in the English or Anglican tradition, have proved more attracted to Pascal's mysticism than Roman Catholics; the latter, if they had sympathies for the Jesuits like Bremond, were still smarting under the wounds inflicted by the *Provinciales*, from which Jesuits have never recovered; if they stood for Thomistic rationalism as conducive to divine grace or resting on that grace, like Maritain and several neo-scholastics, they questioned Pascal's relentless reasoning to humble reason; they deplored his ignorance of St. Thomas and, indeed, of Aristotle, and of most of philosophy before Montaigne. Clement Webb, in *Pascal's Philosophy of Religion* (Oxford Press, 1929), Rev. Henry Stewart in several works, Dorothy Eastwood in *The Revival of Pascal* (Clarendon Press, 1936), and Ernest Mortimer, mentioned above, have looked upon Pascal with warmer sympathy.

The brief sentences, interspersed with quotations from the Scriptures and preceded with the famous word "Feu," which were found sewn in the lining of Pascal's coat after his death have been subjected to many a scrutiny by recent scholars. It was first called, by his sister, Pascal's "memorial," after the words pronounced by God to Moses in the burning bush, in Exodus 3:15. A Benedictine, Dom Pastourel, analyzed those twenty elliptic lines searchingly in a pamphlet in 1930. Abbé Steinmann, in 1954, centered a whole volume on Pascal's mystical experience, representing him as less intent upon proving God than upon finding the traces of God's action and interpreting the

---

[8] J. Maritain, "Pascal apologiste," *Revue Universelle*, August 1, 1923, pp. 184–200. See also H. Bremond, "Pascal et les mystiques," *Revue de Paris*, June 15, 1923, pp. 739–753, and "Pascal et le mystère de Jésus," *Revue de France*, June 15, 1928, pp. 673–683.

signs left by such an action in man and in the world. Marcel Raymond, coolly and lucidly, read between the lines of the Memorial of November 23, 1654, and of "The Mystery of Jesus," which he supposes to have been written soon after, in one of the finest essays on the subject, "La Conversion de Pascal," in Theophil Spoerri's *Überlieferung und Gestaltung* (Zurich, 1950). Father André Blanchet, a Jesuit, agreed with the academic interpreters of Pascal's text that the Memorial, bristling with biblical references, drawn up after, not during, the vision, oscillated between the fear of losing God's grace and the joyful certitude of having found it (*Etudes*, November 1954, pp. 145–166). A curious fragment (No. 524) of the *Pensées* betrays that dual position of Pascal: "There is no doctrine more appropriate to man than that one, which teaches him his two-fold capacity to receive and to lose grace, on account of the two-fold peril to which he is always exposed, of despair or of pride." A professor of philosophy at the Sorbonne, Henri Gouhier, in a substantial essay printed in *Pascal* (Cahiers de Royaumont, No. 1, Editions de Minuit, 1956), dealt with the question: "Is the *Memorial* a mystical text?" He centered his development around the famous phrase from Isaiah 45:15, "Deus absconditus." "Thou art a God that hidest thyself." A Marxist and bellicose thinker, Lucien Goldmann thus entitled a paradoxical interpretation of Pascal *Le Dieu caché* (Gallimard, 1959): with the growth of modern science and of a mechanistic explanation of the world, God became hidden or absent, but still remained present in many minds which clung to the old values. As providence, the Supreme Being no longer was visible or narrated to all eyes by the glories of the heavens; but as a standard of ethical values, He was needed by men. Pascal was not haunted by such a tragic vision of the world as Mr. Goldmann imagines. God, to him, was hidden, because He both illumines and blinds. If He were everywhere and always to be seen, there would be little merit in believing. Faith has to be a disavowal of the intellect. "Credo," said Tertullian, "quia ineptum est." [9]

[9] F. T. H. Fletcher, in *Pascal and the Mystical Tradition* (Oxford: Blackwell, 1954), does not differ essentially from his French predecessors in his analysis of the *Memorial*.

It had to be the fate of a thinker like Pascal, no less rich in contradictions, no less broad in accepting varied facets of truth and in availing himself of every cogent argument in his apologetical zeal, than Plato, Rousseau, or Nietzsche, to undergo posthumous transfigurations whenever a new philosophical climate prevailed. Two currents are therefore discernible in recent French attitudes to Pascal: the Marxist and the Existentialist ones. Henri Lefebvre, one of the most serious minds in the Marxist camp and a fine philosopher in his own right, devoted two volumes to Pascal in 1950–1952. His ambition was to explain the Pascalian apology through the nefarious influence of French absolutism over him. Jansenism is regarded by Lefebvre as a passive form of nascent bourgeois individualism. The Fronde was an abortive revolution of the middle class; after its failure, that class bowed servilely to the Sun King as it bowed to the fatality of evil in this world. The thesis, while much too rigid and paradoxical, has the merit of stressing the possible impact of the Fronde on Pascal and of throwing some light on his political thought. More directly relevant to our consideration of Pascal's religious thought is the stress, placed by Marxists or by Hegelians, on his dialectical way of thinking. "We do not display greatness by going to one extreme, but in touching both extremes at once and in filling all the intervening space" (353). "We must add at the end of each truth that the opposite truth must be borne in mind" (566). Maxims like these and a few others seem indeed to point to a thought which reaches incessantly beyond itself to move to new positions, reconciling or transcending from one to another.

Henri Lefebvre is a relentless attacker of the Existentialists. But the latter encounter fewer hurdles than the Marxists when they endeavor to interpret Pascal according to their doctrine—itself a loose one, and a mood rather than a system. For Pascal does rest a great deal on the primacy of experience, on feeling more than on reasoning. He also proclaims the primacy of existence, in this sense at least, that the existing creature, aghast at his existence, alone and unwanted in a baffling universe, starts from that concrete, lived experience of his existence. He undertakes to discover God through his own need for God. In spite of the famous sentence "Abêtissez-vous" ("Make

yourselves like beasts and tame your bodies in order to believe"),
Pascal fails to deem rites, sacraments, and churches as very important. Kierkegaard, in this respect, will be his direct heir, and a
Scot, Denzil G. M. Patrick, has composed two big volumes on *Pascal
and Kierkegaard*, published posthumously in 1947. Finally, like
modern Existentialists, Pascal depicts the human condition (when
deprived of grace and faith) as absurd; man is not attuned to the
world; he is not resigned to his prison cell; his entertainments are
pallid attempts at forever escaping from himself and from stark truth.
The Existentialist characters, victims of nausea, wallowing in boredom
until the day when they decide to wager, or to commit themselves, are
scions of the anguished libertines whom Pascal's dramatic genius
depicted as searching God. We may expect to read several Existentialist interpretations of Pascal's religion in the years to come.

Delicate as it is to probe individual consciences and to appraise the
sincerity and the intensity of the debates by which their faith may
have been torn, there are even more formidable hurdles facing the
scholar who endeavors to study the beliefs and the religious attitudes
of a whole city, province, or country. Once again, the documents to
be utilized are chiefly literary, and Goethe's reminder must ever be
borne in mind: literature is merely one fragment among fragments;
little has survived of all that was written, and a small fraction of what
was lived has been preserved in what was written. The vast amount of
research done in the French classical century affords several lessons
in that respect.

The authors who wrote abundantly about their faith, or to defend
the religion which was theirs, such as Pascal, Saint-Cyran before him,
Bossuet, Fénelon, and other ecclesiastical orators later, can be studied
in their works. The scholar's equipment is frequently deficient today
since theology has become a closed book to many researchers, since
the Fathers of the Church are seldom consulted and scholasticism is
known but to a very few. A student of the seventeenth century should
have some familiarity with the theological writings in medieval and
Renaissance Latin, among which every educated man then grew up.
Another source of frequent errors is to attribute precise philosophical
significance to formulas which men of letters, seldom philosophers in

the technical sense of the word, used conventionally. Literary scholars are prone to such interpretations: they imagine that they magnify a writer, be he Shakespeare or La Fontaine, Thomas Mann or Albert Camus, when they exalt him to the rank of a philosopher. Philosophers often know better. José Ortega y Gasset, in one of his suggestive essays, advised historians of ideas to discriminate between "ideas y creencias," the doctrines or the ideas held by the thinkers whose systems are expounded in histories of philosophy, and the beliefs, vague, inconsistent, but ardently and tenaciously clung to, which are those of more sentimental and less rigorous men and women. Etienne Gilson offered a similar warning in a suggestive lecture on "La Scolastique et l'esprit classique" in 1929, and that grave historian of scholasticism, unequaled today in his knowledge of medieval thought, boldly concluded: "It would be desirable to restore to our literary history a little more intelligence than it often displays, but it would be chiefly desirable to put a little more heart into it, for it often is through lack of heart that one lacks intelligence" (*Les Idées et les Lettres*, new ed., Vrin, 1955).

The best documented synthesis on the religion of the seventeenth-century writers is that which a former priest become a professor of literature, Henri Busson,[10] gave in 1948, *La Religion des Classiques*. Busson, who had long studied the rationalist currents derived from the Renaissance and, like many another scholar, had been attracted by those men who then thought against the trend of their age and professed libertine unbelief, proved admirably objective in that work. "Never was French Catholicism more Christian," he begins by declaring, reminding us that a Frenchman then was, by birthright and from his infancy on, a Christian and a humanist: religious agnostics and Epicurean libertines themselves have to be replaced in that context. A Spaniard, to this very day, rail as he may against the Church, will with difficulty avow himself to stand altogether outside Catholicism. M. Busson gravely recalls to his readers Montaigne's anecdote, in the course of his Italian travels, on the Roman courtesan who, lying in bed with her customer, would interrupt the rites of

---

[10] The soundest and broadest specialist of the French seventeenth century today, Antoine Adam, is also a former Catholic priest, now teaching at the Sorbonne.

Venus to recite her prayer when she heard the Angelus ring. Writers, long before our present age of self-mortification, were dimly aware of a similarity between their profession and that of venal dispensers of what is euphemistically called "joy" in some languages.

Within the vast realm of Catholicism, Jansenism occupies a privileged place in Busson's study, for literary documents abound where that movement, small in the number of its devotees, great by their quality, is concerned. Racine's Jansenism has been greatly exaggerated, and most, if not all, of the lines of *Phèdre* were some Jansenist inspiration has been suspected—or admired—come straight from Euripides, a pagan unblessed by grace, like Phèdre herself, since, for the Jansenists, no pagan could escape damnation. Mme de Sévigné was sentimentally and intellectually tinged with Jansenism and horrified by the superstitions and the pilgrimages and by the cult of the Virgin Mary practiced in Provence, "the small Barbary" as a contemporary called that province.

The relationship between religion and science in the century of mathematical genius, the seventeenth, is also traced precisely by Henri Busson. Scientists (Huygens, Mariotte, François Bayle, the physician Bernier) were then very close to men of letters, and were seldom totally severed from religion. La Fontaine never disbelieved in divine providence. It is not even sure, in our opinion, that Molière was as Epicurean and irreligious or as detached from faith as he has been portrayed. That Descartes was religious (without either a mystical or a tragic sense of life) is even clearer, at least to this writer. Anguish there was in the seventeenth century in France, but much less sedulously cultivated than it is among us, and the literary fashion did not favor expressing it, therefore exaggerating or analyzing it. The contemporary reaction to Pascal's *Pensées*, published in 1670, may well surprise the modern admirer of the great apologist. Several saw, in those Pascalian notes, stylistic and bombastic hyperboles, which could not coexist with "a pure and simple sincerity." The argument of the wager embarrassed many of the faithful. Pascal's disquietude, cherished by many of us since the romantics, disturbed his contemporaries, for why should not a Christian enjoy peace of mind and seek Christ, through reasoning and reasons of the heart, since he has already found him? Paul Valéry's famous indictment of Pascal is less original than many a modern might have thought.

Several theses have been devoted to Pascal's fame in the eighteenth and nineteenth centuries, but much remains to be done along these lines; for example, a close study of the different editions of the *Pensées* since Cousin's discourse on the subject in 1842, of the order in which they were arranged, and of the notes in which they were commented; or Pascal's influence since 1890 or so on Catholics and unbelievers alike, or even the influence of his imagery, syntax, and rhythm on modern prose poetry. Pascal's influence as an apologist and as a philosopher lies at the center of any study of religious thought in France in the age of the "philosophes." Naturally, deism, atheism, materialism, nascent evolutionism, the attempt to formulate a lay ethics, the struggle against the Church have attracted the attention of most students of the eighteenth century. In a paradoxical work, René Pomeau (*La Religion de Voltaire*, 1956) has attempted to prove that the foe of "infamous" Christianity was, at bottom, more religious than we thought, perhaps even not impervious to some mysticism. Diderot's and D'Holbach's atheism, or endeavor to "élargir Dieu" as Diderot proclaimed in a celebrated exclamation, has not been systematically and comprehensively examined. Laplace's relation to the philosophers of his age and his influence on the cosmological views of many romantics who, like Shelley, died before he did, would also deserve the attention of scholars. Rousseau's religious thought and his religious sensibility have on the contrary served as an object of much debate: all that pertains to Rousseau seems to be charged with electrical force and to arouse passion.

Rousseau's religious attitude was in 1916 the subject of a remarkable French thesis in three volumes, by Pierre Maurice Masson, one of the many French scholars killed during World War I. Little could be added to an exhaustive and subtle work, centered around the well-known pages at the end of *Emile* known as "The Profession of Faith of a Savoyard Curate." P. M. Masson, however, in irreproachable good faith, tended to picture the elusive Proteus that Rousseau was as slightly more Christian and more Catholic than he probably was.[11] He overstressed scattered sentences in Rousseau's remarkable correspondence in which he advised those who sought his counsel to

---

[11] Rousseau himself opposed the two adjectives in a sentence of his ninth *Rêverie d'un Promeneur solitaire*: "I became a Catholic, but I always stayed a Christian."

remain in the religion in which they were born and asserted his own need for religion. "I have religion; . . . I do not believe there is a man in the world who needs it as much as I do" (February 18, 1758). At the same time he purposely wanted to reform all that was antiquated in the Christian legacy which the "philosophes," of whom Rousseau disapproved, had been attacking for fifty years. He also discarded, or omitted altogether, a number of the essential props of Christianity. P. M. Masson could not fail to notice it and was too honest a scholar to conceal that Rousseau's strange Christianity left out doctrinal rigor, the history of Christianity, redemption, and repentance.

It left out even more. Revelation is absent from that faith. The notion of salvation through the grace of God does not enter into it. Redemption is unnecessary because original sin is banished. Nowhere does Rousseau appear to admit the divinity of Christ, or he does it only in poetical terms which anticipate Renan's suave negations. Humility is not a virtue highly esteemed by Rousseau: he preferred fortitude, and he was closer in his ethics to a Stoic than to a Christian. Indeed, he cut off the links between morality and religion, between practicing good because man has first intellectually understood where it lies, and practicing it by instinct and from the heart without the need of intellectual study. The ecstasy which the solitary walker described in a striking passage of his fifth Rêverie, opening the way to Wordsworth and to Shelley, even to Rimbaud, is a pantheistic, not a Christian one.

Nevertheless Rousseau's followers did not err when they hailed him as the restorer of faith. Through his growing abhorrence for the dryness and the sarcasms of the "philosophes," he came to be considered as their antithesis. He knew and felt the New Testament better than they had. He rejected miracles as unworthy of Christ and as an insult to the very reason with which God has endowed man. But he sympathized with man's dissatisfaction with a world from which the divine is banished: "I am stifled in the universe," he exclaims in a letter. He opened the gates to reverie and to emotion, which were two of the channels through which men in the romantic era were to commune with a presence above them. With him, philosophy abdicated its claims to replace religion. Several volumes still need to be written on the impact of *La Nouvelle Héloïse*, of *Emile*, of Rousseau's autobiographical works on the religious sensibility of the French, the German, and the English nineteenth century.

Books of solid scholarly merit appear yearly on Rousseau, the best in the last ten years being those of Groethuysen, Burgelin, Starobinski, and Emery.[12] Rousseau's glory has thrown many of his predecessors into the shade. A curious problem to which scholars have only lately applied themselves is the relative insignificance and the final futility of most, if not all, of the many volumes which in the eighteenth century defended religious faith. For we realize today that France as a whole remained a profoundly religious country throughout the age during which a handful of anti-clericals mocked the priests as impostors and Catholic rites as mummery. Scenes as touching as Chardin's *Benedicite* were lived in every French home: country priests remained almost untouched by the trend toward new ideas which the Encyclopedists were slowly pushing; the revival of religion after the short-lived persecutions of the refractory priests and the cult of the Supreme Being and of the goddess Reason will be sudden and easily victorious because faith had continued to burn within many souls.

Yet not one great book upholding traditional religion, not one moving statement of Christian faith can be found in the whole eighteenth century. The wave of the future, unbeknownst to the contemporaries, carried on its crest only deists, negators, champions of the philosophy of Enlightenment. France did not even have a counterpart to Blake or to *The Vicar of Wakefield* or to Klopstock's *Messias*. That puzzling problem of history of ideas and of history of sensibility has been approached in three solid volumes in as many languages. The first, by Albert Monod, is a patient analysis of the very abundant apologetic literature of the age of Enlightenment, *De Pascal à Chateaubriand. Les Défenseurs français du Christianisme de 1670 à 1802* (1916). Seven apologies of religion appeared, as an average, every year. They passed, as the century grew older, from haughty denunciation of unbelief to disquietude, then to bitterness, and lastly to weariness. Arguments derived from Church Fathers and St.

[12] Bernard Groethuysen, *J. J. Rousseau* (1949); Pierre Burgelin, *La Philosophie de l'existence de J. J. Rousseau* (1952); Jean Starobinski, *J. J. Rousseau* (Plon, 1957); Léon Emery, *Rousseau l'annonciateur* (Lyon, n.d.).

Thomas ceased to carry any impact, while science was altering our view of the world and of men and exegesis was growing bolder; the perspective of history was being enlarged, ethics was cut loose from revealed religion. But except for one or two Protestant pastors who had sought refuge outside of France and for heavy volumes inaccessible to the public at large, Pascal's lesson passed unheeded; apologetics would not start from man's tragic need for God. Rousseau alone was to open new vistas to it. Chateaubriand, in 1802, divined the mood of a new era and stressed the esthetic reasons for Christian faith.

In 1934, Kurt Wais devoted two detailed and learned chapters of his book, *Das antiphilosophische Weltbild des französischen Sturm und Drang, 1760–1789*, to the renaissance of religion and to the interpretation of the soul and the world among the pre-romantics. His dissertation is richer in factual information than in general ideas, but it constitutes a mine of details on the French pre-romantic revolt against the philosophers. But, unlike what happened in Germany and in England in the years 1770–1785, no writer of undisputed stature arose in France in those years. In America, a historian, Robert Palmer, wrote a solid as well as polished work on *Catholics and Unbelievers in Eighteenth Century France* (Princeton, 1939). Wisely, Robert Palmer showed that we cannot understand the "philosophes" aright unless we realize whom they attacked, and how strong were their opponents; for the Church was then rich, well organized, entrenched in secure bastions, impatient of those who questioned its authority—he thus explained why the Encyclopedists had to attack the very foundation of that authority, Revelation, how they intermittently obtained the assistance of the State, jealous of the Church's claim to intervene in politics. The superiority of the unbelievers, however, lay in the talents which they inspired and marshaled behind their cause, and in their awareness of a truth stated thus by J.-J. Rousseau: "One can act upon passions only through passions." The "philosophes" were fired by a passion for man's better future, for his happiness,[13] and for the progress of the race. They offered their contemporaries a new faith to replace an outworn creed. Man would be happy in this world, not in another one, and not individually

---

[13] See Robert Mauzi, *L'Idée du Bonheur au XVIIIᵉ siècle* (A. Colin, 1960).

happy, working out his own salvation in fear and trembling, but through saving other men in fraternal charity along with him.

More and more, historians of literature appear ready to agree that, contrary to a long-standing prejudice once shared in this country by Irving Babbitt and by many a neo-humanist, in Great Britain by T. E. Hulme, T. S. Eliot, and by champions of Anglo-Catholic classicism, nineteenth-century literature in France tapped new and deeper sources of religion than it had at any time since the end of the Middle Ages. A survey of the relationship between a literature which then annexed whole new provinces (history, sociology, criticism) and religious practice, faith (orthodox or, more often, heretical) would require volumes. Much has been accomplished by historians of letters, but much still remains to be done. A few broad lines may be traced here and a few suggestions may be formulated.

André Malraux, in cryptic and imperious developments in his volumes on art, made much of "the end of absolutes," which occurred in the late seventeenth and the late eighteenth centuries; he viewed our modern era as an anguished one, seeking "la monnaie de l'absolu," its "Ersatz" or substitutes, among which art might be the most universal today. True it is that, ever since the Age of Enlightenment and the Revolution, man ceased living in a climate of faith or of conformity. The critical spirit invaded every cranny and recess of our brains or, at any rate, of the brains of a number of intellectual leaders of our culture, for fanaticism passed on from the religious realm to that of politics and fomented nationalism and racism. Renan, echoing German philosophers of the early years of the last century, contended in *The Future of Science* that "the great progress of modern reflection has consisted in substituting the category of becoming for that of being, the conception of the relative for that of the absolute, motion for immobility."

Such widespread relativism made it possible to study ancient and exotic mythologies, the religious creeds and rites of many peoples, both with accuracy and detachment and with profound sympathy. The same Ernest Renan, in the tortured days of his youth when faith was deserting him, jotted down in a psychological essay on Christ: "One must at any cost either explain Jesus or fall at his feet." A few found it not impossible, after prolonged study, to discard much of traditional religion and to worship a disembodied and symbolic Christ, or the divine as severed from a personal God, with deep reverence. Others retained only a sentimental nostalgia for an outworn creed, and a semi-Voltairian fondness for Catholicism as a brake on men's unruly instincts (Balzac, Tocqueville, Bourget, Maurras, Barrès). Others still realized what a service unbelief had rendered religion through forcing it, intellectually, to re-examine its historical, textual, and philosophical foundations, and on the social plane, to win the masses which socialism tempted away from altars allied to the throne.

The social and political history of Catholicism in France, and the history of social Catholicism, need not concern us here, except insofar as they have been echoed in works of literary scholarship. A far-reaching change occurred in the middle of the twentieth century in the attitudes of the Church of France, and it is due in no small part to literature: to novels depicting the condition of workmen totally unaware of Christian values and symbols; to writers like Péguy, Mauriac, Bernanos, Julien Green convinced that religion enters into souls in order to disturb their complacent quietude and to divide them tragically, so that in the quest for God alone some unity will be reached; to intellectual and truly charitable Jesuits and Dominicans who turned magazines like *Etudes, Dieu Vivant,* and *La Vie Intellectuelle* into remarkable literary and philosophical periodicals. This has resulted in the disappearance of all sense of intellectual inferiority among Catholic thinkers; no longer do they feel that the boldest and deepest ideas belong to agnostic scientists or to academic positivists. Fathers Henri de Lubac and Pierre Teilhard de Chardin, laymen like Jacques Maritain, a number of Dominicans abreast of vanguard developments in art and literature, even non-Catholics cherishing their anguished scruples too much ever to rest in the haven of conversion, such as Simone Weil, wield an immense authority in France today. They no longer indulge in polemics with or against unbelievers. They stand close to them, and welcome the challenge of their negations. Monsieur Homais played his part, a useful one at one time, and Flaubert blended sympathy for his anti-clericalism with mockery for his bourgeois pompousness. But M. Homais has few descendants today in the French middle class. The modern negators, often envied by churchmen to whom complacency and mundane religious practices constitute the direst peril to faith, would gladly exclaim, like the father of the child "who had a dumb spirit" in the ninth chapter of St. Mark: "Help thou mine unbelief!"—for there lies the source of their tragic sense of man's fate—and modern men want to be assured, if not reassured, that theirs indeed is an age of tragedy.[14]

Political thought, in France more than in any other land, is, for better or for worse, a branch of literature. It is polemical in character, often hypnotized by problems concerning the form of government or the type of electoral regime to be adopted, rather than by profound structural reforms; and it reaches the common reader far more easily than in happier countries where men are not to the same degree political animals and treat those questions as a game in which fair play is *de rigueur*, not, like the French, as an *affaire de cœur* where foul is fair. With the advent of the nineteenth century, the French ceased to think universally on these matters; they concentrated on the origins, character, and consequences of their own revolutionary upheaval and on national issues. Naturally enough, religion loomed large in their reflections. It so happens that most of the original thinking on its subject, since 1795 or so, has been done by men of the right in politics or by men favorable to religion, without being themselves ardent believers (Tocqueville, Taine after 1871, Maurras). Even Auguste Comte and Balzac, Barrès and Bourget, George Sorel in a more contradictory way, hardly convinced believers, ended by upholding the need for orthodoxy, or at least for conservatism, in religious and social matters. Joseph de Maistre, De Bonald, Le Play, Barbey d'Aurevilly, Veuillot, Albert de Mun are but a few of the many Catholic thinkers whose impact on literature and on French politics was far-reaching. There should be far more scholarly work done on them than has been the case up to now. Lamennais, a warmer and more imaginative writer than any of those conservatives, a spiritual son of Rousseau

[14] For examples of that sympathy, tinged with admiring gratitude, evinced by leading religious figures for unbelievers, see Henri de Lubac, S.J., *The Drama of Atheistic Humanism* (New York, 1949); Raymond Régamey, O.P., *Art sacré au XXᵉ siècle* (Paris, 1952); Jean Lacroix, *Le Sens de l'athéisme moderne* (P. & Tournai, 1958); Adrien Dansette, *Destin du Catholicisme français, 1926–1956* (Paris, 1957); and Walter J. Ong, S.J., *Frontiers in American Catholicism* (New York, 1957).

among the Catholics, an apocalyptic poet in prose, is one of the seers in whom Hugo and Rimbaud might have hailed their precursor. His action on Lamartine, Sainte-Beuve, Maurice de Guérin, and many another romantic or socialist writer was immense. Scholarship has dealt extensively with him in France, but British and American students of literature and of religion have unfairly passed him by.

It is to be regretted that the scholars who have applied themselves to the consideration of French romanticism in its relation to Catholicism should, in most cases, have done so in a spirit of narrow and jealous orthodoxy and have attempted chiefly to point to the deviations which distorted their religion. It is harder in a Catholic country to remain within the Church and to write poetically on God, Christ, angels, or on natural religion than it is in Protestant lands, where those who disbelieve or whose beliefs are vague and unorthodox need not be driven to anti-clericalism. A Swiss-born Catholic scholar, Auguste Viatte, wrote the best-known volume on the subject, *Le Catholicisme des Romantiques* (1922). It is an angry work, severe on the French romantics who, like Lamartine, Hugo, and George Sand, began by being Christian and royalist writers, but soon turned to Voltairianism or to a lax, half-mystical pantheism. Their hopes shifted to a better future for mankind, their allegiance went to progress and man's perfectibility. Hugo, in a poem (a very bad one) in *Les Rayons et les ombres*, in 1840, has indicted the impious eighteenth century and doomed its philosophers to a shameful fate in the eyes of posterity. "Hélas! L'homme aujourd'hui ne croit plus, mais il rêve," he lamented. He was soon to turn into an apocalyptic dreamer himself and to a mystical prophet, intoxicated with God, but not with God as imprisoned in orthodoxy. Lamartine, who still passes for a meek and pious Christian with some naïve readers, has been shown by wrathful Catholic scholars to have become, at the age of forty, a pantheist and a deist, and an admirer of Mohammed's faith even more than of Christ's. In 1847, he characterized Voltaire as "the mystical genius of modern France, the Moses of incredulity," and, as late as 1863, he praised his "just and infallible mind." "The *aurora borealis* of the Gospels" is the phrase he used to laud Rousseau's deistic "profession of faith of a Savoyard curate." Elsewhere again, he baldly strips Christ of his divinity, calling Him "Christ . . . who was, not a God incarnated in a man, but a man divine like a God." Hugo's religion, on which many an exegesis has appeared, was even less orthodox. Baudelaire, to whom the person of Christ was no closer than to Shakespeare (who almost never mentions Him and has little, if any, sense of sin), but whose sensibility was indubitably marked by a Christian education, by fear, repentance, and the need for prayer, and Verlaine, the most shameless sinner among French writers, and the one most sorely in need of God, are the only authentic Christian poets of France before the twentieth century.[15]

It was probably to be expected that, in a predominantly Catholic country like France, most of the scholars discussing the religious attitude of the romantics would treat their dubious orthodoxy with sternness and would upbraid them for turning to Swedenborg, to Milton, to Plato rather than to the Church for their Christian inspiration. True enough, they were haunted by the Devil as much as by God Himself and could hardly rise toward the divine without having first plunged into satanic gulfs. It is equally true that there were many occultists among the precursors of French romanticism and that Gérard de Nerval and Balzac among the great writers, and numerous lesser figures, chose to roam among those strangely confused prophets of illuminism and theosophy, who had discovered symbolist communications between the underworld and the upper spheres, merged dream and real life, man and woman into a weird unity. Religiosity took the place of religion among them. Pantheism was their natural mood and the philosophical attitude most congenial to them, in which, in Hugo von Hoffmannsthal's line, "Und drei sind Eins: ein Mensch, ein Ding, ein Traum."

But scholars from countries where more independence from the dogmas of Catholicism prevails might well, with the added insight which sympathy affords, explore some of the less well known sides of the religious attitude of the romantics and boldly attempt a much

---

[15] Consult Christian Maréchal, *Lamennais et Lamartine* (Paris, 1907), Henri Guillemin, *Le Jocelyn de Lamartine* (Paris, 1936) and "Lamartine et le Catholicisme," *Revue de France*, May 1, 1934; Denis Saurat, *La Religion de Victor Hugo* (Paris, 1929), expanded and modified as *Victor Hugo et les Dieux du peuple* (Paris, 1948); Auguste Viatte, *Victor Hugo et les Illuminés de son temps* (Montreal, 1942) and Paul Zumthor, *Victor Hugo, poète de Satan* (Paris, 1946); Henri Peyre, *Connaissance de Baudelaire* (Paris, 1951), chapter vi on Baudelaire and religion.

needed synthesis on French romanticism and religion. The romantics rediscovered the Bible as well as Dante. A priest who was a very careful scholar, Claudius Grillet, has written two substantial volumes on Lamartine's and Hugo's use of the Bible. But nothing adequate has yet been written on Hugo and Dante, on Balzac's *Comédie humaine*, and Dante's *Divine Comedy*; on Christ in romantic poetry, on mystical and visionary fiction around and in Balzac, on pantheism in Lamartine, Hugo, Maurice de Guérin, and a host of poets and philosophers between Diderot and the Parnassians, on the role of angels in romantic literature, on Platonism in France.[16]

The central influence on the attitude of French writers toward religion in the nineteenth century was that of Ernest Renan. He was bitterly attacked in his lifetime for depriving Jesus of his divinity; then he assumed the airs of an official personage of the Third Republic; he was claimed by anti-clericals and was glorified through several boulevards dedicated to him (as well as to Raspail, Edgar Quinet, Thiers, and, later, Jaurès, Wilson, and Roosevelt), while churchmen and converts vituperated against his insidious dilettantism for a few decades after his death and some historical scholars repudiated his exegesis as unsafe and his stylistic talent as suspicious in a savant. His thought was molded by his German predecessors; it prolonged a tendency of the French romantics, already conspicuous in Benjamin Constant's five-volume work on religion (1824–1831) and in Quinet, to separate religious forms from religious feeling. It pursued Diderot's endeavor to "broaden God," but with far more touching understanding of the sentimental value of religion than the Enlightenment had evinced. It shifted the emphasis from "God exists," as the creator of the universe whom apologetics attempt to

[16] André Joussain's *Romantisme et Religion* (Paris, 1910), satisfactory and intelligently Bergsonian in its age, is now out of date. Auguste Viatte's *Les Sources occultes du romantisme* (1770–1820) is by far the author's most solid work. Pierre Moreau provided useful hints in an article, "Romantisme français et syncrétisme religieux," *Symposium* VIII (1954), 1–17. See also Marcel Ruff, *L'Esprit du mal et l'esthétique baudelairienne* (Paris, 1955); Milner, *Le Diable dans la littérature française de Cazotte à Baudelaire* (Paris, 1960), and a big volume on *Satan, Etudes Carmélitaines* (Bruges, 1948). Ernest Dubedout's *Le Sentiment chrétien dans la poésie romantique* (Paris, 1901) need be mentioned only as a volume not worth consulting today.

demonstrate, to "God will be one day," but cannot be proved and can only be approached through feeling and through a sense of beauty. Orthodox faith resting upon the conventional interpretation of the Scriptures became forever impossible after Renan. But a vaguer, poetically Franciscan or Salesian religion was substituted for it. If rites, dogmas, rigid form, fanaticism were branded as the evil element of religion, sentiment was lauded as its divine part. There may have been some irony in Renan's famous pronouncement, in his preface to one of his *Philosophical Dramas*, "The Priest of Nemi," stating that he had criticized everything but preserved everything and that he and his friends had "provided God with a rich shrine of synonyms." But there was only earnestness and fervor in many other Renanian assertions that religion had been redefined and broadened by him and reoriented. "Most of those whom religion belittles were already little before they adopted it; narrow, afflicted with blinkers with religion, they would perhaps, without it, have been wicked" (*Etudes d'histoire religieuse*, 1857).

Several good books have appeared in America in the last decade on Renan, by Richard Chadbourne and René Galand in particular. But next to nothing has been attempted in the way of a synthesis on Renan's fortunes and influence in France or in English-speaking countries. The field is extraordinarily rich. After a reaction against Renan's dilettantism and what was judged to be his flippancy, by freethinkers and Catholics alike, in the years 1890 to 1920, after some annoyance at Renan's elusiveness and coquettish grace on the part of dogmatists like Henri Massis, Charles Maurras, a reaction set in around 1923, the year of the celebration of his centenary. It had to be conceded that, in a country where the Scriptures were traditionally little read and the history of the Jewish people and of the Christian Church little known, Renan had succeeded in arousing a broad curiosity for things religious and in teaching unbelievers how to regard religion with sympathy, with nostalgia, and with envy. Even Renan's scientific scholarship has elicited praise from specialists like René Dussaud, from Alfred Loisy and Jean Baruzi, both professors of religious history or philosophy at the Collège de France. There is much Renanism in Albert Schweitzer, as there is in the teleological philosophy of Leconte de Nouy and of Father Teilhard de Chardin.

A modern Catholic thinker, Jean Guitton, wrote with sympathy on Renan. Charles du Bos, "anima christiana," who taught, late in his life, at Notre Dame, noted in his *Journal* in September, 1922, that the Renan of all periods, except for the very end of his life, satisfied him altogether and had never lost "Die Helle der Anschauung." "Alongside him, there are hardly any Frenchmen of the nineteenth century who at times do not appear unintelligent." Mauriac, in "le Salut de Renan," *Journal III* (1940), made amends to Renan, whom he had in his youth feared as a monster. "Twenty-seven years after [my early impatience with him], I discover that there is not one line in Renan's intimate papers which does not echo feelings which I experienced, an anguish which I went through, temptations against which I struggled." An English Catholic writer, Maurice Baring, in *Have You Anything to Declare?* (New York, 1937), praised Renan for having brought back many an agnostic to the bosom of the Catholic Church; to him, Renan, curiously enough, taught that "if Christianity is true, . . . then the Catholic Church is its only possible and logical manifestation on earth" (p. 134). A mystical Catholic, Mme Aurel, quoted in *La Vie des Peuples* (February 10, 1923, pp. 137–139), likewise declared: "Renan led me to Christ. . . . I hold Renan for the greatest priest of Jesus, for the one who has brought indolent minds to Christ." Barrès, an agnostic Catholic, who had mocked Renan in his youth, was moved, later in his life, in his *Enquête aux Pays du Levant* (1923) to declare that Renan had Christianized him and others of his generation.[17]

The French literature of the twentieth century appears to hold a magical fascination for teachers and students in Europe, in America, in Australia, in Japan. Books and articles are devoted to it in large

---

[17] See, among many books by scholars which praise Renan's scholarship: James G. Fraser, *Renan et la Méthode de l'histoire des religions* (Paris, 1921); René Dussaud, *L'Œuvre scientifique de Renan* (Paris, 1951); Albert Schweitzer, *The Quest for the Historical Jesus* (London, 1911), chapter xiii on Renan. Other references are to Jean Guitton, *Renan et Newman* (Paris, 1938); Jean Baruzi, *Problèmes d'histoire des religions* (Paris, 1935). André Gide, Henry de Montherlant have obviously read and reread Renan. A little-known and curious writer, a history teacher, born in 1911 and killed during World War II in Italy in 1944, Jean-Berthold Mahn, expressed his admiration for Renan in *Témoignages et lettres* (Paris, 1950). He wrote several historical works on the Cistercians.

numbers in periodicals both scholarly and addressed to the general reader. The many complex questions proposed by the very large place occupied in modern literature by religion and by the unequaled eminence of recent French Catholic writers have been discussed, polemically or seriously—and polemics on religious issues are often deadly earnest in the country of Pascal and Voltaire. The French were Jansenists in their Augustinism even in the Middle Ages and before the obscure bishop of Ypres wrote his *Augustinus*; Sartre and his agnostic friends have called themselves, not without reason, the Jansenists of today, but Jansenists asserting man's unlimited freedom and an optimistic faith in his capabilities, once freed of God, "a useless passion."

A mere survey of the main provinces of that immense realm is all that can be attempted here. First, the relationship of many Catholic and Protestant writers to the Bible, to St. Thomas, and to other medieval thinkers. With André Gide, Charles Péguy, Paul Claudel, François Mauriac, Julien Green, the Bible has become a rich source of inspiration and a nourishment for their inner life. Only for Claudel,[18] whose biblical imagery and whose lyrical commentaries on the Scriptures have been studied at some length, has the subject been granted adequate attention. Jean Giraudoux, Henri Ghéon, André Obey, even the comic writer Marcel Pagnol in his *Judas*, have gone to religious themes for their plays. Pierre Emmanuel, Jean Grosjean, Claude Vigée, and Jean Claude Renard are four of the most gifted modern poets whose inspiration is profoundly biblical. The Thomistic influence has, naturally enough, been felt primarily by philosophers, ever since the *Encyclical Aeterni Patris* of Leo XIII, less than two years after he was elected to the Holy See in August, 1879, consecrated Thomism as the official doctrine of the Church. Among them, Jacques Maritain has profoundly impressed artists and men of letters

---

[18] The religious writers who have studied Claudel from a religious point of view and with sympathy are Jacques Madaule in two big volumes; Klara Maurer in German (on Claudel's Biblical symbolism, Zurich, 1941); Raymond Malter, then J. J. Kim, in *La Table Ronde* (November 1956 and September 1958); Rayner Heppenstall and Joseph Chiari in English, in *The Double Image* (1947) and *The Poetic Drama of Claudel* (1954); Jacques Andrieu, *La Foi dans l'œuvre de Claudel* (1955). Most important is Pascal Rywalski's *La Bible dans l'œuvre littéraire de Claudel* (Fribourg).

through his personality and through his many volumes such as *Art and Scholasticism*, *Frontiers of Poetry*, and *Creative Intuition in Art and Poetry*. There should be room for several works of scholarship on Maritain's friendship with Péguy, Psichari, and other fervent souls in the years 1905–1914. Then on his influence on a score of artists, poets, and novelists, as diverse as Jean Cocteau, Pierre Reverdy, Julien Green, Erik Satie, and Marc Chagall—not to mention Raïssa Maritain herself, one of the genuine mystical poets of modern France. The most substantial volume available thus far is the solid *Maritain et notre Temps*, by Henry Bars, published in 1959. To Maritain in France, to Reinhold Niebuhr in America, to Karl Barth in Protestant Europe, to Martin Buber among the Jewish writers, we owe today a surprising phenomenon which would have appeared unbelievable a hundred years ago: the widespread and profound appeal of theology to the men and women of the second half of the twentieth century.

One of the many claims to originality of those theologians, of Maritain in particular, is that their almost Cartesian attachment to rational evidence, demonstrated with relentless logic, has been accompanied with a deep emotional communion with Christ and a constant sense of his presence both in history and in their own selves. "Tu autem es interior intimo meo," Jacques and Raïssa Maritain, Simone Weil herself, Father Henri de Lubac, Georges Bernanos, Max Jacob, and most of the modern Catholic writers of France might well repeat with St. Augustine. Two of the greatest novelists of the present century are, without doubt, François Mauriac and Georges Bernanos: in both of them, especially in the latter, the conflict which is dramatized is that of man's attempt to reach holiness. Their harrowing question is that which Charles Péguy put in the prayers of his Joan of Arc: "Comment sauver?" Their conviction, however, never swerves from Péguy's oft-asserted axiom: "Il faut sauver." That literature of the years 1930–1960 has been pedantically but aptly called a soteriological literature—wholly intent upon saving baffled and rebellious creatures and upon fitting together the fragments of a broken world.[19]

[19] "Le Monde cassé" (1932) is the title of a play by the dramatist and Christian philosopher Gabriel Marcel, the chief exponent of Catholic Existentialism today. Among the Protestant theological philosophers, Paul Ricœur is the one whose

Three scholars stand out above all others among the numerous ones who have lately undertaken to study contemporary French literature from a religious point of view. Pierre Henri Simon is the one layman among them, but a layman impregnated with faith, able to perceive religious longings in agnostic writers haunted today by the tragic sense of life, but tolerant enough not to convert forcibly those who depict the mystery of a world widowed of God, as another Catholic professor and a prolific writer, Henri Guillemin, has been prone to doing. Simon's books are *Histoire de la littérature française au XXᵉ siècle* (2 small volumes, 1956) and especially *Témoins de l'homme* (1952).

André Blanchet is the most influential literary scholar among the Jesuits today in France.[20] His critical essays in *Etudes* have, in 1959 and 1960, been collected in *La littérature et le Spirituel* (2 volumes). There is not one trace of proselytism in his criticism, not one word of acrimony toward negators like Sartre and Camus. Even in Françoise Sagan's smile, Father Blanchet, with neither irony nor condescension, detects the endeavor of a disillusioned and deliberately dry young woman to be a moralist in the tradition of Chamfort and to lay clear-mindedness as the basis of the formulation of its own values by the youth of today. His most suggestive essays, however, are on Pascal, Claudel, Julien Green, and also on Kafka, Malraux, and Sartre, the richest of all on the Breton Jew, Max Jacob, converted to Catholicism in 1909, put to death by the Germans in 1944, in whom many young Catholics in France today see no longer a clown and an erratic friend of Picasso's youth, but an authentic mystic and a genuine poet.

The most massive work of scholarship on literature and religion to appear since World War II is entitled *Littérature du XXᵉ siècle et*

---

appeal to men of letters is today the most potent. His meditations have centered around the problem of evil. On the soteriological obsession of contemporary French writers, even, or perhaps chiefly of agnostic ones likes Anouilh, Giraudoux, Malraux, Camus, see a youthful but ardent work of criticism by René M. Albérès, *La Révolte des écrivains d'aujourd'hui* (Paris, 1949).

[20] Henri de Lubac is more of a theologian or of a historian of religions (including Buddhism), keenly aware of the social duties of a Catholic today as redefined in Pope Pius XI's oft-quoted appeal to heal the greatest scandal of the modern world, the alienation of the working classes from the Church. See his *Catholicisme. Les aspects sociaux du dogme* (Paris, 1937; new ed., 1941).

Christianisme, by the Belgian priest Charles Moeller (Paris and Tournai, 1953–1960). It consists of substantial essays, sixty to eighty pages each, on Camus, Gide, Aldous Huxley, Simone Weil, Graham Greene, Julien Green, Bernanos, Sartre, Henry James, Martin du Gard, Malègue, Malraux, Kafka, Vercors, Sagan, Gabriel Marcel, Charles du Bos, Charles Péguy, a Spaniard, a Pole, a Russian, an Austrian, and a Dutch girl, Anne Frank. The subtitles of the volumes are: *God's Silence, Faith in Christ, Men's Hope, Hope in God Our Father*. The tone of those essays is apologetic, slightly unctuous, but never self-righteous. Charles Moeller takes it for granted that, if Christendom has almost vanished in the sense that we all live in a secularized world defiled by World War II, by the extermination of millions of Jews in a nominally Christian country, threatened by the rise of Russia and China to the summit of power, there exist nevertheless more profoundly Christian souls than at any time since the Middle Ages.

Strangely enough, Father Moeller is most lenient to unbelievers such as Camus and Malraux; his long (close to two hundred pages long) section on Malraux is perhaps the most thorough discussion of that author in the French language, taking into close consideration Malraux's reflections on art as a substitute for faith. In him Father Moeller hails a man whose tragic imagination is deeply tinged with religious anguish and who, indeed, proclaimed (in an article reprinted in 1955 in *Preuves*) that the capital problem of the end of our century will be the religious problem, posed in terms as widely different from those which are familiar to us today as Christianity differed from ancient religions. Simone Weil appears to him gravely in the wrong, since she leaves out the mystery of love and insidiously wishes to see in the Christian Revelation the fulfillment of the anticipations of her favorite nation, the Greeks, forgetting thereby that Christianity not only corrected, but transfigured, ancient philosophies. By her, and her ilk, Revelation is reduced to a mere philosophy. Purer is the religion of Protestant-born Julien Green, converted to Catholicism through Jacques Maritain, hailed by the Belgian theologian as "a martyr of faith."

Such an attitude toward negators on the part of Christian writers is the most striking feature in the very abundant production of critical and scholarly works being today devoted to the religious problems by the French. There are many antitheists among the negators, but hardly any anti-clericals. Vituperative polemics, once dear to Louis Veuillot and Léon Bloy, has almost disappeared from the writings of churchmen and lay apostles. Marxism itself is considered by them as an atheism pregnant with meanings similar to those of a revelation: the revelation of the wrong of the Church in not having been alerted sooner to the alienation of the working classes in the industrial society. They concede that there is occasionally found among workmen who have never entered a church a spirit of fraternal solidarity and a thirst for justice and even for charity not dissimilar to the impulses which drove the fishermen of Tiberias to Christ. Even modern man's "blasphemous" eagerness to replace God by magnified and glorified man is condoned, when it is not praised, by those Catholic theologians. One of the significant and very solid works of religious scholarship in that realm is by the Catholic Michel Carrouges, *La mystique du Surhomme* (1948). Modern men's dream of becoming supermen, or of portraying such supermen in their writings, in order to fill the void left by the Nietzschean "death of God," is respectfully treated as "mystical atheism" by Carrouges. That revolt of Titans against the divine (E. A. Poe, A. de Musset, Balzac, Baudelaire, Leconte de Lisle, Swinburne, Nietzsche, Gide, Malraux) stems from dissatisfaction with our inadequate conception of God and spurs reformers to purify Christianity and to learn from its attackers even more than from its more timid supporters. Tertullian's statement holds true in our time: "Oportet haereses esse" and, as Pascal, not without embarrassment, confessed: Believing would be too easy if God had permitted only one faith. "We understand nothing in His works unless we start from the principle that He wanted to blind some and enlighten others" (Brunschvicg edition, No. 566).[21]

---

[21] A somewhat similar attitude appears in Michel Polanyi's *Beyond Nihilism* (Cambridge University Press, 1900), and in Father P. R. Régamey, a Benedictine, in *Art sacré au vingtième siècle* (Paris, 1952). On this and allied subjects, see *God and the Writer*, *Yale French Studies*, XII (1953), and by this writer, "Albert Camus, an anti-Christian Moralist," *Proceedings of the American Philosophical Society*, CII (October 1958). To the works mentioned in the preceding pages, the following should be added which might provide the literary scholar with a broader context: *L'Encyclopédie Française*, Vol. XIX: *Philosophie–Religion* (Larousse,

Literary scholars have not been inactive in the vast realm of religion as it is reflected in French literature, or as it molds and often inspires it. In no other country in our century, certainly not in America where fiction and drama keep morbidly shy of religious and metaphysical issues, have speculations on man's place in the universe, on his relation to God, to sin and redemption, to charity permeated the writings of creators and critics alike. Arrogance abounds among the French antitheists of today, curious of Christ; but humility, "the only wisdom we can hope to acquire," according to T. S. Eliot, abounds equally, and tolerance for the agnostics or for the members of other faiths, allied to fervor for their own, marks the Catholic intelligence today in France, the country which is, more than ever, in that respect, "the eldest daughter of the Church."

Through such scholarly study of religious writers and of their characters, seldom edifying but often tragically torn, as in Claudel, Mauriac, Bernanos, and in Dostoevsky before them, history has gained a new insight into the unconscious, the contradictions of souls, harrowed by remorse or exalted by prayer, the phenomena of imitation sweeping across whole layers of people; it has learned how to make room for fear, anguish, guilt, benevolence, and all that, in any civilization, lies deep beneath the economic factors or the rational explanation of people's behavior. The modern literary historian, like the modern historian in general, realizes that history is a failure if it does not conjure up for us the manner in which people once lived, and therefore *felt*. Documents, arrays of facts, even books do not enclose the sensibilities of the people who preceded us. As R. G. Collingwood put it in his *Idea of History* (1946), "History lives only as a present interest and pursuit, in the mind of the historian when he criticizes and interprets those documents, and by so doing relives for himself the states of mind into which he inquires." The historian of literary works concerned with faith or with unbelief, with emotional and passionate forces, must, to a greater degree than perhaps any other, be a creative scholar.

1957); Adrien Dansette, *Destin du Catholicisme français* (P. Flammarion, 1957); William Bosworth, *Catholicism and Crisis in Modern France* (Princeton University Press, 1961); Martin Turnell, *Modern Literature and Christian Faith* (London: Darton, Longman and Todd, 1961).

9 | ROMANTIC POETRY AND RHETORIC

FOR MORE THAN half a century in France, and for a slightly shorter time in Great Britain and America, romanticism has been the target of the critics' onslaught. Romanticism *in se*, as a view of life and especially as a vindication of the rights of imagination and of emotional values, fared rather well under the repeated blows which it was dealt. We contend, in the essay which follows this one that it could well be called "le mort vivant" and that a resurgence of romantic moods was conspicuous in the recent literature of France and of England. Romanticism considered historically, in its European manifestations of the early nineteenth century, has suffered the fate of all that is but one phase in a long evolution: its novelty has worn off and the beginning of the modern age has been pushed later in time, around 1860–1870 in literature, or earlier, around 1680–1715 in the history of ideas.

Yet the obloquy heaped upon romanticism by its theological, philosophical, and political foes has on the whole redounded to the glory of that movement. The German romantics, perhaps the truest of all (Hölderlin, Novalis, Kleist, even the philosopher Schelling), have never counted a larger band of enthusiastic zealots than they do today. English romanticism suffered more from the recent organized attempt to encompass poetry within a set of criteria evolved from Dryden and Pope, or from Donne and Marvell, or even from Herbert and Crashaw. Yet neither Coleridge nor Keats nor even Wordsworth suffered in the process. Shelley bore the brunt of the attack, and he has weathered it victoriously. Teachers trained in irony, paradox, structure, and ambiguity remark that they do not have to put up an apologetic plea when asking their students to read *Adonaïs*, "Hymn to Intellectual Beauty," not even "I Arise from Dreams of Thee." Byron himself has won again, if he ever had lost it, his fascination for readers of his biography, of his letters, of *Don Juan*, and even of his earlier poems.

But the romantic movement of Latin countries proved more vulnerable. The Spaniards have never been oversensitive as to the place ultimately to be assigned to Espronceda, Zorilla, or Larra, and to an era of their literature which was not especially conspicuous for its "hispanidad." The Italians are forced to answer "Manzoni, alas!" when questioned as to who is their greatest novelist, but they know that their truest glory lies elsewhere. They have remained justly proud of Leopardi, but they still debate whether he was romantic or classical. Many of them would not too regretfully proclaim, as one of their critics did in 1908 in entitling a little book thus, that *Il Romanticismo italiano non esiste* (by Gina Martegiani). On the whole, the Risorgimento, not romanticism, holds the chief place in the cultural history of their early nineteenth century.

Things went otherwise in France, where, between 1875 and 1910, academic criticism had established romanticism as a great national movement from which fiction, criticism, history had sprung. French anthologies of modern poetry ritually opened with the big four (Lamartine, Vigny, Hugo, Musset) galloping as the fiery French *quadriga*. The novelists of the romantic era were the last to be acknowledged as classics. They have fared best with posterity (if one excepts George Sand). The 1949–1950 celebration of the double anniversary of Balzac's birth and death was a true apotheosis. Stendhal is even dearer to the youth of France, and he may well some day be hailed as their truest romantic: for he is cherished for his worship of passion and for his sentiment, for his melancholy and his shyness, for his poetical conception of his characters, and for the poetical vibration of his style, he who was strangely insensitive to poetry.

Michelet, the arch-romantic among the French, is admired by many Frenchmen today as their greatest prose writer, which he may well be (Sartre *dixit*, in *What Is Literature?* p. 119). Two other names might be added to his as embodying all that was most genuinely romantic in France between 1820 and 1850—those of Berlioz and of Delacroix. Never had Berlioz captured such a share of our musical programs as he has lately. As to Delacroix, he (not any more than Géricault and even Chassériau) had never suffered from the anti-romantic reaction. The impressionists, Cézanne, the Fauves all paid him their tribute, and no fresco has yet rivaled the admiration which goes to his ceilings at Saint-Sulpice or at the National Assembly.

Only the attacks against romantic poetry had struck home in France. We are not taking seriously the naïve teachers who absorbed, without any grain of salt, the pompous and stilted pages, à la Brunetière, of Thierry-Maulnier's *Introduction à la poésie française*. It was an entertaining "canular" to cut the romantics into shreds and to erect as the giants among French poets Garnier and D'Aubigné (in whom rhetoric reigned supreme) and (a disturbing index to the compiler's poetical taste) Charles Maurras! But even genuine and judicious scholars have, since 1920 or thereabouts, aligned themselves with the foreign critics of French romantic poetry.[1] They have scored its lack of purity, to which moderns have been made peculiarly sensitive by the prolific priest who, fretting and vaticinating on his academician's tripod like a new swooning Abbé Trissotin, set up Valéry's verse, Racine's "La Fille de Minos et de Pasiphaé," and even Musset's "La Blanche Oloossone à la blanche Camyre" as the arche-types of purity. They echoed Mallarmé's claim (regularly mis-interpreted, as Aimé Patri showed in *La Revue Musicale* of January, 1952) that poetry should "reprendre à la musique son bien" and should neither name objects nor formulate statements, but suggest. French

---

[1] Paul Hazard, in a polished but not over-profound essay, "Les Caractères nationaux du lyrisme romantique français," in *Quatre Etudes* (New York: Oxford University Press, 1940); Louis Cazamian, in "Le Romantisme en France et en Angleterre," *Essais en deux langues* (Didier, 1938) and "Retour d'un infidèle à la poésie française," *ibid.*; the author of the present article, who does not lay any claim to being judicious, pointed out the deficiencies of French romantic poetry as compared to English in *Shelley et la France: Lyrisme anglais et lyrisme français au XIXe siècle* (Cairo, 1935), pp. 155–170. Margaret Gilman has a very penetrating article on the subject in *Yale French Studies*, No. 5: *France and World Literature* (1950), pp. 14–26.

romantic poetry was also charged with being deficient in mystery, reluctant to submit to the pantheistic ecstasy or to the semi-mystical experience which Rousseau had revealed to Wordsworth and Shelley, which Rimbaud was later to recapture. The hint that they are logical rationalists even in religion, poetry, gastronomy, and politics always irks the French. Lately they have cast envious eyes upon the divine, or subhuman, madness which engulfed Hölderlin, Lenau, Nietzsche, and they have gloried in Antonin Artaud among the moderns, and in Nerval, who, because he wrote six, at the most seven, beautiful and mysterious sonnets, has been disproportionately magnified into a major poet. Both were, at any rate, authentic madmen, and a third was added when Cocteau coined his epigram on Hugo: "a madman who believed he was Victor Hugo."

Our purpose is not to reopen a momentous debate in a brief article. Our conviction is that the delirious enthusiasm for Baudelaire at first, then for Rimbaud and Mallarmé as the only authentic poets of modern France, has run its course. These poets are immensely great, especially for those who, like the sexagenarian author of these lines, first discovered them before thesis upon thesis, textual analysis piled up upon over-subtle deciphering of their enigmas had converted them into pillars of academic criticism, overgrown with adhesive learned gloss. But they do not epitomize the whole of French poetry, and no example is perhaps more perilous than theirs for poets of the future. Indeed the posterity of Baudelaire has hardly been a prolific one in twentieth-century France: Reverdy has occasional Baudelairean accents and he stands as an isolated exception. The surrealists have proved strikingly cool to Rimbaud; Claudel, with all his admiration for the poet who had served as the angel of the Annunciation to the future convert, is very remote from Rimbaud's *Illuminations—* mainly because he is an eloquent *vates* rather than an illuminated visionary. Valéry sedulously denied that Mallarmé had ever influenced him much, or that Mallarmé could ever have exercised any influence through his poetry. There is far more of Hugo than there is of the trio Baudelaire-Rimbaud-Mallarmé in the best poetry of France at mid-century: in Claudel and St. John Perse, in Michaux and Emmanuel, in P. J. Jouve and Claude Vigée, in Audiberti and Pichette. There is even a little of Sully-Prudhomme in Supervielle and not a little Musset (wedded to Anna de Noailles) in Aragon. Eloquence is a hydra and it would have taken many Verlaines to wring its ever renascent necks. Besides, wringing its neck successfully would obviously have meant, for poetry itself, decapitation. French poetry has not yet lost its head.

What was lacking in the romantic poetry of France in the first half of the nineteenth century? Many answers have been proposed, none of which is wholly satisfactory. Music primarily, might we say, and that affinity with folk poetry, with the simplicity of ballads which we cherish in Coleridge occasionally, in Goethe's ballads, even in Heine, or in Lenau's "Postillon" or "Drei Zigeuner." But it is most doubtful whether the music of Swinburne, even that of *Christabel*, and that of all but a few German ballads by Schiller and Goethe constitutes an authentic claim to superiority over the French for the poetry of England and Germany.

Other critics have laid the blame on the French passion for the general, which detracted from the directness of their lyrical poems in Lamartine, Hugo, and Vigny, and tended to turn spontaneous lyrical effusions into ample and well-ordered developments dubbed meditations, contemplations, or philosophical poems. Much, it is true, was thus lost. Lamartine's Elvire in "Le Lac," Vigny's Eva have no individual personality. But is Emilia Viviani or Jane Williams more sharply characterized by Shelley, or Ulrike, the girl who inspired seventy-four-year-old Goethe with his most pathetic love and to whom we owe the Marienbad elegy? A case could easily be made for meditative as against narrowly personal poetry; and the old-fashioned identification of lyrical as personal, short, and musical is no longer accepted by most of us. T. S. Eliot made the latest attempt to explode such a narrow conception of lyricism in his 1953 National Book League Lecture on "The Three Voices of Poetry." Romantic poetry strove for the general and the universal far more than the poetry of Donne and Herrick, or of Théophile, Maynard, and other seventeenth-century French poets had ever done. Indeed, one of the most arresting definitions of romanticism is the following one: "The truest essence of romanticism is to make the individual moment or the individual situation absolute, to universalize and to classify it." As the style may lead one to suspect, that definition was not proposed by a Frenchman, but by a German romantic, Novalis. It reads as No. 970 of his *Fragments* (Minor edition, Jena, III, 363).

Margaret Gilman, in the interesting article mentioned above, offered an ingenious explanation for the inferiority of French romantic poetry. That poetry did not strike roots in a national tradition, for it was, unhappily, a revolution rather than a revival, and it did not rest on a body of thought around imagination: hence it lacked a content, and relied upon feeling rather than upon vision. The first point seems to us a stronger one than the second. We doubt very much that the achievement of English lyricism from Blake to Coleridge and Keats was due to their rhapsodic but highly confused statements on behalf of imagination. The English painters of the romantic era, who also raved about imagination, produced very mediocre paintings. We have similar and even stronger doubts where Baudelaire is concerned and his unconvincing tribute to the "reine des facultés." We are still sorely in need, however, of a history of the concept of imagination in France through Dubos, Diderot, Marmontel, Delille (who, like Akenside, wrote a poem on imagination), to Vigny, Baudelaire, and surrealism. Margaret Gilman has died too soon, but she had already treated some aspects of it. But the conclusions to be drawn as to the baneful effects on poetry of the lack of an adequate theory of imagination must doubtless remain highly problematic.

The villain of the piece, who has incurred most of the blame for the deterioration of the French romantic poets in the estimation of lovers of poetry, is eloquence. The French are, so Caesar declared of the Gauls, a nation of expert talkers. They are, or were until lately, trained in writing Latin or French discourses, broken into the rhetorical devices taught by Isocrates, Cicero, and Quintilian. They are also somewhat histrionic, and flourish most conspicuously when they have a public, in wit, in comic observation, and in oratory. Rhetoric was instilled or dinned into their ears from a tender age, at least until the era of symbolism. Therefore their poets were rhetoricians.

There are many flaws in such a line of reasoning. Rhetoric taught as a separate discipline disappeared from French syllabi in 1885 (see E. Chaignet, *La Rhétorique et son histoire*, 1888). Mallarmé, Laforgue, Verlaine, Rimbaud had been instructed in it no less, indeed far more, than Lamartine and Vigny, who had been indolent schoolboys. So had all English and German poets of most of the nineteenth century. But is there in truth much less rhetoric in the English or German romantics than among the French? We doubt it. The very first sentence of the first of Novalis' *Hymns to Night* is a most rhetorical question. The sixth and last of those *Hymns*, "Sehnsucht nach dem Tode," teems with exclamations, rhetorical interrogations, and even amplifications. Hölderlin's "Der Archipelagus," which Gundolf shrewdly interpreted, his "Brot und Wein," which has more elegiac tenderness, and indeed all of the poet's prophetic hymns, such as "Der Rhein" or "Patmos," are as rhetorical as Pindar once was, or as anything in Hugo. Schiller, who acted to Hölderlin as a rather stilted mentor, did not fail to advise him, in a letter from Jena on November 24, 1796, to be on his guard against "a hereditary fault of German poets, the prolixity which often crushes a very felicitous thought under an endless development and a deluge of strophes." He held up to his young admirer an ideal of parsimony, clarity, and simpl; ity.

The rhetoric of each of the great English romantics would deserve a study. It is present in Keats, not only in his long poems, but in his most perfect stanzas:

> Who are these coming to the sacrifice? ...
> What little town by river or sea-shore? ...

and in the second stanza of the "Ode to Psyche," invested with sensuous appeal; or in "Where are the songs of Spring? Ay, where are they?" Shelley is far from being the worst culprit (if guilt there be) among the romantics. Coleridge's "Ode to the Departing Year," "France—An Ode," even the splendid "Dejection. An Ode" make skillful use of all the traditional devices of rhetoric. Wordsworth did likewise. And few Frenchmen, not even Corneille, certainly not Hugo, have ever established a poem or a tirade on a framework as impeccably logical, as obviously solid and bulging with "if," "therefore," "and so," "nor less, I trust," "once again," "thrice repeated," "not for this I," "nor perchance if I were not thus taught," "nor perchance if I should be," etc., as has Wordsworth in that magnificent description of an ecstasy, "Lines Written Above Tintern Abbey."

An anthology of the most eloquent passages in French poetry might include "Le Lac," "Ischia," "Paroles sur la dune" (and, if it were an anthology of bad poetry, a sorely needed one, "Le Dernier Chant de Childe Harold," "Rolla," and the "Lettre à Lamartine," even some of the most atrocious poems of Hugo such as "Regard jeté dans une mansarde" in *Les Rayons et les ombres*). But it should also comprise "Bateau Ivre," Mallarmé's "Toast funèbre" and even "Prose pour des Esseintes," samples from Claudel's odes and hymns so numerous that selection would prove embarrassing, reams of verse from La Tour du Pin, Emmanuel, Milosz, and others, even one third of Paul Valéry. The peril for the anthologist would be to decide what to exclude from Lautréamont and, indeed, from St. John Perse. André Breton remarked in his recent and very rich volume, *La Clé des champs* (Sagittaire, 1953) that the cast of Apollinaire's thought is revealed by his favorite leitmotif, "Il y a," just as Perse's key formula is "Celui qui," which opens the floodgates of his sumptuous census of men's multifarious and nonutilitarian activities. "Celui qui," introducing a balanced series of enumerations, is a device straight from Bossuet, to which Lamartine (in the passionate and musical eloquence which concludes "Ischia") and other romantics resorted, as they did to "Puisque, puisque," cumulatively proving that "il faut aimer sans cesse après avoir aimé," or to the "maintenant que" of "A Villequier" and "Paroles sur la dune."

The loss, or, to use the untranslatable French word, the *déchet* in symbolist poets (when, like Verlaine, Henri de Régnier, Verhaeren, Vielé-Griffin, they were imprudent enough to write more than one volume) is frightening, as the *déchet* in Claudel, in Jouve, nay, even in Valéry is likely to be. It is probably more considerable than the similar waste in the so-called great romantics. And we are led to wonder whether the most original and durable achievement of French romanticism was not, in verse, its eloquence. De Quincey, who wrote a long essay, "On Rhetoric," in 1829, quoted Bacon's definition of the duty and office of rhetoric as "to apply reason to imagination for the better moving of the will." He himself, unashamedly borrowing Wordsworth's definition of great poetry, saw in eloquence "the overflow of powerful feelings upon occasions fitted to excite them."

Poetic eloquence at its best is characterized by an abundance of feelings or of ideas emotionally experienced, by that saturation which is often found in the powerful creators; then by an intoxication with one's powers, that romantic imperialism denounced tirelessly by Seillière, which leads one to impart some of that overflow to others. Persuasion was a noble art among the ancients, and eloquence was, in Aristotle's word, its handmaid. Eloquence requires the mastery of a number of rules and devices which rhetoric taught. I. A. Richards, Kenneth Burke, and Jean Paulhan have rehabilitated the word "rhetoric" among us, and transformed its content. But they have not as yet trained a generation of college students—or of philosophers, social scientists, and politicians—to ponder sufficiently over the warning uttered by Pericles to his countrymen, as reported by Thucydides: "The man who thinks but who does not know how to express what he thinks is on a par with him who has no idea at all." Dialectics, which for the Greeks was the counterpart or the complement of rhetoric, has sprung into fashion again since Hegel and Marx. Rhetoric may not have too long to wait for the rehabilitation which is due to it. It had been associated with sophistry. In actual fact the Stoics viewed it as a virtue and as a branch of ethics which taught how to discriminate between good and evil, as Jean Cousin recalled in his voluminous study of Quintilian (Boivin, 1935, I, 780).

The poetics which stressed images above all else was for a time beneficent. It ended, however, by belittling poetry and by leaving it with a dwindling audience of over-subtle aesthetes. Many a younger poet today would gladly echo the concise remark of one of them: "Images seem to me means, not ends" (Randall Jarrell). The isolation of poetry from the main stream of life and its divorce from reality have been concealed from some of us by the fervor of a few for Hopkins, Mallarmé, or the later Yeats. Professors still succeed in inflaming their students, who are at the receptive and romantic age, with the love of esoteric poetry. But such love hardly ever survives their graduation from college. Adults are irretrievably divorced from poetry as they are not from music or painting: the niggardly place granted to verse (most of which hardly deserves the name of poetry) in our magazines today bears witness to the failure of poets and interpreters of poetry to enlarge their scant band of readers, in spite of a marked growth in population and in the size of the literate and of the college-graduated public. It is our fond belief that the radio programs grossly underestimate their public when they grant, in America at least, such a miserable place (when it is not a glaring absence) to the reading of poetry. Those of us who do not totally despair of the future of literature in this age of mass media hope that the poetry which has a content, because it embodies a passionate understanding of human emotions ("Wer das Tiefste gedacht, liebt das Lebendigste," proclaimed Hölderlin), and which has wind or breath ("le souffle" which Jean Prévost has searchingly analyzed in his *Baudelaire*) may survive the curse cast upon it by the tenants of purity and of form or pattern divorced from content.[2]

Space is lacking for a detailed analysis of the original eloquence, "the good one," which is occasionally found, among much dross and much immature declamation, in each of the leading romantic poets of France. One example alone may be given here. The *Harmonies* is probably the least successful volume of Lamartine's youth (excluding the later *Recueillements*): "Your 'gloria Patri' diluted in two tomes," wrote to the poet one of his detractors. Yet three or four poems in it scale heights to which French lyricism had never soared before, and they are the eloquent ones—among them this fragment from "Novissima Verba" in which the poet, casting a backward glance at his life in a supreme farewell (he survived that crisis of

---

[2] Marcel Arland, a refined and perspicacious critic who has usually been more devoted to Marivaux or Constant than to the romantics, has, as had Claudel before him, lamented the distrust of eloquence in recent poetry. "Many poems today lack that broad flow, that deep murmur in which, sparkling as they may be, images and lovely details can both be fused and seek their exact value. Without them, a poem may be a succession of pleasing fragments, but not the living thing which a beautiful work must be. 'Prends l'éloquence et tords-lui son cou.' For the last sixty years, we have been doing precisely that; but we overlooked the fact there is a certain kind of eloquence which no great work can do without. Distrust of eloquence has brought about distrust of poetry itself. . . . Luckily, eloquence can survive many deaths" (M. Arland, in *Essais et nouveaux essais critiques*, Gallimard, 1952, p. 130).

melancholy of 1830 to die only in 1869), pays the following tribute to love and woman, by whom alone living was justified.

> Amour, être de l'être, amour, âme de l'âme,
> Nul homme plus que moi ne vécut de ta flamme!
> Nul, brûlant de ta soif sans jamais l'épuiser,
> N'eût sacrifié plus pour t'immortaliser!
> Nul ne désira plus dans l'autre âme qu'il aime
> De concentrer sa vie en se perdant soi-même,
> Et, dans un monde à part de toi seul habité,
> De se faire à lui seul sa propre éternité!
> Femmes, anges mortels, création divine,
> Seul rayon dont la nuit un moment s'illumine,
> Je le dis à cette heure, heure de vérité,
> Comme je l'aurais dit quand devant la beauté
> Mon cœur épanoui, qui se sentait éclore,
> Fondait comme une neige aux rayons de l'aurore,
> Je ne regrette rien de ce monde que vous!
> Ce que la vie humaine a d'amer et de doux,
> Ce qui la fait brûler, ce qui trahit en elle
> Je ne sais quel parfum de la vie immortelle,
> C'est vous seules! Par vous toute joie est amour,
> Ombre des biens parfaits du céleste séjour,
> Vous êtes ici-bas la goutte sans mélange
> Que Dieu laissa tomber de la coupe de l'ange,
> L'étoile qui brillant dans une vaste nuit
> Dit seule à nos regards qu'un autre monde luit,
> Le seul garant enfin que le bonheur suprême,
> Ce bonheur que l'amour puise dans l'amour même,
> N'est pas un songe vain créé pour nous tenter,
> Qu'il existe, ou plutôt qu'il pourrait exister,
> Si, brûlant à jamais du feu qui nous dévore,
> Vous et l'être adoré dont l'âme vous adore,
> L'innocence, l'amour, le désir, la beauté,
> Pouvaient ravir aux dieux leur immortalité!

These thirty lines, the magnificent long ode on "Les Révolutions" composed in 1831, and, in spite of several flaws which the poet carelessly left in it, his powerful poem on his daughter's death, "Gethsémani" (1834), rank in our eyes among the truly great achievements of French lyricism. They all belong to the eloquent type of poetry which Lamartine, around and after 1830, recognized as the one best suited to him. On September 22, 1835, after delivering a speech at Mâcon, he wrote: "I now see the effective truth of what I had always felt: that eloquence was in me more than poetry, the latter being only one of its forms." He similarly noted later, of one of his favorite Girondins, Vergniaud, that "his imagination first overflowed in poetry before it burst out into eloquence."

Such a dynamic kind of poetry may appear verbose, too sumptuously ample, too prone to approximate and to skirt the inevitable image or the strikingly concise and enigmatic line. It is entitled to its rightful place in France, however, alongside the more fashionable finds of Valéry, less eloquent but in no way less rhetorical (indeed far more "arty" and tricky) than Lamartine's rolling periods.

> Qui pleure là, sinon le vent simple à cette heure? . . .
> N'entends-tu pas frémir ces noms aériens,
> O Sourde!

and the exquisite but most rhetorical and artificial questions addressed in the presence of "La Dormeuse":

> Quels secrets dans son coeur brûle ma jeune amie? . . .
> De quels vains aliments sa naïve chaleur
> Fait ce rayonnement d'une femme endormie?

We refrain from mentioning Valéry's more obvious failures, such as "La Pythie" and the bad stanzas (there are several such) of "Le Cimetière marin." Static poetry occasionally creates delightful miniatures and delights in serpentine folds and volutes. It appeals to the feminine half of ourselves which confesses, with Mme Emilie Teste: "A good part of the soul can enjoy without understanding; it is a large part in me." But the invasion and the conquest of our whole being by a surge of poetical eloquence carried by an "élan vital" are not to be easily banished from the kingdom of poetry. When all is said, if French romanticism had been more similar to the best of German and English romanticism, we should deplore it today. For it would probably have spent all its force between 1820 and 1840, and have dried up or crushed the rest of French poetry, as came to be the case in Germany from Heine to George, in England from Tennyson and Browning to Yeats (Hopkins being for all practical purposes absent until 1918).

Instead, just as the French Renaissance, blossoming long after the Italian Renaissance, timid, awkward at first, borrowing lavishly and slavishly from the ancients and from beyond the Alps, turned out to be the slow dawn of a perdurable and original classicism which outlived the earlier attempt of Italy, French romanticism in 1820–1840 was only one phase by which literary history, taken in as it often is by manifestoes and debates, has been hypnotized. The so-called romantic movement of 1820–1840 was in fact only one wave (and probably the most timid, the most classical or pseudo-classical one) in the long history of French romanticism. The first, now conveniently termed pre-romanticism (1760–1775), was far bolder and more authentic in everything but poetry. The second was the timid ripple of *Atala*, Mme de Staël's novels and criticism, *Obermann*, in 1800–1810. The third one began, in the pattern which Malraux has proposed as the law for all artists, by imitating pseudo-classical models before it became aware of its own originality.[3] Only on and through the stage could the liberation of French literature occur, after 1827–1830. Parnassianism, Baudelaireanism, Bovarysm were, in our view, chiefly a new and fourth romantic onslaught, carried on by a liberated generation which no longer had to vituperate against classicism to conceal how close it was to it. Symbolism was, especially in its precursors, the most revolutionary of those successive romantic waves, and psychologically the most profound.

Yet too many of the symbolists appear to us today as failures: they were satisfied with a languid and nerveless poetry, poor in intellectual content, distrustful of motion as well as of eloquence, fearful to commit itself to the great issues of the age. They paraded the word "mystery," and attempted to put mystery by force everywhere; but they seldom yielded to the marvelous and failed to follow up that "renascence of wonder" which an English writer glorified as the achievement of romanticism. Such at any rate is the charge of André

---

[3] One of the very best works on romanticism which made this point (of romantic poetry being a supreme neo-classical achievement) is the old study by Emmanuel Barat, *Le Style poétique et la révolution romantique* (Hachette, 1904).

Breton, in an essay on "Le merveilleux contre le mystère," in which he praises the best of the romantic accomplishment against an overrated symbolism.

Romantic rhetoric is not to be equated with the sense of wonder or with poetry, to be sure. But we believe that, after half a century of vituperation against eloquence, many lovers of poetry and many poets have become aware of the perils of a poetics evolved from an indiscriminate repudiation of French romanticism. Valéry's poetics, which his poetry often contradicts, has led several younger poets, unable to read the professor at the Collège de France with the required irony and to see through the finery of an aged coquette, to an impoverishment of their gifts. Claudel, that inveterate romantic in revolt against romanticism, may well have been wiser when he tirelessly called modern poetry to the task of attempting the slow, progressive commotion of the whole man, alone worthy of a truly catholic poet. Curiously enough, he thus met with another literary potentate, the pontiff of surrealism, whose poetical achievement, from the cascade of amplifications of "L'Union libre" to the rhetorical invocations of the "Ode à Charles Fourier," has not been averse to eloquence. Eloquence is after all one of the ways in which literature, and poetry in particular, can escape the perpetual nightmare of art—immobility which is death—and capture that prerogative of life: motion. One of the shrewdest critics of modern French poetry, Gabriel Bounoure, rightly said: "Tout poème est un itinéraire pour l'âme. Il n'y pas de poème immobile."

ROMANTICISM AND FRENCH
LITERATURE TODAY
LE MORT VIVANT*

THREE QUARTERS of a century ago, romanticism was under attack
in France and in Great Britain. The papers then read before learned
associations reflected the trend of criticism in the decades before and
after World War I. Their authors advocated the unanimous discarding of such an abused and misleading term as romanticism, at least
in its singular form. They gravely branded modern literature as
disloyal to humanism and crudely disrespectful of Emerson's "inner
check." One of the pontiffs of that era had decreed in one of his papal
bulls, appropriately enough uttered in *The Sacred Wood*: "There may
be a great deal to be said for Romanticism in life, there is no place for
it in letters." The French adversaries of romanticism, Pierre Lasserre,
Ernest Seillière, Charles Maurras himself, appeared through the
tinted glasses of American neo-humanists as worthy champions of
classicism, although restraint, discipline, the golden rule of *ne quid
nimis*, and the wisdom of humility had certainly been denied these
impetuous prophets of the past. Young scholars, envious of the in-
defatigably productive Baron Seillière devouring two or three romantic
imperialists every year in as many annual volumes, taught in some
American seminars that the French had repudiated their arch-villain,
Rousseau, and had meekly repaired to the fold of their one true

* This essay was originally read as a paper at the request of the group General
Topics II of the Modern Language Association of America at its meeting of
December, 1952, in Boston. The general title proposed was "The Influence of the
Romantic Movement on Modern Thought."

tradition: classicism. Professors, dismayed by the rebellion of the "lost generation," found some solace in the thought that Western Europe at any rate knew better and was, as the phrase has gone for a hundred years, "on the verge of a classical renaissance."

Twenty-five years have elapsed since the rather cool celebration, in Paris, of the centenary of the *Préface de Cromwell* and of the markedly academic commemoration of romanticism in 1927. The pendulum has swung back. The anniversaries of the deaths of such romantics as Chopin, Chateaubriand, Balzac, and the one hundred fiftieth anniversary of Victor Hugo's birth have been celebrated not only with éclat, but with warmth and spontaneousness. Indeed, the peril is at present in the dearth of detractors of Balzac and Hugo, which might well indicate that they are no longer feared and fail to arouse passionate enmity. Berlioz is more often heard in concert halls than ever before. Stendhal is cherished, not for being a cynical and calculating psychologist, dissecting the mechanics of love and worshiping cold-blooded energy, as he was deceptively pictured by an earlier generation, but as the most soft-hearted, the most naïve, tender, and shy of all the romantics. Surrealism, as rapturously romantic a movement as France had seen since 1830, set up Lautréamont and Rimbaud, both scions of romanticism, as its demigods, and never has their fascination held greater sway. In 1951, a questionnaire sent to the twenty-year-olds elicited their preferences among living writers as topped by Malraux, Claudel, Montherlant, Cocteau. Among nineteenth-century writers, the favored ones were Stendhal, Verlaine, Rimbaud—then Musset.[1] Valéry, Gide, and those who might have passed in 1925 for the foes of romanticism came far behind in the tributes of the young. Indeed, Valéry's one book of the last two decades which won him the renewed affection of the public was *Mon Faust*, his most Dionysian work. Gide never sided with the anti-romantics, not even with Jacques Rivière's nonpolitical but scathing condemnation of romanticism in his 1913 articles on the novel of adventure. "Romanticism," Gide used to repeat to the young, "ruins only the weak ones," as he had once said of that other form of romanticism, Nietzscheism.

In Great Britain, the last fifteen years have strangely aged the neo-

[1] Robert Kanters and Gilbert Sigaux, *Vingt ans en 1951: Enquête sur la Jeunesse française* (Paris, 1951), p. 129.

classical fervor of the twenties. The imperious pronouncements of T. E. Hulme (whom a premature death in World War I probably prevented from shaking off continental influences) appear very crude today. The *Criterion* has played its part—a healthy one—in British criticism, but it has not influenced literary creativeness to any noticeable degree. W. H. Auden's distrust of emotion and of romantic values was belied by his highest poetical achievement, which, in our opinion, was to be found in the last and very Shakespearean lines of *The Ascent of F 6* and in his *Christmas Oratorio*. Romanticism reigns again unchallenged in Stephen Spender, who has written intelligently and discriminately upon it,[2] in Dylan Thomas and David Gascoyne, in George Barker, in the pathetic figure of Richard Hillary "falling through space," in Francis Scarfe and Derek Savage. The latter, in *The Personal Principle* (1944), announced: "We are moving toward a new Romantic movement," and he did his best to herald it. The former, publishing in 1942 his essays and manifestoes on the liberation of poetry entitled *Auden and After*, had likewise boasted of the romanticism of his contemporaries. "This is a fundamentally Romantic generation, filled . . . with a great mythological conception of themselves as martyrs, born into one war and fattened for another." Among the young writers whom he hailed as the torchbearers of the "new emotional revival" were those who have aligned themselves under the group of the New Apocalypse: Henry Treece, J. F. Hendry, Nicholas Moore, G. S. Fraser. Their doctrinal views, ebullient and combative, have been loudly expressed in their anthologies, *The New Apocalypse* (1939) and *The White Horseman* (1941). In 1949, Stefan Schimanski and Henry Treece brought out *A New Romantic Anthology* at the Grey Walls Press and offered entertaining and confusing definitions of the old antithetic terms: classicism and romanticism. "Classicism is a pair of parallel lines, meeting nowhere. . . . The Romantic artist is the advance-guard of human sensibility, who leaves the artistic world richer than he found it. . . . Romanticism is the soaring spirit, that spark of the Creator, which will flash one day out of the tired eyes, to glimpse and enjoy the Paradise that God intended." Indeed, the romantic impulse seems to fill not only the

---

[2] Stephen Spender, "Romanticism of the English Romantic Movement," *English Review*, XIV (March 1947), 288–300.

impetuous South African Roy Campbell, who staged a post-war return with his *Collected Poems* in 1950, having forgotten little and learned only a bit more, but Alex Comfort, Stephen Watts, Mervyn Peake, Padraic Fallon, Roy McFadden, and many of the promising young talents of Great Britain today. With them, the adjective "romantic" is no longer derogatory. They brandish it as proudly as others did "classical" or "baroque" a decade ago.

If one generalization about the bewildering and contradictory American scene may seem valid, it is probably that the divorce between the so-called creative writers and the scholars or critics is more final in the literature of America than in any other. The main and the most original body of academic criticism in the last twenty years has upheld classical or Augustan standards; in no country have not only Pope and Johnson, but Aristotle and Longinus, been more frequently appealed to. Irony has been the goddess worshiped with due "high seriousness" by the teachers of poetry. But the influence of these critics upon the actual writing of fiction, drama, and poetry has been apparently insignificant, even though most poets, renouncing the Bohemian haunts and the ungentlemanly irregularities of their European counterparts, have in the United States been tamed by an academic rank and residence on a university campus.

The cult of Scott Fitzgerald and that of Hart Crane, the fondness for violence in all the novels which have pictured World War II, the wild rebellion of *The Catcher in the Rye* and of *The Air-Conditioned Nightmare*, the adolescent obsession of many writers with their own ego and their conception of literature as a purge (but hardly a purifying one) are unmistakable romantic features. More than anywhere else, the writer in America may complain of being unacknowledged, vent and nurture his anguish, mistake inebriation for inspiration, hark back to lost values and collective myths which he does little to recreate. Even when he attempts to rejuvenate conservatism, as does Peter Viereck, he does so with passionate romanticism. Muriel Rukeyser, Winfield Townley Scott, and most of the poets represented in John Ciardi's *Mid-Century American Poets* have stressed the emotional power of the poem as constituting its main power. Randall Jarrell, one of the most gifted and most lucidly critical of these poets, shrewdly detected in modernist poetry (that of Pound, Tate, Stevens, Cummings, Moore, etc.) "an extension of romanticism, an end-product in which most of the tendencies of romanticism have been carried to their limit."[3] Henry Miller, who represents many of the deep-seated American trends because he unwillingly caricatures them with such aplomb, formulated his romantic creed in his "critical" volume, *The Books in My Life* (1952): "Be what thou art! only be it to the utmost!" Feeding one's hunger, one's thirst, or one's greedy revolt, and always in vain, as Hart Crane expressed it in his sonnet on Emily Dickinson, "You who desired so much—in vain to ask—/ Yet fed your hunger like an endless task," seems to be a familiar pastime with those American romantics whom Europe, which had restrained its own romanticism temporarily, hailed with naïve exultation just before and after World War II.

The French anti-romantic reaction of 1910–1930 has nevertheless brought several beneficent results. It shook many professors of literature from their lethargy and drove them to sift all that was immature, juvenile, rhetorical in romantic writers in order to concentrate on what was truly great, or great for us moderns, in Lamartine, Hugo, Balzac. Our perspective on these writers and several others has been totally modified since 1930 or thereabout. The foes of romanticism had, moreover, and shrewdly, centered their attacks not on the literary theories of the French romantics, but on their moods and particularly on their refusal to face reality, on their melodramatic expression of emotion, and on their confusion between sentiment and sentimentality. They flung barbed arrows at the romantics because they envisaged them as venomous and contagious, which was the surest way to make them appear seductive to a younger generation. They were men of passion themselves and most unreasonable champions of reason. Their vision of a monarchist, Catholic, and classical France, purified from the Northern baneful mists and imparting its standards and its rules to Europe, was in itself another "Arcadian dream," one of the most pathetic delusions ever entertained by

[3] Randall Jarrell, "The End of the Line," *Nation*, February 21, 1942, p. 222.

Frenchmen. Wisely had an amused and perspicacious observer of Maurras, the Englishman Basil de Selincourt, declared of him: "It is possible to hate Romanticism romantically."[4]

The romantics of 1950, thanks in part to a clear-sightedness which they owe to the debunking of romanticism by their spirited neo-classical predecessors, differ from those of 1830. They are not escapists: they do not picture the world as very different from what it really is or expect a utopia to be ushered in tomorrow. They are not so shockingly or blatantly sentimental as to inscribe their initials on the bark of trees, nor do they threaten or commit suicide with the earnestness of a Berlioz or of a Kleist. They do not refuse to face what their parents and other "sex educators" have gravely described to them as "the facts of life." Women, even in the most romantic novels of our time, no longer behave like the heroines of Balzac or of George Sand. Modern romantics do not limit romanticism to a literary revolt against the rules and to a sonorous but often uninformed cult of Shakespeare, Ossian, Byron, and Schiller. Indeed, they find fault with French romanticism for not being romantic enough. Their preference goes to the most mystical of the German romantics, to Blake, Keats, and even Coleridge and Shelley, but no longer to Byron and Scott. The late Edmond Jaloux, Albert Béguin, and many of their followers, disappointed by the inordinate amount of classicism lingering in French romanticism, have curiously looked across the Rhine toward genuine romantics who actually died from love, metaphysically rationalized every one of their changes of heart for a Caroline Schlegel or a Bettina, metamorphosed their yearnings for a thirteen-year-old girl into the mystical pursuit of a blue flower, knocked at the ivory gates of mystical dreams and of insanity. French critics heaved a sigh of relief when they could show that insanity had prowled fairly close to Hugo and Balzac, had actually snatched Nerval and some minor epigoni of the all too sane French romantic movement.

The most valuable service rendered French romanticism by the onslaught of its opponents has been to help it outgrow its most grievous fault: its fondness for rhetoric and for a sumptuous screen of

[4] Basil de Selincourt, in a subtle essay on Maurras entitled "A French Romantic," collected in *The English Secret and Other Essays* (London, 1923).

painted or high-sounding words which intervened between the readers and the landscape, the scene, or the feeling described. It is not unnatural for a writer to be in love with language and to play caressingly with words as a painter does with his color tubes. Joyce and many another Irishman, Thomas Mann, Faulkner, are no less enamored of words than Giono, Audiberti, Michaux, and Céline. But the French romantics had too often ignored the price of brevity and the virtue of economy. Their exuberant wonder at having freed language from the shackles of "bienséances" and at having democratized all the words in their dictionary carried them to a new Ciceronian lavishness. They erred in picturing the world without in gaudy hues, but they failed to probe the world within as relentlessly as Racine, Pascal, and even Marivaux and Laclos had once done. But their very excess in setting up that painted veil between their readers and their object or their own selves, after its early fascination wore off, helped the French value discretion and "pudeur" all the more. One of the ablest of the younger French critics, Gaëtan Picon,[5] sensed the crucial significance of the renewal of language attempted by the romantics, soon followed by a revulsion against the exuberance and rhetoric and by the present obsession with silence:

> With Romanticism the word "literature" slyly begins to alter its meaning. The classical language is then worn out. . . . Romanticism creates a new language, which proved to be, as we well know, a sumptuous and fecund rhetoric. But, at the same moment, it discovers that man matters more than his language. As the modern world opens, the obsessions of modern man outshine those of the writer. From then on, literature becomes an impatient and impassioned effort to populate with new truths and new values the expanse which the disappearance of old creeds had just surrendered to the desert. . . . From Romanticism stemmed an attitude of impatience and contempt toward language. . . . Language, stretched tautly toward something other than itself, rushes to its own destruction.

A whole volume, or probably several, would be required to survey the pervasive romanticism of recent French literature. Such volumes,

---

[5] Gaëtan Picon, "Métamorphose de la Littérature," *La Gazette des Lettres*, September 4, 1948; reprinted in *Panorama de la nouvelle littérature française* (Paris, 1949), pp. 251–252.

if they could be written, would suffer from confusion and arbitrariness, like all that has been written on that indefinable and elusive phenomenon. For romanticism cannot be reduced to one single common denominator. Every revolution in letters and the arts since 1800 or 1820 has been romantic, that is to say, a continuation of one or another of the multifarious aspects of the great invasion of Europe by literature and of literature by poetry which shook the beginning of the last century—even realism, even the Parnassian movement in poetry, and certainly symbolism, naturalism, Fauvism, expressionism, Dadaism, surrealism. An observer of his own times, stressing living literature rather than criticism or literary history, can only claim to perceive the particular color and shape assumed by the latest romantic wave and its importance relatively to the whole mass of literature being produced.

(1) The "mal du Siècle" was not killed or cured by the "embourgeoisement" of the nineteenth century under Louis Philippe and Guizot, Queen Victoria and Bismarck. Marcel Arland, Daniel-Rops, and their contemporaries, who reached their early twenties with the end of World War I, revived the phrase and took stock of their "inquiétude." The generation which is at present reaching the age of thirty or thirty-five seems no less prone to self-pity, melancholy, and broods complacently over its coming into the world too late or too soon, just as Musset once did or Arnold standing near the Grande Chartreuse. In fact, the phrase "le mal du Demi-Siècle" has been coined to characterize the new disease of the years 1951 and following. Several heroes of recent French novels are new Hamlets or new Dostoevskian characters, carrying their hearts in a sling, afflicted by the immensity of the tasks to be accomplished, and blaming their ill-fated time for their own cowardice or flabbiness. Such are Molloy journeying to the end of the night of the absurd in Beckett's novel, Jean Cayrol's heroes, Dhotel's Bernard le paresseux in the novel which goes by that title, the pitiful and diseased "apprenti" of Raymond Guérin, the lamentable introspective and murderer à la Dostoevski in Le Clec'h's *La Plaie et le Couteau* (a new Heauton Timorumenos), the self-analytical protagonist of Zéraffa's *Le Commerce des Hommes*, the wavering and hesitant painter in Brincourt's *La Farandole*. They occasionally regret, and so does their

exasperated reader with them, man's inability to give himself a kick in his own pants. They seem nostalgic for the years of the Resistance movement which, like the Napoleonic Wars to their predecessors of 1810, had temporarily given a purpose to their lives and turned them into leaders of men. They had then framed grandiose projects for French reconstruction and for an idealistic revolution; but peace came and an uninspiring cold or tepid war. They learned over again the lesson of all revolutionaries, formulated by Péguy after the Dreyfus mystique and by Lamartine in Jocelyn's famous meditation on revolutions: "Malheur à qui les fait! Heureux qui les hérite!"

The psychology of the new "demi-solde" of 1945–1950, the unemployed and disillusioned hero of the Resistance, as it appears in the recent French novel, is strikingly reminiscent of the romantic moods of some Stendhalian and Balzacian characters. Only the present "mal du Demi-Siècle" probably goes deeper and will not be so easily displaced by the successful ambition and the conquest in love of our modern Julien Sorel and Rastignac.

(2) Again, not unlike the generation which followed the Revolution and the Empire, the present one seems to center its meditations upon the significance of history and its own position in relation to the particular challenge, as Arnold Toynbee calls it, presented by its predicament. Joseph de Maistre, De Bonald, Saint-Simon, Auguste Comte, Michelet, Tocqueville, Lamartine, Balzac, and Hugo had all been obsessed by the baffling catastrophes of the Terror and of the twenty years of war which led them to interpret God's mysterious designs in a new way or to negate them altogether and search for a purely human law in the unfolding of history. Our contemporaries have exchanged the theocratic terminology for the Marxist one. Only a minority of them accept the deterministic dialectics unreservedly. But the indirect triumph of Marxism which, like the vogue of Kierkegaard, has helped send many Frenchmen back to Hegelianism, has been to impose its terms and its categories upon modern thought. Malraux's *Psychology of Art*, Emmanuel Mounier's, then Albert Béguin's, essays in the periodical *Esprit*, the 1952 literary event which was the acrimonious debate between Sartre and Camus in *Les Temps Modernes*, avidly amplified by the whole of the press, are but a few among the many manifestations of the new concern with the attitude

of man toward history. The torment of the past, absent from classicism and an integral part of romantic psychology, again afflicts our contemporaries. Even those who, like Sartre, asserted that one must write for one's own times, implied disregard for posterity but were by no means unconcerned with the past. Never has the pronouncement of the leader of another Hegelian generation, Renan, himself the witness of the abortive revolution of 1848, proved truer than it is today: "History is the true philosophy of our time. . . . Each of us is what he is only through his historical system."

(3) Pessimism, which was once an outgrowth of romantic melancholy broadened into a systematic and would-be objective attitude, characterizes much of modern letters, in America no less than in France or in Italy. The romantic pessimism of the younger generation does not lament in poetry reminiscent of Shelley, Leopardi, Heine, or Vigny that the world is wrong. That would be implying that it could have been or could be right, or good. Its key word is the absurd. From Camus to Beckett's nightmare, in which Molloy and Molloy's rescuers wander, with many imitators of Kafka and followers of Dos Passos and Faulkner, the theme of man's incongruity and dissonance (in the etymological meaning of absurdity) in a universe in which he is a stranger and "de trop" fills recent literature. In the face of the once acclaimed myth of progress, our age has set up the Freudian "Todestrieb" as a far more romantic force. Disintegration fascinates those moderns, more than half in love with death. "We are the Romantics of clear-sighted disappointment, the great decrepits," proclaimed the most nihilistic of their mouthpieces, E. M. Cioran, in 1950 in his somber *Précis de Décomposition*.

(4) But pessimism, when driven to such lengths and expressed with such fervor, is the other facet of an intense but easily frustrated illusion: that it is worth man's while to vituperate against his fate, and that things could be different from what they are. Along with the absurd, the concept of revolt is the other pole of the present age's vacillations; and no word renders the central mood of romanticism more adequately than the word "revolt" and all that it connotes.

All the forms of the romantic revolt have been revived by contemporary writers: the literary revolt is no longer directed against conventional rules or academic standards, but against literature itself.

Jacques Rivière, once again the most lucid observer of his own era, sympathetically watching the Dadaist antics, had coined the phrase "the crisis of the concept of literature." That crisis has been reopened by Blanchot, Picon, and younger critics, and it is in full swing in our midst. The writer, like the bourgeois, suffers from an unhappy conscience. He seems bent upon wrecking all that smacks of literature and of written style in his craft and attempts to adhere as closely as possible to the colloquial spoken language. "La littérature ou le droit à la mort" is the title of Blanchot's longest critical essay in *La Part du Feu*. French literature apparently aims at its own self-destruction so that, phoenix-like, it may be reborn.

The romantic revolt of 1940–1950 is also social, or rather antisocial, and suffers from its isolation. Many a reviewer has lately remarked upon the renewed fascination of the Mediterranean for modern English writers,[6] just as in the time of Shelley and Byron. The post-war American authors have found their Mecca in Italy. The French are migrants and exiles, unable to accept integration in a society composed of "salauds," the new term for Philistines. They read avidly about those who joined a group or served a cause for a while: T. E. Lawrence, Saint-Exupéry, Ernst Jünger, even that caricaturist of the adventurer, Malaperte, only to agree with Baudelaire that the greatest delight about joining a party is in the thought that one may betray it.

But the essential aspect of the new romantic revolt today is metaphysical. Malraux and Camus are its greatest prophets. But Giono and Bernanos, Breton and Eluard, Char and Ponge, Anouilh and Sartre, are also romantic rebels. "To live is not to be resigned," declared Camus very early. And every one of his later works, *The Plague* or the ideological essay on man in revolt, have vindicated, in terms often reminiscent of Camus' truest ancestor, Vigny, man's assumption of his humanity against the divine. "In order to be a man, refuse to be God."[7] Others, Malraux notably as early as *La Tentation*

---

[6] For example, the author of "Poetic Impulses of Our Time" in the *Times Literary Supplement*, August 29, 1952.

[7] Two of the most beautiful and most moving essays by Camus on his position, which deserve to be better known, are his *L'Exil d'Hélène* in *Permanence de la Grèce, Cahiers du Sud* (1948), pp. 381–386, and his splendid "The Artist as Witness of Freedom" in *Commentary*, VIII (December 1949), 534–538.

de l'Occident and Sartre in terms which denote a close reading of his predecessor, have in contrary (though in fact parallel) terms defined the ambition of modern man as self-deification. Two volumes of criticism have stressed this Satanic or Titanic character of modern literature, and many more will doubtless follow, for no aspect of French letters since Sade, Hugo, Lautréamont, and Rimbaud is more characteristic than this attempt to drive the Nietzschean death of God to its most tragic consequences. They are *La Mystique du Surhomme* (Paris, 1948) by a Catholic essayist, Michel Carrouges, and *La Révolte des Ecrivains d'aujourd'hui* by R. M. Albérès (Paris, 1949).[8]

(5) The same critic and novelist, Albérès, had, in an earlier and youthful essay, sketched a *Portrait de notre héros* (Paris, 1949). Every generation should thus be attended by patient doctors who would feel its pulse, listen to its heart, translate its dreams, and draw the portrait of the favorite hero or heroes into whom it projects itself. There is little doubt in our mind that such a portrait, in 1945 or 1952, would be found to present striking similarities to Manfred and Don Juan combined in one, to Hernani's "force qui va" and Fantasio, to Balzac's Raphael, and even to Julien Sorel at his trial. Our picture of modern man as novels offer it owes much to our times, to concentration camps and the fear experienced as well as aroused by Germany, Russia, and other tyrannies present or to come. It has also been molded by Kafka, Julien Green, Graham Greene, Faulkner, by Camus' first novel, and by an English novel which has profoundly and deservedly impressed the French, Malcolm Lowry's *Under the Volcano* (1947). The new hero is a hunted man—hunted by the police state, by war, by sex, drug, drink, fear, madness, and other masks worn by fatality. "It is no accident," wrote Camus in the article of *Commentary* referred to above, "if the significant books of today, instead of being interested in the nuances of the heart and the verities of love, get excited only about judges, trials, and the mechanics of accusation; if instead of opening windows on the beauty of the world, one carefully closes them on the anguish of the solitary."

---

[8] One hardly need be reminded of the most famous cries of Byron, Poe, and of Musset's "Qui de nous, qui de nous, va devenir un dieu?" Lamartine keenly described in a letter of May 27, 1819, his own age as one "in which men want to become gods."

Anguish, the Kierkegaardian "Angst," is, without doubt, the emotion expressed with the most relentless consistency and the most forceful originality in recent French literature. Feebly, the modern hero has called for an answer from some provident presence above.

"Mais le ciel reste noir, et Dieu ne répond pas," exactly as in Vigny's "Mont des Oliviers." The conviction asserts itself in the new romantic that there is no way out of his concentrationary universe, that the discrepancy between man's aspirations and the conditions meted out to him by life is total and beyond remedy. But (and like the romantic pessimists of a hundred and twenty years ago) the recent writer is proud of that anguish which designates him as a chosen vessel to protest against God or God's absence. "One would have to be blinded by much Pharisaïsm," wrote Sartre, "not to find in anguish itself the formidable mission with which every one of us is invested." Malraux, Anouilh, most of the younger novelists, and the most desperate of all those writers, Blanchot,[9] all echo such a cry. But the pride they take in their anguish, which sets them apart from the "salauds" and from selfish hedonists, does not doom them to passive acceptance. Sartre has repeatedly stressed the Jansenist character of his generation in France, and Malraux in 1945 asserted that the leading French writers of his day were aligned, even if they rejected faith, with the Pascalian tradition. A Jesuit periodical once hailed Camus as a Pascal without Christ. An aphorism such as this one in Camus' letter to René Char in *Actuelles* indeed reminds one of Pascal as Vigny and the romantics interpreted him: "The greatness of man lies in his decision to be stronger than his condition."

If, as our modern romantics like to repeat, there is no hope of alleviation of their metaphysical anguish, if there is indeed more bitterness in their despair and less easy solace found in glittering words than

---

[9] Maurice Blanchot wrote in *La Part du Feu* (1949): "L'art et l'œuvre d'art . . . affirment, derrière l'espoir de survivre, le désespoir d'exister sans cesse" and in his "récit," *L'Arrêt de Mort* (1948): "se perdre, il le faut; et celui qui résiste sombre, et celui qui va de l'avant devient ce noir même, cette chose froide et méprisante au sein de laquelle l'infini demeure." It would be worth while studying the romantic cadences and overtones in recent French prose.

in the men of 1820–1840, three paths have lain open before them which have led them to temper the artificiality and the humorless histrionics preying on most romantics.

The first is irony. Musset, Hugo, Nerval, Stendhal, and even more Byron, the Germans like Tieck, Jean-Paul, and Heine, had woven it into their romantic attire. Jean-Paul, commenting upon Schlegel's assertion that poetry was to become romanticism itself,[10] added that the same was true of the comic element. "Alles muss romantisch, das heisst, humoristisch werden." Irony as an antidote to sentiment or as a disguise for passion is everywhere in the works which can be called romantic around us. The sense of the humorous, or, as the French say, of the "cocasse," which T. S. Eliot and his followers admired in Laforgue and which some described as a mark of classicism, has been woven into the literature that has followed in the thirties and forties. In this sense it is fair to contend that romanticism contains the classicism which preceded it as classicism was, or will be again, romanticism tamed and assimilated. The "art de pudeur et de modestie" in which Gide saw the essence of classicism coexists with intensity and passion. "It is ironical philosophies which make passionate works," declared Camus. Malraux, the early Giono, Claudel, had something theatrical and tensely exalted which is not easily palatable to the young novelists and poets of 1950. Valéry jokingly remarked to a confidant[11] that Claudel, for all his greatness, lacked elegance and economy. "He uses a crane to lift a cigarette." Irony has been the saving grace of Giono's delightfully Stendhalian novel of 1951, *Le Hussard sur le Toit*, of Montherlant when he has consented to temper his egocentrism, of Sartre, Queneau, Anouilh, and of Vailland, Curtis, Merle, and most novelists of the last decade.

The recent romanticism came after an era of debunking of love as the great theme of literature. The death of love was for a while lamented by observers of the new literature as was the death of God. Love certainly had to resist many onslaughts: that of homosexuality and that of eroticism in particular. A scientific or a Jansenist hatred of love envenomed many a book by Proust, Mauriac, Montherlant,

[10] Jean-Paul Richter, *Vorschule der Aesthetik* (Hamburg, 1804), I, 179.

[11] Dorothy Bussy, "Some Recollections of Paul Valéry," *Horizon*, No. 77 (May 1946).

Jouhandeau, Sartre. Malraux proposed, in a preface to the French translation of *Lady Chatterley's Lover*, that an end be put to the myth of love so that the new myth of sex could be forged. Laclos was acclaimed as the prophet of eroticism, a lucid control of the heart and cultivation of the senses from which idealizations would be banished.

There again, the legacy of the years which seemed to have discarded "l'amour-passion" is not being repudiated, but assimilated and outgrown. Modern romantics are not likely to pretend that lovers have no lips or to wax rapturous over chastity. The role of the senses in love is taken for granted and often described in recent French works with a clear-sighted sanity which was lacking in Stendhal and Balzac. But many signs point to a reintegration of sentiment in the description of love and even of "pudeur," that envelopment of the body by the soul, as Nietzsche defined it. The twenty-year-olds questioned by Robert Kanters and Gilbert Sigaux in the book quoted above in footnote 1 did not answer very differently from the young men of 1830: "One does not have the woman one loves. One makes love to those whom one does not love. It devours one's heart." Anouilh's plays revolve around pure and disinterested love as the one redeeming feature in a world of corrupt adults. Julien Gracq, crowned by the Goncourt Academy in 1951, proclaims unabashedly his admiration for the Graal legend (as do numerous moderns) and for the "exalting and despairing formula: I can live neither with you nor without you" (Preface to *Le Roi pêcheur*, 1948). Several of the novels published since 1950 have turned against the distrust of sentimentality and the annihilation of passion other than physical. Such are Pierre Emmanuel's sensuous but rapturous *Car enfin je vous aime* (1950), Paul Colin's *Les Jeux sauvages* (1950), Guy Le Clec'h's *La Plaie et le Couteau* (1952), Dominique Rolin's unrestrained *Moi qui ne suis qu'amour* (1950). J. B. Rossi's *Les Mal-Partis* (1950), which has been compared to Radiguet's *Diable au Corps* and is perhaps superior to it, likewise glorifies a sentimental passion felt by an adolescent for a nun, and Robert Margerit's *Le Dieu nu* (1951) is the most poetically romantic of all. The author characterizes his story, which plays deftly with a faint suspicion of incest but is a hymn to the "naked god" of the Phoenicians, Love, as "an ardent and chaste lesson." André Breton, who, since he founded surrealism, has paid tribute to the romantics as the high priests of the marvelous and of love, may be proud of his belated influence over the latest crop of French novels and poems.

In a third manner it may be contended that the analytical lucidity of the modern worshipers of the ego, all grandsons of Rousseau, Constant, and Stendhal, is being absorbed by the new romanticism. The place of the words "sincerity" and "authenticity" has been paramount in the French critical vocabulary since World War I. One may be coldly sincere through destroying the delusions of the heart and through a scientific control of oneself by a never failing intellectual lucidity. Another sincerity may be reached through the acceptance of the risks of passion and the exaltation of feeling, duly accepted but not restrained by the brain. Lucidity, that word which denotes the highest possible praise to a Frenchman and even to a Frenchwoman, is easily attained and therefore hardly valuable if it does not have to pierce through mysteries or to probe dark abysses. It should be gained through a painful struggle with turbid emotions and conflicting impulses from the flesh, from the unconscious, even from those pristine, archetypal forces deposited in us by "timeless dynasties."[12] It must be conquered and not passively received through deliberate exclusion of most of life.

No concept has obsessed French writers of the years 1910 to 1930, guided by Rivière and Gide, so persistently as the quest for the type of sincerity which is not dissection or exclusion of feeling, hypocritical disregard of the sensual and erotic side of our nature, but which is the discarding of all extraneous borrowings and of the trappings of our

[12] Richard Wilbur, the young American poet, has expressed the poignancy of things clear in striking lines in "Clearness," *Ceremony and Other Poems* (New York, 1948):

> There is a poignancy in all things clear
> In the stare of the deer, in the ring
> of the hammer in the morning.
> Seeing a bucket of perfectly lucid water
> We fall for imagining prodigious honesties
> And feel so when the snow for all its softness
> Tumbles in adamant forms, turning and turning
> Its perfect faces, lettering in our sight
> The heirs and types of timeless dynasties.

inner life, and the courageous acceptance of the truly authentic. The French generation which followed in 1940–1950 has fallen heir to that cyclopean task of clarification. Of romanticism as it shook the early nineteenth century, it rejects the pathetic fallacy, the pantheistic overflow of human feelings over nature, declamatory pomposity, and the willful self-delusions of the heart. The novels and plays of today do not condescend to justify the behavior of characters through the rights of passion, as George Sand once did, or through the corruption of a society which must be trampled under foot by post-Napoleonic upstarts. Their bête noire is bad faith, the unauthentic social comedy and mundane pursuits of another age. Their favorite heroes are outlaws, as in the so-called romantic age, though less glamorous ones: Camus' Meursault, Bernanos' murderers, Malraux's adventurers, Sartre's Genet, comedian and martyr, thief and pederast. But they all reject insincerity, intellectual comfort, the complacency of the characters of 1900 who could wallow in adultery and corruption to their heart's content, provided they retained the outward show of respectability. Anouilh's plays tirelessly harp upon that string, that love between fully clear-sighted and sincere persons alone justifies the present world, otherwise teeming with the impurity and ugliness of sentimental and social lies. Indeed, sincerity, often devoid of charity and not averse to brutality, is the one pedestal upon which a new morality seems to rest for the writers of the last few years whom Albérès has grouped in his book on "la Révolte."

A moral and "uplifting" conclusion would be out of place in a semi-learned, semi-literary essay on the survival and expansion of romanticism today. Yet the search for a new ethics is everywhere present in recent volumes, among Existentialists as well as among the epigoni of surrealism, among the Marxists, and among the Catholics. This ethics is not one of diffidence of all that is impulsive and irrational in man, of curbing the manifestations of original sin in us, as T. E. Hulme, Maurras, Seillière, and other neo-classical advocates attempted to formulate thirty years ago or more. Gaëton Picon, a clear-sighted analytical critic himself, wisely concluded his 1949 *Panorama* of recent French literature with these words: "Classicism would never have died, if it were possible for us to bring it to life again." The modern ethics is, in Albérès' characterization, a Promethean and soteriological ethics, and

French literature today is indeed both: a literature of revolt against man's fate and one of salvation, for the world is out of joint, as it has always been since it was created, only a little more so at the present time.

It would be difficult for a literature which, more than any other, prides itself on feeling the pulse of its own age, not to be romantic, that is, unquiet, torn by anguish, rebellious, scornful of an order that is crystallized inequality, obsessed by the powers of death and disintegration. But the attempt to set up new scales of values is even more conspicuous than the revolt against the outworn ones. The "death drive" has seldom triumphed over the "love drive" or over the impulse to assert life with all the more gusto as life is insulted as being unprofitable, tragic, senseless, incessantly threatened, and therefore doubly attractive. The new romanticism cannot be rightly opposed to classicism. As Mario Praz put it, the two words should not be considered as antithetic for they connote two conglomerates of varied elements which are of different orders or lie on totally diverse planes. "There is such a thing as a 'Romantic Movement' and classicism is only an aspect of it," wrote the author of *The Romantic Agony*. Recent French literature, highly imperfect, richer in scattered talents than in genius, too often bent upon "épater le bourgeois" or shocking the rare creature who is still capable of being shocked or "épaté" in 1968, is nonetheless a courageous and constructive literature. It does not adorn reality, it does not fly into escapist refuges, it does not shy from its task of answering the challenge of the modern world with virile lucidity and with hope in the Miltonic "dubious battle" being fought by man at the dawn of a new half-century. It is thus not unworthy of the role which literature in France seems to have assigned to itself ever since the seventeenth century, and even more so since 1850–1860: that of replacing religion and ethics for many minds. Of the best works of today, it will probably be said that, in their passionate but clear-sighted portrayal of man and of his condition, they have not derogated from the nobleness of the stark but manly masterpieces of an earlier age, now used as classics in the training of youth and praised in following terms by the Protestant septuagenarian Jean Schlumberger:

Just as Sparta inflicted upon its young men, through a whipping in front of the altar of Diana, an ordeal of endurance, we submit ours to the reading of *L'Education Sentimentale*, *La Terre*, or *Les Fleurs du Mal*, and we refuse to consider as virile a mind which flinches from such a contact. No country of the world, except the America of today, imposes such an initiation upon its youth. If some cry out in protest that art, the ends of which are exultation and joy, should not, except in a monstrous paradox, be utilized as fasces of rods, the retort is clear: if some moral or religious disciplines have, without irretrievable damage, been allowed to lapse into disuse, it is because art has taken over part of their former task.[13]

[13] Jean Schlumberger, *Jalons* (Sagittaire, 1941).

11 | THE RESPONSIBILITY OF MASS MEDIA

MY SUBJECT—the responsibility of mass media—is of such tremendous importance that no man whose profession is that of educating the youth and of interpreting the heritage of the past to those who will be entrusted with the building of the future can remain unconcerned by it. The foreign-born intellectual, who, not impelled by any historical tragedy, by any threat of exile or of destitution in his own land, has freely elected to come, teach, and write in the United States, feels inclined, even more than native citizens, to proffer advice and to blot out the stains which tarnish the image of his promised and adopted country. He may prove more severe than some complacent or blasé Americans to the failings of this land of the free and of much-vaunted democratic opportunities. His justification is that he still nurtures an ideal for America as the country whose destiny today is, thanks to technology, to deepen and to spread culture without diluting its essence overmuch. No other country has yet so fully and so generously accepted, without always formulating it with clarity and without invoking ideological principles from which to deduce it, a predicament which may be defined thus: to refuse to allow too many people inside its own frontiers to remain afflicted with poverty and with spiritual and intellectual destitution, or else those barbarians of the interior might, in time of stress, turn angrily against the culture from which they would have felt excluded; to refuse just as stubbornly to let the privileged ones on our planet become ever richer and culturally favored, if the underprivileged people, emerging out of backwardness in darker continents, fast multiplying in numbers and frustrated in their nascent aspirations, were to remain barbarians of the outside. The responsibility of mass media today concerns the three fourths of mankind rising to consciousness in Asia, Africa, South America. Those new techniques can achieve much to help them climb to a reasonable level of understanding of themselves and of others. Through mass media (cinema, radio, television, books, newspapers, and magazines) is formed their image of the West and of America.

Through trial and error, through vicissitudes of generous idealism and noble behavior followed by lapses into idol-breaking of the American better self, such as the Harding presidency and the so-called McCarthy era witnessed, this country's manifest (but at times obscured) destiny is to lead the world toward more consciousness. Its best minds are, probably more ardently than anywhere else, eager for the truth which once was, and is, to make men free. The faith in education is more widespread and intensely lived than in most nations today, excepting perhaps Russia; the freedom of the mind, and even from prejudices, is greater than elsewhere. The acceptance of the burden of foreign aid by a majority of Americans has placed them at the front rank of the citizens of a world community who are ready to share with others. The faith of other nations in this country has not been seriously shaken by the new self-assertiveness of affluent Europeans or by the overemphasis, in mass media and in American literature, upon squalor, sex, and crime.

On the other hand, a number of the most earnest minds analyzing American culture here and now do not conceal their dismay: creativeness is often lagging behind the zeal to imitate, to process, to conform; freedom all too often degenerates into license and duties are seldom accepted as the necessary corollary of rights which are used and abused. The breakdown of Puritanism and of traditional ethics has left many young people without guidance; the invasion of literature and of life by sex hardly seems to have brought much enjoyment of life, or less freedom from remorse and anxiety. Sex crimes are more frequent than in most other civilized countries. Mental health has not been achieved in spite of our unearthing of complexes or of our attempts to picture the surrounding world as a fine abode to which we should be complacently well adapted.

The concern of those of us who realize that time is more urgently of the essence now than it ever was is due to the process of acceleration of history which has suddenly launched fifty nations on the path to self-government and to technical modernization. The possibilities for those lands in Asia, Africa, the Americas to turn to chaos, cruelty, mutual and self-destruction are just as wide open as their possibilities for good. The impact on them of our example, even more than that of financial or technical aid, can be immense. The picture of greed and venality in American business and politics, of built-in autocracy and selfishness in labor unions, of juvenile delinquency, of brain-washing or slumber of the minds systematically fostered by mass media can have unforeseeable baneful effects abroad and retard the emergence of young nations out of semi-barbarism to such an extent that the peace and survival of the world will be in jeopardy.

At home, the evils which the critics have denounced in mass media, especially of radio and television and, to some extent, movies, should be squarely faced. They have often been denounced in anger, or denied with some hypocrisy by those who had a vested interest in seeing present conditions endure. The mass media industry is today powerful and courageous enough to welcome candid debating of pros and cons by third parties. Its own public image may well be dependent upon its ability and will to reform. Gilbert Seldes, in 1950 in *The Great Audience* (New York: Viking Press), rightly declared in his examination of the mass man's being created by mass media: "At stake is simply the future of this country as a creative democratic society."

No elaborate historical account is necessary. Since the invention of printing at the end of the Middle Ages, the discovery of the cinema, then of radio and television, has clearly constituted the most momentous event in the history of man communicating with other men. Even the advent of a cheap press with the American and the French Revolutions, then with the telegraph, and the wide use of advertising in Europe and the United States, in the years 1830–1850, did not match the revolution of our century in importance. The Revolt of the Masses, which the most eminent of living Spanish philosophers, Ortega y Gasset, traces back to those decades a hundred and thirty years ago, has turned into a triumph—or perhaps a Pyrrhic victory; for their tastes, their demands, their minds have been manipulated by a few who were not over-anxious to lead those masses to preferring what was best in them. James Gordon Bennett, of the young and aggressive *New York Herald*, founded in 1844, then declared bumptiously: "Books have had their day. The theaters have had their day. The temple of religion has had its day. A newspaper can be made to take the lead of all these in the great movements of human thought and of human civilization. A newspaper can send more souls to Heaven and save more from Hell than all the churches and chapels in New York, besides making money at the same time."[1]

> 'Tis an awkward thing to play with souls,
> And matter enough to save one's own,

in Robert Browning's words in "A Light Woman." Radio and television have been vituperated against by many a lay preacher as soulless machinations playing with souls. Behind those declamatory vituperations, what are the cool arguments presenting the case of their detractors?

First, the defenders of the printed word, traditionally devoted to Gutenberg's invention as the greatest service ever rendered to civilization, their memories echoing with many a touching message on reading books and the spiritual profits to accrue from it, have mourned the new tyranny of images replacing the words read and presumably pondered over. True it is that the chief advantage enjoyed by a reader of newspapers, magazines, and books is lost by the radio or television audience. The latter cannot interrupt in order to go back and reread. It cannot pause to assimilate, jot down a remark, discuss it with others. The stumbling blocks encountered in reading would send back the more curious minds to a dictionary, to a reference; they made an active reading necessary, just as the study of ancient languages, through which elites used to be trained, forced the young to realize how words looked in a language other than their own and to struggle, with some profit for the intellect, before fully grasping what Plato, Cicero, Virgil, or even what Shakespeare and Milton meant and expressed. Since the new cult of the images is hardly likely to lose its devotees, brought up in a world of comics, of illustrations, of art reproductions, it should be the task of education to offset any perils

[1] Quoted in Eric Barnouw, *Mass Communication* (New York: Rinehart, 1956).

inherent in that return to the visual through a greater stress on languages at college and on difficult reading later. Modern literature abounds in difficult works and their difficulty seldom discourages readers, or buyers. Languages force us to discover how diverse are, in a different context, words which may look superficially like those we use in politics, trade, and even in conversation. Many ideological, and not a few political, divergencies are doubtless due to words misunderstood.

The next butt of the arrows aimed at mass media is their facility. There was, to be sure, no especial virtue in the old-fashioned European way of multiplying discomfort for the wife or the servants in a home, of accumulating rules, red tape, and customs barriers in old countries, except that the exasperation vented against such hurdles may have made men less bored and more meek as mates to put up with, women too concerned with such minor obstacles to have enough energy left for making scenes or seeking old-fashioned trysts. But we are told by austere moralists that we cease to prize what we secure too easily through the mere pushing of a knob. Our lurking sadism is fostered by the impatient turning of a button and cutting off of a preacher's sermon, an educator's admonition, or a woman's screaming or giggling. The truest evil is the spread of fragmentariness around us and inside us. The line from Yeats's "The Second Coming" has become an apt motto for our modern moralists: "Things fall apart. The centre cannot hold." We tend to spin around in a welter of unrelated news, insensitive to their apparent discrepancies, unable to perceive the link between today's events and yesterday's occurrences. The whys and the wherefores elude us and we seldom can foresee the possible consequences of today's happenings. We lack the context in which to replace a crisis taking place in Indonesia, Peru, or Cuba. It used to be said that the mark of the educated person was to be hardly surprised by events. The more news is thrown at us every hour on the hour, dinned into our ears through a process of repetition which defeats its own purpose, the more bewildered we seem to be about what happens in Korea, the Congo, Cyprus, De Gaulle's France, or in Canada and Venezuela. Similarly, hundreds of courses in current events in our schools and colleges since 1920 or so have failed to turn out a generation more adept at understanding world affairs and at anticipating events than our grandfathers ever were.

"Surprised by joy"—Wordsworth coined the apt phrase as an opening to one of his sonnets. But the chief delights in life, if they surprise us, have also been prepared by imaginative expectation. How many biographies have described to us that mood of tense excitement in which, "impatient as the wind," a boy or a teenager first experienced the joy of "a first acquaintance with poets" like Hazlitt, a first visit to the theatre to listen to La Berma in *Phèdre*, a first visit to a land of legend, an early love. One of the faults of mass media, so easily within our reach if we only absent-mindedly press a button, is that they are not preceded by that imaginative preparation. No state of grace invades the viewer or the listener before the epiphany or visitation from outside or above fulfills his expectant dream. He does not meet the awesome event halfway as we do when we go to a concert or a theatrical performance, even to a live lecture. Repetition and monotony are the rule. The news, the canned music, the desiccated jokes are given over and over again to satiety. The onlooker misses the thrill of the crowd around him, vibrant with admiration for its sport or art idol, pitiless to the idol's failings, uncertain over the outcome of the fight being waged. Passivity and boredom ensue. Never was it so true to repeat with the late Dean Inge of St. Paul that the role of boredom in the world is grossly underestimated. The passive, if not sadistic, indifference with which catastrophes, crimes, the persecution of minorities, the hunting of outlaws or heretics are watched by many bodes ill for the revulsion of our moral conscience in the presence of deeds which, in our age, have equaled the hideous circus games watched with equanimity by the Romans.

Some endeavors have been made by the organizers of a few television shows to turn, in part at least, the young people watching them into participating actors—through games, questions, a sense of suspense. The fear of many parents and teachers remains great, however, and not altogether unfounded, that generations of watchers of the little screen may constitute a nation of voyeurs. The more ominous prophets of despair in our mass age, like Robert Maynard Hutchins, have even envisaged the day when, "under the impact of

TV, . . . people can neither read nor write, but will be no better than the forms of plant life."[2] The same stern critic of facility at all levels of education once sarcastically surmised that when our astronauts land on Mars or other planets they may well discover that there once was intelligent life there and persons who preceded our own globe in the discovery of, and addiction to, radio and TV by a thousand years. They had then been reduced to the death in life of mental apathy.

Conformity soon follows in the wake of passivity. That evil has lately become the bugbear of educational sermonizers in America; it is the conformist theme of many commencement speeches to indict conformity. We seem to fear that individualists in America are no longer rugged enough and much too ready to flock into organized groups and be reassured in their anxiety and insecurity by the surrounding presence of others who think like them, or abdicate thinking at all. In the eyes of a Latin, accustomed to countries where the unifying and bureaucratic power of the central government requires, if it is to be offset at all, some disobedience on the part of the citizens, such a civic or social behavior on the part of North Americans offers pleasant advantages over their own secret leaning toward anarchy. The working of democracy is smoother in the United States.

But it may also become so smooth as to be taken for granted and provide hunting grounds for lobbyists, persuaders of wealth, and demagogues. Mass media have radically altered relations between a ruler, or a candidate for office, and his people. In relatively small countries like England, Germany, or France, statesmen and politicians have been quick at taking advantage of the radio, then of the television screen, and the old political parties or the local and regional dissents have been stifled or profoundly upset. In a vast continent spreading from the Atlantic to the Pacific, there is little in common between an electoral campaign which required weeks before taking a would-be President through thirty states, and the televised debates of 1960 or '64, with experts gravely rating a President or his opponent according to their grading book of TV efficiency. But messages on the state of the Union or on the budget or on racial integration are no longer invested with the solemnity which, before

[2] Quoted in Charles A. Siepmann, *TV and Education in the U.S.* (UNESCO, 1952).

the advent of audio-visual media, engraved them in the memories of patient readers and provoked discussion on their import. Words broadcast from the White House are not clearly differentiated by the listeners or the viewers from an inquiry into the underworld with glib gangsters posing for the audience freely offered to them or from commercial shows.

The danger to which many a guardian of the traditions of democracy in our age points lies clearly in the realization by industrialists and salesmen that they were presented with a prodigious mass market in which their ever expanding production might find new outlets if only new needs could be aroused. The aim thus became to level the people down to the condition of passive buyers of mass products, often unwanted and in any case threatened with accelerated obsolescence. According to the harshest critics of mass media, the insidious purpose of the producers of goods and of their advertisers thus became to organize a systematic decline of attention. Clifton Fadiman, who coined that phrase, indicated their purpose as "attracting the attention without actually engaging it."

Things are not quite so bleak. The incessant growth of loud publicity may well defeat its own purpose in the end; it is directed at an equally growing resistance to the waves of aerial words destined to wash our brains. A sheep is not an altogether ignoble animal, and gregarious flocks have been known to be led by good pastors toward a good purpose. "A Nation of Sheep" was an easy catchword to serve as a title for a rather unconvincing and shallow book. Still an educator should be the first to insist that, as forces around us tend to obliterate our power of active attention and our critical reaction to the exasperating claims of publicity, his duty is to encourage mental effort in the young.

The history of Europe and America since World War I is, in that respect, a disheartening one. In Russia, in Fascist Italy, in Hitlerian Germany, critical attention and the saving graces of humor or, better still, of irony gave way with ghastly ease to the malignant or pompous propaganda which manipulators of opinion borrowed from commercial publicity. France, which had traditionally boasted of its Voltairian irony, of its sharp wit, and of a healthy disrespect for its rulers, fell prey to inane slogans before and during the days of Vichy, and occasionally since then. The McCarthy era, as it is much too glorifyingly termed, showed conclusively that it could happen even in a country unravaged by war and fearless of any foes. The history of the behavior of Americans during the Korean War is not a glowing episode in American annals. It was told in part and with the help of official Army archives in a book by Eugene Kinkhead entitled *In Every War But One* (New York: Norton, 1959). The sad exception designated by the title implied that "in every war but one that the United States has fought, the conduct of those of its servicemen who were captured and held in enemy prison camps presented no unforeseen problems to the armed forces." But in the Korean War of 1950–1953, twenty-one of the Americans captured resolved to remain with the enemy. One out of three American prisoners proved guilty of some form of collaboration with his captors. Not one American prisoner escaped to make his way back to our lines. Thirty-eight per cent of the 7,190 prisoners literally allowed themselves to die in captivity (and these deaths could not be ascribed to Communist maltreatment; prisoners were not subjected to brainwashing), a higher proportion than that of the more cruel and more primitive Revolutionary wars. In contrast, the 229 Turkish prisoners withstood indoctrination by their captors one hundred per cent; half of them were wounded; not a single one died in captivity. Prisoners of other European contingents also resisted Chinese propaganda with more stubbornness or more critical diffidence. Officers of other contingents displayed greater ability to lead and to perceive and define the aims of the war. None acted as spies for the enemy.

The lesson has been wisely and courageously drawn by the American Army; as a result, it issued a new "Code of Conduct for Members of the Armed Forces." It was realized that presenting the Army to recruits as essentially a well-paid career, affording security, good food, ample time off, and recreation hours for TV and movies, is tantamount to underestimating the devotion to their country, the generosity, and the adventurousness of young Americans. Youth is the age of heroism even more than that of pleasure. It is also the age of intelligent discernment, provided education has fostered some healthy spirit of criticism and the publicity of mass media has not altogether dimmed it.

The perils of mass media, when and if unchecked or not lucidly faced, are made all the graver by the new phenomenon altering the daily pattern of our lives today: the steady growth of leisure time. The men at the top, the managerial group and the business executives, those new Christs of the modern world, as one of their own ilk has called them, martyrs to their plurality of jobs and to their interlocking directorial boards, devoured by stomach ulcers consequent to their sandwich lunches, obsessed by the restless urge to plan and to lobby and perhaps to buy politicians and keep them bought, torn between their complaining, abandoned wives at home and the alluring obedience of their secretaries at the office, are the most pathetically devoid of leisure among today's creatures. But it is reckoned that free time for other and normal men has well-nigh doubled today from the scant amount allotted in the past to working men. A total of two thousand working hours a year (at approximately forty hours a week) will soon be the rule, as compared to four thousand or more a hundred years ago. Retirement is provided at a relatively early age in many professions. Leisure will soon constitute the one benefit that most of us will be certain of enjoying at some time or other, and education should probably prepare us not so much for our probable jobs as against them and for the wise use of leisure. Aristotle contended that politics was the best use men could make of leisure, but the example left by Greek politicians of old is hardly a cogent one. Excitement, in spite of newsmen and radio commentators and television shows of candidates for office kissing babies and smiling to little girls and lavishing gilt words to conceal their thought (or the absence thereof), is seldom present and even more seldom contagious in modern politics. Something else has to be devised. The issue is not just economic (to prevent the extension of "moonlighting" and of unemployment) and social (boredom being conducive to restlessness and a cause of revolutions) but also moral. Work was for centuries in our civilizations the rock foundation of morality. A vacuum is to open up when work ceases to absorb twelve or ten or eight of every twenty-four hours. If mass media are to fill it, they should not fill it with hot, or polluted, air. "Today," wrote recently an impartial specialist on communications, Dean Theodore Peterson of the University of Illinois, "the typical American spends more time looking at and listening to the mass media than at anything else except his work or sleeping, and the typical youngster leaving high school has spent more time in front of a TV set than in the classroom."[3]

In the face of such perils, one of three attitudes can be assumed. The first, and perhaps the easiest one, is to join the loud chorus of angry vituperating voices and to denounce the new wasteland of our half-century, as Mr. Newton Minow did, with singular courage. That American tradition of wrathful young and old men rising against the debasement of the people contrived through the evil use of "the monovocal, monopolistic, monocular press" as a *New Yorker* moralist has branded it (A. J. Liebling) goes back to Thoreau and to the noble admonitions of Walt Whitman in his *Democratic Vistas*, to Upton Sinclair and to both conservative neo-humanists and idealistic liberals in the 1920's. It has withstood the interested and naïve objurgations of those who, like a vice president of CBS (Mr. Victor Ratner), exclaimed in their grief: "To criticize radio, why, that's un-American!" No less empirical a statesman than President Hoover himself once declared confidently that "the American people never would stand for advertising on the air."

But the railroad, the airplane, the cinema in their heroic beginnings had met with similar skeptical distrust and self-righteous denouncing by the moralists of 1830 or of 1910. Such criticism may make for good volumes of satire of a brave new world or of social criticism of our power elite and of our affluent society and its perfidious persuaders. Those best sellers indicting mass media and American business, curiously enough, flourish far more vigorously in America than they do in any other "capitalistic" or prosperous society. In no other literature is the businessman and the conformist dweller of suburbia so consistently caricatured as in the literature of the United States. Indeed, with serene confidence in the ineffectuality of such indictments of their power or with humble and masochistic ability to laugh at themselves, the American businessmen and their sons and daughters in college appear to be enjoying the unfair picture given of them in literature and the arts far more than the Victorian British or French

[3] Theodore Peterson, "Why the Mass Media Are That Way," *Antioch Review* (Winter 1963–1964).

bourgeois, trembling at the people's disaffection and at the ghost of a new revolution, even pretended to do in the days of Flaubert and Karl Marx.

A second group might consist of the optimists. Their enthusiasm for the mass media may be due to their vested interest in them, to their awe before the bigness of such an industry, to their naïve worship of any new technological invention. They argue that their concern is to provide the people with what they seem to want, or put up with, not with what they *should* want or *might* conceivably welcome if it were offered to them. The most thick-skinned among them mince no words about their scorn for the intellectual, in general, that ineffectual creature whom a President of the United States characterized as "a man who takes more words than is necessary to say more than he knows." Not a few of those enthusiasts of the mass media profess the American religion of the worship of youth. A large number of listeners and watchers, a large number of movie-goers are recruited among the people under twenty or twenty-five. Not unnaturally, the mental level of many shows and of the advertisements inserted in them will encourage the young to keep their schoolgirl complexion, persevere in mental boyishness, and eschew the realities of mature life. The glorification of youth long was the religion of a country which set itself up as the young country as against the old and more cynical lands less rich in opportunities.

Between the pessimists and the optimists stand, as always, the meliorists. They know the futility of posing as the perpetual laudators of a past which is irretrievably gone, in which the "interpretation of culture," as T. S. Eliot called it, was accessible only to a few. They nurture no snobbish contempt for the "bread and circus game" once denounced by Juvenal and for its multifarious proliferations in our midst. They do not even mourn the fact that intellectuals in America are less hallowed than in France or Germany; the record of the intellectuals in those countries, in politics and in morality, has not, after all, been altogether admirable. A number of traitors, collaborators, racial persecutors, or passive supporters of the Hitlerian regime or of Stalinist ruthlessness arose among the philosophers, writers, and artists of Western Europe.

Those meliorists, on the other hand, well know that, among the optimists who would proclaim that all is well with the big and the little screens are in fact to be found the most discouraging pessimists, who do not care to reform or improve, and lack faith in the capacity of the countrymen to prefer what in themselves is not necessarily the most mediocre. In all pursuits of life, and particularly where the arts are concerned or where the improvement of men through education is at stake, criticism is the lifeblood of creation. Too many of the pessimists, systematically sulking at mass media, have recently been recruited from the ranks of the academics. Those self-styled liberals can also be the most stubborn and prejudiced of misoneists. They cherish their mental comfort and hate to let it be endangered by the inroads of the vulgar or by the vitality of a technique or of an art which questions their placid habits. The Renaissance humanists who first consecrated the term "humanists" with a revered halo had likewise turned their backs against popular culture and cherished a churlish pendantry. Their descendants were guilty of failing to do justice to Van Gogh and Wagner and to Hardy and Zola.

The meliorists, among whom many teachers should today be found, would be better inspired to acknowledge the inevitable ungrudgingly and to play their part in orienting the development of the mass media, just as Tocqueville and other aristocrats understood, after the Napoleonic Wars and the advent of the mass age, that the wisest course of action was to accept democracy as inevitable and to bring out its potentialities for good. Like Aesop's tongues, the cinema and television may become a tool for stultification or an instrument for betterment. It would be idle to ignore some cogent facts and figures: Frank Stanton, president of CBS, recalled in 1963 in a small booklet, *Books and Television*, some striking details: novels heretofore so seldom purchased as Stendhal's *The Red and the Black* and Henry James' *The Turn of the Screw* were suddenly bought by the thousands because a lecture on TV had commented on the first and a television play had been based on the second. Book sales in general were more than doubled during the decade when TV spread to the American public; borrowings from public libraries suddenly multiplied. Alexander Wollcott's "Town Crier" sent thousands of readers to novels by Faulkner and Dashiell Hammett. The sale of arduous volumes of anthropology, sociology, philosophy, literary criticism in paperbacks has certainly not been hampered in Britain and the United States by the phenomenal and parallel growth of mass media; those low-priced volumes themselves are indeed mass media. In countries whose culture long afflicted Americans with a sense (often unjustified) of inferiority, such as France, at the very time when television was reaching fifteen million Frenchmen out of forty-five, classics were being purchased in larger numbers than ever before. The firm of Gallimard launched a series boldly called "Idées," with difficult volumes by Camus (*The Myth of Sisyphus*), Sartre (*Portrait of the Anti-Semite*) selling at once over one hundred thousand copies. Other firms, up to then highbrow in their offerings, such as Payot and Plon, similarly reached the common reader with reprints in fifty thousand copies of volumes, long deemed forbidding, by St. Theresa, Karl Marx, or S. Freud. In the face of such crops of statistical evidence and of the experience of any of us who visits today booksellers' windows or record and picture shops in average cities or watches attentive crowds in museums, observes the musical culture of the many, the sulking denouncer of mass media as necessarily nefarious may well be silenced. He bears his share of guilt in the divorce between the academic intellectuals and the majority of Americans. Mr. Edward Shils, a social thinker at the University of Chicago, put the case squarely and fairly in a remarkable essay, "Mass Society and Its Culture" in the number of *Daedalus* devoted in the spring of 1960 to "Mass Culture and Mass Media":

> There is no doubt in my mind that the main "political" tradition by which most of our literary, artistic, and social-science intellectuals have lived in America is unsatisfactory . . . The intellectuals cannot evade the charge that they have done too little to ameliorate the situation . . . In America, the intellectuals have not felt bound by any invisible affiliation with the political, economic, ecclesiastical, military and technological elites.

The issue of the responsibility of mass media has become far too momentous to allow for any fruitless controversy between the intellectuals and the producers, the tenants of elite culture who fear any dilution of a rare and precious essence once viewed as theirs alone and those who, in business as in politics, are only too ready to echo the phrase of Ledru-Rollin, one of the promoters of universal suffrage in France in 1848: "They are my troops and I am their leader. I must follow them." Nothing less than the structure of our democracies is at stake. American psychological preparation to enter World War II; resistance in occupied Europe; the trend, probably irreversible, toward referendums as against elections in several democracies; the weakening of parties and the personalization of political power, conspicuous in France and elsewhere today, would never have occurred or developed as they have had it not been for radio and television. Those who hardly ever noticed advertisements or posters "cannot choose but hear," like the wedding guest in *The Ancient Mariner*. Through the display of gadgets, products, furniture, or the allurement of exotic tourists' paradises, as the French Minister of Information Alain Peyrefitte (himself a graduate of the Ecole Normale Supérieure and an academic converted to mass media) put it in "La Révolution audio-visuelle" (*Revue de Paris*, December 1963), a novel conception of happiness has permeated the masses. The celebrated cry of Saint-Just, who perished on the scaffold at twenty-seven, "Happiness is a new idea in the world," has become truer now than during the Terror. But how can that happiness be preserved from degenerating into complacency and apathy, the plaything of greedy corruptors or of debasers of the people?

It is our contention that, in this second half of the twentieth century, after the shock of World War II, the challenge of the Sputnik and of the Lunik, the awakening of many Americans to grave flaws in their educational system, the debates about the unfavorable image of this country entertained by the rest of the world, America realizes that science and culture, the understanding of foreign countries and the need to evolve more intellectual leaders here and now are imperatives for her continued claim to greatness. More is being done financially and materially for the universities than at any time in any country. Scientists and scholars enjoy a more effulgent prestige than has ever been the case. They guard the coveted gates to college entrance as jealously as mythological figures at the strait entry to paradise. They hold the key to the decrease of unemployment. An enormous power is today invested in the scientific institutes, law schools, universities of America: that power can no longer be underestimated by politicians, by Hollywood, Broadway, or Madison Avenue. Professors, aware of their greatly expanded role, no longer alienated or underpaid, courted by institutions, business, magazines, and foundations, have ceased to feel alienated in a technological and mercantile society. While scandals have displayed the susceptibility to corruption, or to conspiracy to maintain unduly high prices, in union bosses, electricity magnates, pharmaceutical advertisers, and sugar lobbies, the academic profession has not seen its reputation for integrity tarnished. Of all the pursuits of life, theirs is perhaps the one whose practitioners are least likely to sell its soul for a mess of pottage. It is up to them to serve the community and civilization through wise use of their influence. Their duty is to remain critical but also to be cooperative and constructive. If much is unsatisfactory with the most universal of mass media, radio, and television, what can be attempted to make them less faulty?

The first recourse, even in countries where "unfettered free enterprise" is a sacrosanct motto (more honored in the breach than in the observance, however), is to the federal government. The power vested with mass media is today so frightening, since it reaches everyone in their homes, equalizes the rich and the poor, the children and the adults, makes women as abundantly informed and as politically wise as men, can foster hate or fraternity, war or peace, that it cannot be left altogether to uncontrolled private enterprise. We all know that, outside electoral language and the circumlocutions of boards of directors, there is not, and cannot be, such a thing as totally free enterprise. Through its budget-making function and its defense outlays, its foreign aid and its welfare duties, the central government guides and directs the economy of the nation. A revolution has quietly occurred in the last twenty-five years in universities: their medical schools, their scientific faculties, their engineering departments, to a lesser extent their psychological and sociological research has come to be financed, often up to 75 per cent, by government grants. Neither Oxford nor Cambridge, neither Harvard nor Yale can be truly called private universities, if the source of their funds is considered. Free they have remained, since no strings are attached to many of those grants. Nevertheless their research may insidiously be oriented toward the projects most likely to be endorsed on a higher level; a sense of gratitude or tact to the source of their funds may curb any tendency toward irresponsibility, perhaps even toward heresy, perhaps even toward adventurous originality.

Still the fear of government interference is an almost morbid one in the United States. The word "socialism" causes eyebrows to frown and flesh to creep, even though this country's best allies are often to be found among socialist governments abroad. Through its assistance —not, perforce, to any private companies, but to central and often authoritarian governments, in Africa, Asia, and South America—the manifest destiny of the United States in the present decade has become to help the spread of socialism in underdeveloped countries. Social legislation and restraints to the power of bigness to pressure the little business and the little man are more effective in America than in all but three or four northern countries of Europe. Justice Earl Warren, when he was governor of California, is reported to have hinted once, "What the Government does for us, we call social justice. What it does for our neighbor, we call socialism." The Federal Communications Commission, if it is not able to accomplish all that Mr. Minow dreamed at one time for it, commands power and respect. It would achieve far more if public opinion were behind it and were better enlightened on some of its goals and policies.

The conviction of the foreign-born author is that the distrust of government interference with the mass media, like the distrust of any federal role in education, the arts, and letters, is the lingering remnant of a prejudice which constitutes an insult to American honesty and to the intellect and sense of justice of senators, congressmen, and federal administrators. Any middle-sized city in Germany supports an orchestra, an opera company, a museum, literary events, through public funds. Subsidized French theatres in France have seldom evinced partiality or dishonesty. Ministers of culture have been, and should be, criticized: but no one in several old countries, justly proud of their cultural heritage, questions the claims of the government to appoint museum and theatre directors, to subsidize mass media, to develop television channels. To do otherwise would be considered tantamount to turning democracy into plutocracy and to leave a whole area, on which the intelligence and the morality of the young may feed, to uncontrolled publicity. If private companies fail to provide enough time on the air for the disinterested, and financially profitless, cultural entertaining of the adults, if they choose to maintain children in amused and passive infancy instead of helping them become their better, and hopefully their truer, selves, cities, states, and the central government would find themselves constrained to intervene. The pressure of public opinion might well force them to do it. Trial and error there would be. Mistakes would be committed, as they have been by ministries of fine arts in France when they refused to accept Seurat's paintings for the Louvre or to buy Cézannes and Gauguins when they should have done so. Criticism would be and should be vocal. But the United States government is in no way less able to select competent and honest administrators for the arts or for the supervision of mass media than are the governments of Scandinavian countries or of Great Britain. The BBC, which is not government-controlled but a monopoly operating under the supervision of a board appointed by the British government and acting autonomously, is envied by a growing number of radio audiences in America. A few, all too few, of the British offerings of literary quality have been emulated or reproduced in this country. Still, a larger number of influential TV watchers than is probably realized voiced their hope that more performances of *Hamlet*, *Hedda Gabler*, *No Exit*, the plays of Shaw, Strindberg, or O'Neill might be given in America, as they were on the BBC. Those persons of influence, who cannot be suspected of socialist leanings or conspiracy to undermine the old-fashioned laissez-faire dear to readers of Adam Smith, after watching many a federal intervention in education, science, and business which the country has no reason to regret, cannot be convinced that control necessarily follows support. Systematic distrust of the eventual mistake or imagined perfidy or venality of the very persons whom the American people have elected to their legislatures, to Congress, or to the White House is a strange mental attitude to hold for citizens of a democracy called upon to offer a model for much of the world.

It is, in our eyes, just as strange that there should be so little communication and mutual confidence prevailing between the firms which run the mass media and those among the cultured audiences who criticize them constructively and hope to improve them thereby. No great country can long suffer, without grievous losses and the jeopardizing of its stability, a rift between business and the intellectuals, between bankers and the professors of economics training the bankers of tomorrow, between the politicians and those who prepare the political minds and the internationally informed citizens of tomorrow. Some of the mishaps of the 1929–1939 decade, when business lost the confidence of the intelligent public of America and disgruntled intellectuals felt alienated and attracted to leftist causes, arose to a large extent from the lack of understanding between the two groups. Sooner or later, the two hundred thousand teachers in this country who teach J. M. Keynes, David Riesman, Freud and Kinsey on the sexual liberation, William H. White, and Vance Packard, who lecture every year on American novels unanimously picturing the gross brutality and the utter futility of wars, will have instilled their views into the minds of the young, whose fathers may have been stubborn sticklers for the old economics, the old sociology, dutiful "chairmen of the bored" . . . and providers of funds for the colleges where their ideas are being ridiculed.

A growing conviction has spread in the minds of those who teach the American youth and lecture to intelligent and eager audiences of college graduates and others that the American public is being grossly underestimated by those who have taken charge of the movies, the newspapers, the cinema, the radio, and television. The retort that marketing surveys and questionnaires prove that the public is given what it wants and that sponsors care only for large numbers of people "exposed" to their publicity claims is a fallacious one. Serious doubts have been voiced before the Oren Harris Subcommittee on Investigations in the House of Representatives which examined methods of measuring television audiences. Mr. Vance Packard, who wrote on "New Kinds of Television" in the *Atlantic Monthly* of December, 1963, reported, "The subcommittee heard weeks of damning evidence of slipshod use of varying hundreds of meters or diaries to indicate national or regional viewing habits." He added, "There was also testimony that the pressure of the rating services on their fieldmen to cut corners tended to result in a general underrepresentation of people of above-average intelligence, income, and sophistication. . . . Some fieldmen working in apartment areas favored approaching building superintendents because they were always home." In some parts of the country, the supposedly "representative" viewers of a hundred thousand people or more were two dwellers of slum houses—who of course had had no education.

There are, on the other side, thousands of us today in America who may claim to be in close touch with the youth of the country and with publics avid for adult education who have refused to stop growing after twenty-five. They buy the paperback volumes, the records, the illustrated art volumes now enjoying such an immense popularity. Their ability to influence others through conversation, example, and the prestige of their being college graduates is out of proportion, in a positive sense, to their number. They can testify to the greed of American youth for knowledge, information, for beauty and art, for music of quality and movies which are not infantile. The cry is loudly heard for more creativeness in education and in home pursuits, for rejuvenated cities, for finer school, and church, architecture. What other countries, with a huge majority of illiterates only half a century ago, like Russia, have been able to achieve in improving the taste of their masses does not lie beyond the range of the United States, where education is also a religion. We educators are aware of our faults: we may be ponderous, overserious, prone to sermonizing any captive audience rather than lively enough to captivate them, naïvely convinced that people will placidly tell themselves that what bores them instructs them and improves their souls. But we deserve the confidence and esteem of the big companies which own and run the mass media; we are ready to meet their claims halfway, to make the classics alive, to divest ourselves of our intellectual snobbery and of our pedantry when addressing audiences of millions instead of our few obedient students. We can serve the communications industry instead of being tempted to meet it with strictures and suspicion. But the industry would gain if it invited us on its councils, consulted us on how to raise public taste and habits without infringing upon their freedom, and how to decrease the widespread suspicion of their motives as well as the growing weariness with the excesses of advertising, eventually defeating their purpose through the irritation they engender.

The government may be expected to face the problem of mass

media with more energy; the companies may be persuaded to assume their responsibility more seriously; educators and intellectuals, through voicing their concern, are doing a service to society. Ultimately, however, the solution is up to the public itself. "We can get what we like, or we shall grow to like what we get," remarked George B. Shaw. Only loud public demands can eventually force any improvement. This country graduates half a million young men and women from college every year, twice that number from its schools. The pool of persons who have received a good education must be reckoned today around fifteen million people and is constantly being enlarged. Those graduates should be moving forces in their communities. The time is past when the only heroes of our population were athletes or tough guys. Trained intellects are respected also, and scientists, and artists. Teachers have endeavored to train the minds and the tastes of their students during their college years; they can testify to a genuine and widespread interest in the youth for ancient drama, modern history, problems of ideas, for science but also for the arts and for the classics in several languages. Do the same young men and women who sincerely admired Goethe, T. S. Eliot, Joyce, Camus while in college suddenly weary of intellectual effort and gloat on trash?

If the eagerness to continue, not learning in particular, but enjoying one's taste and intelligence and the flexing of one's mental muscles has not survived college graduation or the advent of middle age, teachers are at fault. They have abdicated too meekly before the young, professed the cult of childhood and youth first established by J.-J. Rousseau with such zeal that they have nurtured the childish psyche of boys and girls and retarded their mental growth. "Youth's a stuff will not endure," Shakespeare warned in *Twelfth Night*. It is but a stage toward maturity and not especially pleasant to be absorbed in lingeringly while the prospect of growth and mature confidence lies beyond. Sellers of suits, of sports clothes, of musical machines, proprietors of motels in Florida and Bermuda, publishers of *Mademoiselle* and of its competitors among magazines may have hit upon a great commercial idea when exploiting the market of the teenagers. Educators and parents would be more respected if they had refused to follow suit. Not a little of the brashness of the modern adolescents, often leading to youth gangs and to delinquency, is due to the young's lack of respect for the minds and behavior of their elders: the latter have striven hard to share the tastes of their teenagers, to behave like them, to watch the same shows, read the same books. But they have thus refused to place at the disposal of those who come after them the example of their experience and whatever wisdom may accrue to age. They have not stimulated in their progeny or in their pupils the eagerness to go on reading, thinking, learning, in a word, maturing. "Ripeness is all," remarked gloomily *King Lear*'s Edgar. The difficulty is to know how to ripen without rotting or doting, or practicing the worst form of dotage, which is to simulate retarded development.

Two pleas may be offered in conclusion to those who are in a position to influence the American public and who wish it to obtain mass media worthy of the hopes nurtured in many an American heart. The first is that less conformity, less sickening banality, and more courageous dissidence may mark the newspapers and the movies, the radio, and the television of this country. The melting-pot concept may have been a necessity when the new continent was being populated with millions of heterogeneous immigrants with no common ethical or cultural background. It has provided manufacturers and salesmen with a huge mass market ready to absorb the same products. A certain American courtesy kept the educated citizens of this country from disagreeing openly with each other. The two political parties pathetically attempt to formulate platforms and policies with a semblance of disagreement, wrapped up in elaborately harmless circumlocutions. Students in school and college, journalists, radio commentators learn how to argue the pros and cons of every issue, and the public may have imagined for a time that such sophisticated debates, granting a voice even to a southern segregationist, to a pseudo-Nazi, or to a socialist was a sign of fair play—and cleverly turned those advocates of minority groups into innocuous creatures.

But the consequence has been an increasing indifference to any issue, the conviction that any moral reaction is out of place and that any cause may be argued for and against anyway. Observers of this country who have its future at heart, Arnold Toynbee and Adlai Stevenson among others in the last few years, have expressed their fears at the mental stagnation which the stress laid by mass media and too many educators upon conformity tends to foster. We have, they exclaimed, a need for "creative heretics," for men and women with conviction who are not afraid to be dissenters. Eric Barnouw, in his book *Mass Communication* (New York: Rinehart, 1956), quoted a spokesman of the National Council of Churches at a meeting of religious broadcasters, asserting: "Any one of you here can reach with your voice at one time more people than Jesus did in His entire ministry." However, Eric Barnouw adds, Jesus achieved more in part because He represented a small and most controversial minority. Religion in America has not gained from being paid lip service to, in a very insipid fashion, on every broadcast. Many are the priests who contend that vigorous dissent from unbelievers and would-be reformers has, on the contrary, immensely enhanced Catholicism in a country like France, and invited the Church to reform. Historians of Germany have frequently pointed to the severest flaw in that country: not to have had, since Luther, enough dissenters. Questions should be raised on mass media even on the structure of society, even on the Supreme Court and the sacredness of the American Constitution. Justice Black declared in 1943: "The authors of the First Amendment knew that novel and unconventional ideas might disturb the complacent, but they chose to encourage a freedom which they believed essential if vigorous enlightenment was ever to triumph over slothful ignorance."[4]

A Frenchman cannot help being a moralist. Since he does not enjoy Malvolio's reputation of being virtuous, he cannot be suspected of wishing the end of all cakes and ale. But the last and more earnest plea made by this author, and scarcely an original one at that, is that the public vigorously voice its request that sex and crime be at last given less prominence on TV shows. The harm done by that ridiculous overemphasis to American prestige in Asia, South America, Europe is incalculable. If average creatures in those countries are shrewd enough to realize that neither literature nor the screen faithfully portrays life as it is, they cannot help reasoning that those displays of blood and lust do offer American viewers what they have been made to believe they want and that the owners of mass media do not think they deserve

---

[4] Quoted in Charles A. Siepmann, *Radio's Second Chance* (Boston: Little, Brown and Co., 1947) pp. 131–132.

anything else. Are they altogether to blame if they imagine America to be a land of sex perverts, of rapists, or of impotents who like to dream of the sadistic aggressiveness of which they are not capable?

The debate is an age-old one. Censorship is unavailing and unadvisable if imposed from above to audiences which would resent being treated as children. Publicity given to lurid stories of drunkenness and crime; to biographies reducing Sinclair Lewis, Eugene O'Neill, Dylan Thomas, or even Toulouse-Lautrec to nothing but the condition of alcoholics; films and shows displaying drug addiction; novels with a preference for misfits, retarded adolescents, and idiots (from William Faulkner to James Purdy) have themselves become an addiction. No one will advocate a return to Puritanism. But many may wish that sonorous and respected voices, in Washington, in Hollywood, and not just at commencement ceremonies recalled to the American public that it has a right to expect something else from those who control its mass media. American males are not so lecherous or inflammable as their providers of entertainment and of publicity would have them believe. Women are not just perpetually uncovered cover girls, screaming mothers, frustrated "subterraneans" emerging out of Jack Kerouac's stories, or empty-headed baby dolls. The wit who hinted that the creed of our mass media, where the portrayal of women is concerned, may be summed up in a new evolutionist formula: "Men sprang from the apes, but women sprang first" was more serious than he realized. The portrayal of women in fiction, magazines, and the screens of the United States, with never one creature of that sex ever lovable or likely to serve as an ideal for the dreams of the young, is a national shame.

Murder, war, greed, from Clytemnestra to Lady Macbeth and Phaedra on to modern fiction, have naturally always constituted the theme of tragedy. Life has always had to be lived in the face of death. But André Malraux, the French minister of culture, proclaimed it in vibrant tones before the French National Assembly when he presented the budget for the services over which he presides, that art had traditionally presented the victory against fate and death along with man's defeat under the blows of the gods. A few of his words may not be out of place when transported to the country in which the future of man's fate has long been envisaged as the most hopeful.

Our age has witnessed the birth of the great techniques of dream: the cinema and television, considered not as means of information but as instruments of fiction. . . . A century ago, three thousand Parisians attended the theater every night; today three and a half million of them enter the world of fiction every evening. . . . We cannot allow machines for dreaming to appeal only to the least human, the most organic and animal in man: sex and death.

There have been cultures which consumed more than they created, which assimilated but seldom invented. Others, the Jewish culture, the Greek, the French, the American have created also. They feared not dissidence, turmoil, adventure, the contemplation of death; but they sided with what in man creates as against what destroys. The mass media today, provided their public firmly wants them to, can bring forward man the creator and not man the destroyer to all those who have faith in the future of culture and of intelligence in a democracy.

12 | EXCELLENCE AND LEADERSHIP HAS WESTERN EUROPE ANY LESSONS FOR US?

THERE ARE at least three subjects (and probably a dozen more) on which no wise man should ever attempt to write: love, genius, and leadership. Of the three, the last is the most mysterious and the most unpredictably and capriciously feminine. No amount of training, no sedulous nurturing by the family or the social group, no long line of ancestry piously dedicated to the eventual flowering of a leader, not even the stern flexing of intellectual muscles or the cultivation of character through cricket, baseball, warfare, or flogging has ever proved a sure means of developing leaders. Few teachers have with any degree of certainty been able to predict which of their pupils would some day march ahead of the common herd and mold events. Fewer still among the school or college friends of future leaders have perceived, or acknowledged, the germs of that indefinable quality in them. Many who graduated very young and were laden with the richest promises from Harvard, Oxford, or the Ecole Polytechnique have turned out at forty-five to have left their future behind them. Others, like Winston Churchill's successor at the head of the Conservative party, happened not to be served by their health or by circumstances and missed an opportunity which seemed to be theirs for the asking.

History, which affords us a comfortable insight into the mistakes of others, may explain actions long after the event, but the decisions through which some men become leaders while others are crushed in defeat cannot in most cases be anticipated. Léon Blum, one of the most intelligent observers of events and an actor gifted with keen foresight in some of them, remarked in a volume of memoirs on the Dreyfus Affair, published a year before he took over power in France in 1936:

> The aligning of individuals with one or another of the two camps surprised me no less than the very emergence of those camps. I was young, and experience had not yet taught me one thing: that the most fallacious of all the operations of the mind is to calculate in advance a man's or a woman's reaction to a really unforeseen ordeal. We are almost regularly mistaken when we claim to solve such a calculation through applying psychological data already acquired, thus prolonging the logic of the known character of past life. Any ordeal is new and every ordeal finds a man who is also new.

In no country have as many volumes on the subject of leadership appeared as in the United States. The reading of most of them is a dismal, when it is not a ludicrous, experience. They dissert at length on the necessity for candidates for leadership to make friends, to co-ordinate, to get things done, to lead "the strenuous life" once dear to Theodore Roosevelt, to learn how to conduct conferences. The last item must be a source of considerable embarrassment to many men of affairs: for they are laboriously advised to decorate their conference rooms with "irenic green," also favored by insane asylums; to promote "togetherness" through calling everyone by his first name; to devise well-planned recesses, during which background music should be played softly; not to hang modern abstract art on the walls, for it makes uneasy "those who don't know what the garish splotches mean." Data are then gathered to prove that, among other attributes, leaders enjoy a taller stature than ordinary mortals. Bishops average 70.6 inches, but preachers in small towns only 68.8; university presidents rise to a 70.8-inch average, presidents of small colleges have to be content with 69.6; sales managers average 70.1 inches, salesmen a mere 69.1. Shades of Napoleon, of John Keats, of Stalin, who never reached the height of even a sub-salesman or of a dean of a very insignificant college!

The perusal of a few such volumes should be enough to convince anyone who is not a worshiper of statistical data and of factual surveys that leaders are indeed mystery men, born in paradise or in some devil's pit, but that they never must have become leaders through the study of books on management or of treatises on the making of higher executives. The process by which excellence is reached, or aimed at, in countries of Western Europe and through which leaders ("principi," "Führer," "élites," "chefs" in the countries where the word "leaders" is without an equivalent and the word "leadership" as untranslatable as that of "commonwealth") are prepared, cannot be described methodically and accurately. Schools for leaders have at some time or other been attempted, from the Order of the Templars and the Turkish janissaries to the German Ordensburg seminar under Nazism, the Communist party in Russia, and the short-lived *écoles de cadres* in Vichy France. It would be an insult to American democracy to hold them up as examples. Leadership can but be a broad ideal proposed by the culture of a country, instilled into the young through the schools, but also through the family, the intellectual atmosphere, the literature, the history, the ethical teaching of that country. Will power, sensitivity to the moods of an age, clear thinking rather than profound thinking, the ability to experience the emotions of a group and to voice their aspirations, joined with control over those emotions in oneself, a sense of the dramatic and even the pliability of a *commediante*, such as Bonaparte evinced at will, are among the ingredients of the power to lead men: they are not easily absorbed through education, not even through imitation.

But conditions can perhaps be created under which potentialities for leadership would not be stifled and might even develop faster or ripen more fully. And although leadership and excellence are far from synonymous, we may take it for granted that few would quarrel with the need to stress quality versus sheer numbers, and excellence rather than adjustment to life and its mediocrity, in education today. It is highly questionable whether European countries have produced more or greater leaders than America has over the last sixty years, relatively to the population. Even in diplomacy and foreign policy (fields in which many Americans seem to be afflicted with a complex of inferiority over their achievement and like to moan over their fumbling), the record of Britain and France between the two World Wars, that of Germany before and under Nazism, that of Litvinov,

Molotov, Stalin himself, and their present successors is in no way more enviable than that of the United States. Statesmen, generals, admirals, business organizers and executives, during World War II and since, have in this country led with as much (or more) foresight and decision as those of any other land. Educators and scientists have rated second to none. A European-born professor in America may deplore the smaller role granted here to intellectuals and the emphasis on a democratic process which at times seems to fear elites and to balk at eliciting leadership from the masses. Bold would he be, untruthful probably, and tactless to boot, if he advocated any wholesale import of Western European methods of aiming at excellence in a very different environment.

But this country has now long been mature enough to know that learning from the past is what distinguishes the civilized man from the animal or from the uncivilized; that many of the boldest moves in art and literature have, in our own century, come from a rediscovery of a phase of the past (Egyptian art, Romanesque sculpture, medieval philosophy, Greek tragedy). America's capacity for digestion, moreover, is such that she can devour what tempts her in other cultures and easily assimilate it. Rome, France, Germany, Russia, Japan once proceeded thus at the height of their vitality. A survey of several realms in which progress in fostering excellence could be achieved in America, owing to the example of other democracies, may be not without some utility. Those realms are education, the sciences, letters and the arts, and the place of the intellectual in society, insofar as it may be assumed that leadership is a virtue which highly developed intellectuals may possess more than other groups of citizens.

Education in Greece and Rome, then in the countries of Western Europe, differed from education in America in that it never was aimed at the vast mass of the people, indiscriminately; it never had to mold into a nation with one language and one civic ideal, into a conformity of tastes, of behaviors (and of buying habits) a motley crowd of peoples who had broken off ties with their native land and had come, to a large extent, from the less cultured segments of the populations of Eastern and Southern Europe, of Ireland, of Scotland, or of Germany. For a long time in the nineteenth century and the first decades of the twentieth, the goal of education at the secondary level was to prepare leaders for the professions—the church, the army and navy, diplomacy, administration. Scholarships have always made it relatively easy—even in Britain, where access to Eton and Harrow, Oxford and Cambridge, was through a strait gate—for the children of poorer families to receive a solid general and technical culture. Still, secondary education in a *lycée*, a *gymnasium*, a private or a grammar school in England was sharply separated from primary education. Those who came from the affluent classes of society enjoyed an advantage over the boys from poorer homes; it was due to conversation with their parents, to reading facilities at a time when public libraries for children were unheard of, to ampler leisure, and a cultural tradition in their family. Nine tenths, or probably 95 per cent of those who made a name as scientists, statesmen, or intellectuals were from the gentry or the middle class.

The number of positions to be filled by the youth thus trained, in engineering, in administration, in diplomacy, in the liberal professions, failed in our century to increase proportionately to the ever growing mass of young men—lately, also, of young women—eager to occupy such positions. A feature of our age is the reluctance of men with even a mere smattering of education to be content with the trades by which goods are actually produced, metals extracted, the earth tilled, or the cattle raised. Marketing, salesmanship, insurance, transportation of the goods produced by the unhappy people who know no better, and promotional work of every kind hold more attraction for any man who has gone to school. Such a man bolsters his ego through signing papers brought in an "in" basket and gravely shifting them to the "out" one. The result has meant an intense competition to enter the tertiary sector of an economy and a stress on degrees, diplomas, hurdles at every stage. Every young Frenchman, Italian, or German from the middle class and everyone who covets entry into the middle class has therefore to undergo competitive examinations at every stage, from the age of eleven to eighteen or twenty. The grades given by teachers would, if translated into an American scale, range from ten or fifteen to seventy-five or eighty. Barely 40 per cent of pupils reach the average of fifty (out of a maximum of a hundred). Nearly 60 per cent of the pupils at the end of their secondary studies fail in the final examinations which open up the gates of the universities. The whole of secondary education, in France especially (and the Russian system was organized along the lines of the Napoleonic university), but also in Britain, where scholarships to Oxford, Cambridge, or Liverpool are in keen demand, is geared to university education and to stiff competitive examinations on a fixed syllabus. The results are not altogether felicitous. A majority of French children study mathematics, theoretical physics, thermodynamics, history, Greek and Latin according to programs imposed by the ministry, and for a very few, for admission to the Ecole Polytechnique, the Ecole Nationale d'Administration, or the Ecole Normale Supérieure. One alone out of five or ten candidates to these bastions of the intellectual elite forces entry into them. Those who fail fall back upon less glamorous professions: often they wander into business. But a sad wastage of potential talent occurs, for the line which separates the candidate who reaches the thirtieth rank, where thirty only are admitted for the whole country, from the thirty-first is necessarily a very tenuous one. At the present day, the countries of Western Europe have awakened to the need of training not just three thousand engineers for a country of forty-five million people, all men versed in the arcana of theory and with a highly trained intellect— but fifteen thousand. The tyranny which the prestigious French Grandes Ecoles exerted over the country has had to be relaxed, and their demanding requirements have been waived in new, rivaling institutions designed to stress empirical rather than abstract knowledge.

The very severe competition for the positions of leadership to be won by the graduates of those celebrated Ecoles spreads to all levels of education. Little time is spent or lost on sports and games. The waste which according to many American educators prevails in the last year of high school in this country is avoided: the years with which secondary education ends, at the ages of sixteen to eighteen, in continental Western Europe, are on the contrary the most arduous and the most severely competitive. Philosophy, as the crowning discipline completing the earlier study of languages and of history, or mathematics and the physical sciences for the scientifically minded students, occupy the last year. In every one of the three terms into which the academic year is divided, "compositions," more solemn and more feared than tests are in our system, take place in every subject. Emulation is in no way supposed to be contrary to equalitarian democracy; students are ranked as first, second, third . . . twentieth, and little sympathy is poured on the last ones for having tried their meagre best and failed. Such a system is exacting, but bracing mentally. The ranking at examinations is done without any regard to the identity of the candidate: his name is not revealed to the examiner, who should never be the same teacher as taught him in class. In Oxford and Cambridge, in Stanford or Yale, some leniency may be evinced by boards of admission, if not by professors, to sons of the nobility or of the rich or to those of influential alumni, on the theory that since they will belong to the ruling class anyway, because of birth or money, and may have funds to dispose of, they might just as well be exposed to some education. More democratic equality prevails in the continental nations. Education at the advanced level is the only key which can open the locked treasures of influential positions: it is already professional. It could not deserve the strictures of R. M. Hutchins, who condemned the conception of a university as "a waiting room in which a student must consume his time in harmless triviality until he can go to work." Far from being looked down on as undemocratic or as a breeder of complexes, the will to excel is taken for granted and the desire to do so is instilled into every child: he naturally aims at belonging to the elite—an elite which is cultural rather than social.

Along with universal competition at all levels, accepted as a matter of course in old countries, where there are far fewer positions for white-collared workers and for executives than there are able candidates to fill them, the abhorrence of specialization characterizes Western European education. Scientists, humanists, philosophers, doctors, army leaders, men of affairs, in France in particular, but also in Italy, Austria, and Germany, have repeated that "general culture" is essential to anyone who will be called upon to lead, to initiate ideas, to envisage a problem as a whole, and to devise imaginative solutions for it. Scientists like Claude Bernard, Pasteur, Henri Poincaré, Einstein, or Freud were not only widely read persons but also men whose solid humanistic culture never slowed down in their later scientific pursuit. It is commonly contended that the ability to range over the past stimulates boldness to grapple with the future and that a scientist, a manager, or an industrialist can only gain as a leader if he is aware of the motives which have always moved men. Henri Bergson, in one of the earliest addresses he gave, condemned specialization as a form of laziness, more fit for the animal which does one thing to perfection, but one only, than for men.[1] Julian Huxley would agree; in *New Bottles for New Wine*, he reassesses the myth of progress and declares that "specialization—in other words one-sided adaptation to a particular mode of life—eventually leads to an evolutionary dead end." A general like Lyautey, who displayed rare talents of organization and had begun his career with a revolutionary article on the social role of the officer, reflected assiduously on leadership and trained a number of leaders in Morocco. According to him, the need and the function of anyone who would command was "the technique of general ideas." The conviction is sacrosanct with most continental European educators. Any leader must eschew imitation, revolt against narrow-mindedness, prove adaptable to new situations, and be able to generalize from his experience. Such men exist in more empirically minded countries, like the Anglo-Saxon. But it may be confessed that a circumscribed outlook, a sense of bewilderment when deprived of their usual and reassuring environment, a parochialism or a timidity, whenever the conversation turns on ideas or on general political or philosophical problems, too often mark most American men when in contact with their European counterparts. The influence which American leaders today should wield in world affairs has been sadly impaired thereby.

The defect goes back to the schools, and it is not easy to remedy, even today, when American schools have incurred severer blame than they had for a whole century. Diversity is the rule in American education when compared to that of Europe: there is no ministry of education, no common standard, no way to persuade some fifty thousand school boards that they should raise their sights, make their syllabi harder and less immediately (and deceptively) practical, pay

[1] For references and titles of works alluded to in the text, see the bibliography at the end of this chapter.

their teachers more generously, and recruit better ones. The fear of federal authority imposing itself on the states and of politics (with its accompaniment of lobbying, favoritism, venality) is so ingrained in America that a reversal of the trend is not likely to occur. Yet we may well have reached a stage today when a rapid mutation has become indispensable. A much larger share of national investments should go to the improvement of the schools, or else the chance to have more leaders, more scientists, more statesmen emerge from American democracy may well not be seized. If the prejudices against the tyranny of the central government over states' rights is too strong, the universities, both private and state, will have to assert themselves: the general desire to go to college is such, the desire to enter a graduate or a professional school later is also such that universities and colleges for the first time in history can impose higher, national standards on American education. Less premature specialization and narrowing down, a wider perspective of history, more intellectual independence, and a greater propensity to envisage one's subject in its relation to other fields would probably contribute effectively to solving the predicament in which America finds herself today. Today, four or five continents are clamoring not only for experts skilled in practical know-how, but also for teachers, lawyers, diplomats, men of affairs also endowed with "think how" and able to adapt the lessons of American success to very different cultures and to proud and sensitive peoples. The number available of such men is far from adequate. With our college population of four to six million, we have failed to train enough potential leaders.

If the examples of ancient Greece and of three or four Western nations in Europe today can be conjured up, their lesson, as we may presume to interpret it, is as follows:

First, we have underestimated the role of the teaching profession, probably the most important as well as the most difficult in any country. With the school age prolonged until fourteen or sixteen, only those teachers who have some intellectual power, mental curiosity, and some breadth can fire boys and girls with the impulse to go on studying. It will be a revolution in the mores of this country when teachers are paid as much as lawyers, doctors, and businessmen, when scientists are as respected as millionaires and become the Florida or Georgia weekend guests of Presidents: but such a revolution cannot long be postponed. It is positively paradoxical and well-nigh absurd to see a businessman surrounded with awe in his community, admired as a civic and church leader, courted by ever hungry college presidents, because he has discovered a new cosmetic, a new pharmaceutical pill, skillfully advertised a new girdle, or built a new electrical appliance, while teachers, preachers, and scholars are discreetly scorned and politicians treated with even less discreet contempt as men necessarily ready to be bought and perhaps not even loyal enough to stay bought.

The revolution in the minds of Americans will have to start from very high up—in Washington, Hollywood, Wall Street. Universities should provide the example. Their presidents go about clamoring for better schools, a more generous recognition of the intellectual, more respect for the humanities and for an ideal of a good life as preferable to an affluent one. But none of them has yet dared add a few educators, an eminent scientist or a poet, some representatives from his faculty to the businessmen, financiers, and lawyers who, almost exclusively, sit on his corporation or board of trustees. As a result, those trustees, timid in all that pertains to education and to science, exercise no leadership over the faculty and are lamentably devoid of constructive views on education. They are considered by the faculty as potential money-raisers or as convertible donors (to be converted from potential to actual ones by a persuasive president), seldom as inspirers or leaders. Those who teach and those who do not are thus kept separate as if they belonged to different social strata or different planets. Historians of French culture are wont to stress the advantages in prestige which accrued to literature in France when the Academy was founded, with archbishops, ambassadors, princes, and dukes sitting at the same table, defining words for the same dictionary, side by side with dramatists, poets, and grammarians. A similar intellectual and social gain would be effected if scholars and educators could explain their points of view to trustees of their institutions and learned from those men of affairs what the world expects from education.

Second, a consideration, even a cursory one, of the training which appears in Western Europe to produce excellence oftener than in

America would soon, in our opinion, lead to denouncing the lack of an ideal for the child to aim at. Many a leaf here could have been stolen and pondered from the works of ancient Greece. But, even when classical studies were more widespread than they are today, we had failed to derive or to apply lessons from Greek education. Distinguished scholars, among whom Werner Jaeger is preeminent, have pointed to *paideia* as the key to "the unique educational genius which is the secret of the undying influence of Greece on all subsequent ages." The Greeks, for the first time in history, conceived civilization as the deliberate pursuit of an ideal and proclaimed that education meant, as Werner Jaeger puts it, "deliberately molding human character in accordance with an ideal." In that ideal, *arété* or virtue in a broad sense was primary, while utility was relegated to the background. The man who drew near to that goal of *arété* was legitimately proud of the ideal he was pursuing. In the *Iliad* (VI, 208, and XI, 784), first Glaucos in addressing Diomedes, then the aged Nestor in discoursing on Achilles, repeat the admonition, "Always be the best and keep well ahead of the others."

Such an educational ideal was transmitted to the Italians of the Renaissance, to the French ideal of the *honnête homme*, to the British concept of the gentleman. The faith which these three nations have in their educational ideal (and which the French, more than the others, have turned into an actual cult, not devoid of arrogance toward the less fortunate beings whose culture is not French) leads them to this day to establish schools wherever they go: French imperialism has always been more cultural than economic. Except for a number of missionary colleges they have founded in the Near East or in Africa, chiefly for the natives of those lands, Americans have not usually carried their educational ideal with them when living abroad. In no realm probably are they afflicted with such doubts amounting to a genuine complex of inferiority as where their educational institutions, especially at the secondary level, are concerned. The culprit there is equalitarianism. The French, to be sure, have long ago made a fetish of equality; but, after proclaiming that all men are born free and insisting with Rousseau on a political and social system which corrects natural inequality through equality before the law, the French have never doubted that intellectual gifts were unequally spread and that efforts had to be most unequal on the part of some men as compared to others. Equality should not result in the disregard of quality. An American who has an important position on *Time* magazine, has written most discerningly on what he terms *The Waist-High Culture* (1959), Thomas Griffith, himself an alumnus of a western state university and no snobbish admirer of Europe, very sensibly remarked (pp. 180–181):

> The legal fiction of universal equality is a denial of the truth of an inequality of merit; but worse, it is also a repudiation of the value of unequal effort, and we may wonder how many American school children have demanded less than the best of themselves for fear of the unpopularity that goes with wanting to excel. . . . Of all the wastes in American society, not the cutting down of forests but the stunting of intellectual growth is our most costly squandering of resources.

Two other lessons might well be learned anew from the examples imparted to us by the people whose thinking centered around training the leaders of society, the Greeks: first the relative disregard of technique and the stress upon self-expression and communication with others, then the high value set upon maturity and manhood as opposed to childhood. We live today in a technological civilization, and no modern man in his senses can advocate a purely literary education which would ignore science and the Baconian necessity to understand nature, and thus to obey it, in order to command it. But technology has also broken up our lives and our world into shreds while appearing to simplify them. The same author quoted above, Thomas Griffith, warns us after assessing the "waist-high culture" of his country: "Technology and comfort add nothing to our characters, and may increase our problems while weakening our ability to confront them."

Most men build only parts of a machine or of an object; very few ever construct a whole or create inventively. The corrective to such a technological civilization lies in fostering a keener zest for literature and the arts, which to the Greeks embodied the expression of all higher culture. The absurd prejudice that those who do should not be overly concerned with expressing themselves, and that distinction in writing and speaking implies an inability to do, should be eradicated. There are, after all, only two ways of governing man: one is through violence and tyranny, and it brooks no discussion, scorns persuasion; the other is through speeches (fireside chats, radio talks, television debates, parliamentary discourses, United Nations jousts of eloquence). The word *logos* appositely designated both speech and reason with the Greeks. To them, the cultured man was one who could express himself and persuade others. The Sophists, the greatest of Hellenic educators, in spite of the poor reputation with which Plato has afflicted them, asserted it, and Thucydides, who was not remote from them, lent to Pericles the famous pronouncement (II, 60): "The man who can think and does not know how to express what he thinks is at the level of him who cannot think."

The nonchalance with which those who should lead us today treat the English language in the country of Jefferson and of Lincoln, their affectation of familiar, if not vulgar, speech, and their disregard for grammar and for simplicity and terseness or their preference (alas, sincere) for slipshod and barbaric jargon have become one of the chief impediments to their potential influence on the masses. Woodrow Wilson, quoted by Ordway Tead in his volume on *Leadership*, rightly laid stress on the power to exhort, "to creep into the confidence of those you would lead," as a prerequisite to political leadership. The power of the spoken word has, if anything, grown in the last two or three decades. Our leaders in business, politics, diplomacy, and education are nevertheless least fitted for what they will have to perform almost daily: expressing themselves forcefully so as to teach, convince, and enlighten others. Oral examinations should be given in our schools from the age of twelve up.

We pride ourselves on having discovered the child and, since Rousseau and Wordsworth, then with Freud and our psychoanalysts, we have been fond of repeating that the child is father of the man and that much of what men and women are, or of what they fail to become, is to be traced back to their childhood or to their infancy, or to the crucial months which preceded the traumatism of their birth, when they basked in the maternal security to which they will hark back ever after. Enormous gains have thereby been achieved by child psychology. Education has endeavored to adapt itself exactly to the capacities of the child at every stage of his progress. Every adolescent has been treated as a network of problems, and his neuroses or his whims have been surrounded with awe. The teacher of teenagers enters the class-room as he would a psychiatric hospital; the parents, fearful of asserting their own influence on these youngsters in their critical stage of metamorphosis, secretly to make themselves alike to their progeny, whose complexity and scorn for the elders baffle them, raise their hands in despair and pray that the adolescent may "go steady" and thus find "stability" with a friend of the opposite sex, since he fails to discover it in the home. The whole shift of interest from the man to the boy has brought us a fascinating crop of novels and plays written by, for, or about adolescents.

Meanwhile, the therapy of sublimation and the ideal of transcending that adolescent phase are being ignored. Through treating every child and every teenager as a potentially unbalanced person, through evincing a ridiculous punctilious respect for every manifestation of his personality and every mumbling of his self-expression (before there is much to be expressed), through our fear of stifling a potential Mozart or a Rimbaud in our schoolboys, we have failed to assist the child to develop into a man, to strive to become a leader. It is high time the trend should be reversed. There again, the Greeks and the Romans (it may be less invidious to invoke them than the French or the Russians) did differently, and perhaps no less well. *Paideia*, with them, consisted in the training of the man, in the preparation for *humanitas* and in the molding of a *vir*. Childhood and adolescence were only a momentary stage, to be transcended—not ends in themselves. Education, as Nietzsche also wished it to be, was a liberation from all that hampers the unhappy individual who is not yet a grown-up. A system which produced Pericles, Demosthenes, Plato, Euripides, Phidias, and Euclid or, in another place and age, Hamilton, Jefferson, Washington, Franklin, and Marshall cannot have rested upon altogether wrong psychological assumptions.[2]

---

[2] Henry Steele Commager is among several thoughtful Americans who today voice their objections to the "social law" of the prolongation of infancy first formulated by an American, John Fiske. "Americans," he notes, "have perhaps carried the practice to excess. A rich nation can doubtless afford financially the prolongation of childhood and youth well into the twenties, but a sensible people will not permit the growing waste of years and of talents involved in our current educational practices." See the bibliography.

The present state of scientific leadership or of literary creativity obviously cannot be surveyed in the compass of a single article. Our remarks must needs be limited to whatever profit the examples of other Western countries may afford us and what mistakes they may help us not repeat in our turn. Here again, neither in science nor in the arts and letters is excellence, or eminence, less often reached in the United States than in other democracies. The wave of breast-beating and of chauvinistic spite which followed Russia's recent scientific feats was ill-considered. While the scientific spirit is one of free inquiry which sooner or later calls everything into question, it is also true that when scientists have been prevented from speculating on the absolutes of philosophy or of politics, either because the political regime under which they lived (Richelieu, Louis XIV, Napoleon, Communism) frowned upon such inquiries, they were thereby enabled to devote more attention to their purely scientific disquisitions. It would be a fallacy to believe that Fascism, Nazism, Stalinism, or Chinese Communism, because they are tyrannical regimes, are necessarily deprived of great scientists—or of great writers. Moreover, any revolution suddenly brings wholly new layers of people to literacy, to culture, to self-consciousness; it pushes those new elites to the summit from which the former privileged groups have been dethroned, and thus taps new sources for leadership (political, military, administrative, intellectual), as France did between 1789 and 1800 or even 1815. America hardly stands in need of a revolution to spur its conquest of space.

But she might well do with a number of relatively minor reforms, the effect of which could be far-reaching. One would be the general adoption of the metric system. Another would be to elicit more scientific vocations through the teaching of scientific courses in the last years of high school and in the first two years of college by truly competent and inspiring teachers. As things stand, hardly any American student in the large universities ever enters into contact with a scientist of repute until he reaches graduate school: and many wander toward law, or business, or the compiling of statistics for insurance groups or for accountants, for lack of an incitement toward scientific research with which a gifted teacher would have provided them. A third measure might consist in de-emphasizing the mania for collaboration which has become characteristic of American science: too many papers are signed by three or four authors and show all the defects of multiple authorship. The young may gain some prestige from having their names bracketed with that of an elder statesman with whom it is to their interest to agree; the older scientist may unwillingly appropriate the ideas of the younger men or, worse still, may entrust their assistants with all the drudgery of firsthand experimenting and thus lose contact with essentials, and gradually emigrate into an administrator's office. But the history of science, even in the century of Becquerel, Planck, Einstein, Fleming, Morgan, and Pavlov, should remind us of the way in which most of the epoch-making discoveries were made—through "the lone musings of genius," by solitary men who did not necessarily submit to the way of life of businessmen, working at regular hours in an office or a laboratory, surrounded by assistants and secretaries and dictating machines; their capacity to dream, to disregard organized order and a conventionally neat and sterilized desk, to listen to the whims of fantasy and to the knockings of chance at a well-prepared mind was more beneficial to them than the fear of audacity which cramps men working in gentle compromise and in the affected cordiality of "togetherness." Cooperation is obviously necessary where the complexity of science has become infinite and the mass of accumulated knowledge is doubled every fifteen years: no scientist can be an island any longer. But he can still retain some individual personality in the presentation of results reached in a collective undertaking, and set nonspecialists afire, or a-dreaming, with the poetry of science.

Warnings of far-seeing scientists in Britain (Sir Lindor Brown) and in America (Egon Orowan among others) have pointed to another reason, linked with that passion for working together which has kept science in those countries from bold pioneering: the fascination with organization on a grand scale. An American professor of mechanical engineering like Egon Orowan, conceding that many of the fundamental steps forward in science have been taken by Europeans or by Americans who had been trained in part in Europe, wonders whether "the strict Roman organization of life can be adopted without losing the Greek fertility in new ideas." It may be excessively complimentary to the Russians or to the Germans to compare them with the Greeks, while to be assimilated to Rome has in our age become curiously derogatory: Corneille, Rousseau, and Danton thought otherwise. But the harrowing question in our civilization is: "Have not American universities been less successful than others in escaping the suffocating grip of the social assembly line?" (Orowan). In the past, it was not uncommon for a Claude Bernard or a Chevreul to continue working fruitfully in his laboratory long past middle age. Nowadays, as the same author observes,

> An unusually able scientist is on the scrap heap sometimes at the age of 30 or 40: he becomes director of research of a large unit, or head of a large department, a dean, or an important committee man oscillating between his home town and Washington, D. C. . . . Not that he ceases to be useful; but he is doing work which many others could do equally well or better, and he has to abandon work, usually more important in the long run, in which there is no substitute for him.

The implicit model which business life proposes to, and insidiously imposes upon, scientists, social scientists, and humanists alike lies at the source of that evil. In business, the goal is to be an executive, that is, a person who tells others to do the work and whose importance is measured by the number of people under him, if not by the number of telephones on his desk. If Pasteur or Einstein had likewise been lured in mid-career to an executive job or to a position with one of the large foundations, if Beethoven after his First Symphony had been appointed director of musical creation at an academy of music (the suggestion is Egon Orowan's), if Toulouse-Lautrec had been made visiting artist and critic at some American art school, the world would be much the poorer by it. Our affluent society, and perhaps our whole system of free enterprise in intellectual life, even the generous tax deductions which permit the proliferation of foundations (often of four perfunctory or semi-lunatic ones for one of great usefulness) constitute a danger to the emergence, and even more to the persistence, of leadership in intellectual life in America. Great names are utilized to go and wheedle funds out of foundation officials when, as in some other countries, they might be left alone as honored members of an Academy while state officials took over the work of raising or distributing funds. While in countries with a more centralized organization young researchers and professors are assigned positions by the government, and the mature scientist or the artistic creator or even the great professor of literature may enjoy the privilege of seldom answering his mail and of refusing to attend committees, an incalculable amount of time is devoured in America by the writing of letters of recommendation. The placement of his graduates is the elder professor's heaviest burden. The same young man will commonly apply for five different grants every year; and the master who numbers one hundred such former students among his followers would betray their democratic claims on him if he refused to write five hundred letters. No wonder if at forty-five an American scientist or an American humanist feels all creativity in him dried up and mournfully allows himself to become an organization man, invested with a semblance of power, since he assists in the distribution of funds and of promotions made possible by the wealth of others, but painfully aware of his own abdication. In no other country is it taken for granted so placidly that after forty-five or fifty a writer or a scientist has little left to contribute and had better consent to the role of a "lost leader."

Any attempt to speculate on the relative creativity or the relative degree of excellence displayed by writers, painters, musicians, critics, and scholars in America and in Western Europe would require a volume in itself. The present writer has already expressed himself on the subject elsewhere. Suffice it to say that sheer creativity is certainly no less remarkable today in this country than in Britain, France, or Germany. If formal excellence is often lacking or less sedulously pursued than in other cultures, if the inner life of fictional or dramatic characters is less persistently explored, and if the portrayal of passion is seldom mature, those three glaring weaknesses of American letters are compensated for by greater vitality, more epic audacity, and a less egocentric cult of literature and of its practitioners by authors and public alike. The serious gap from which American culture suffers most is the inability of critics to create a public of connoisseurs around the writers, which alone might, through the understanding and prestige which that public would provide, offset the attraction of money and of Hollywood royalties.[3] The critics themselves and the

[3] The reader whom the subject may interest is referred to my *Failures of Criticism* (Ithaca: Cornell University Press, 1967).

professors in the many realms covered by the vague denomination of "humanities" are often mortified by their awareness of not wielding the influence which in Tsarist Russia and in the liberal countries of Western Europe was, or is, that of their corresponding numbers. Those who think, who are at least as numerous and as outstanding as any in Europe, suffer from not influencing those who act.

To be sure, the gulf between theory and practice is ever vast and deep. Professors of political thought are not necessarily successful as politicians, or even as counselors of statesmen. Theoretical economists can err strangely in their contradictory prognostications, and their frequent lack of contact with either politicians or business life reduces their voices to so many unheeded cries in a wilderness. Men of action do not object to inviting thinkers and academic scholars in order to have it explained why they act as they do; then they continue doing it with a strengthened good conscience or with a bad one painlessly silenced. Great financiers and effective secretaries of the treasury in this country or in Europe, great statesmen such as Clemenceau, Churchill, or Roosevelt were often men whose political philosophy, if ever expressed consistently, would have appeared childish to professors of law and Ph.D.'s in government and economics. Their thought was contradictory, often improvised at the prompting of circumstances; but they were able to size up events, to divine trends, to interpret the aspirations of the masses, and to guide them.

Intellectuals are not by necessity incapable of action: Disraeli, Lenin, De Gaulle, Salazar were after all intellectuals, and so once were Pericles and Caesar. Woodrow Wilson, himself a trained intellect and a stern moralist, wrote in his youth a very revealing essay which he read (he was then thirty-four) as a commencement address in Knoxville, Tennessee, in 1890, and again at Oberlin, in 1895. He, like many others who have helped make history, had in himself the dual personality of a man of thought and of a man of action. He soon perceived the weakness of intellectuals: they do not stand as close to the mass as those who act. They cherish proportion, restraint, academic grayness, niceties of character; they tell others what they should do, but they do not "creep into their confidence" in order to persuade them. He added:

Leadership, for the statesman, is interpretation. He must read the common thought; he must test and calculate very circumspectly the preparation of the nation for the next move in the progress of politics. ... No man thinking thoughts born out of time can succeed in leading his generation, and successful leadership is a product of sympathy, not of antagonism [pp. 42 and 53].

Even earlier, while he taught at Bryn Mawr in 1885, he had yearned for a statesman's career and written to his fiancée to that effect, confiding to her: "I love the stir of the world." He proclaimed in his inaugural address at Princeton in 1902: "We are not put into this world to sit still and know; we are put into it to act." Few statesmen indeed have achieved as much as Wilson did in domestic reform and imaginative mapping of the future during his first presidency. His countrymen may well be proud of having had in this century the one intellectual who also could act with foresight and, until the ill-fated last years when the art of compromise deserted him, could translate independent meditation and loftiness of purpose into deeds.

The lessons of continental Europe in this domain are not altogether admirable, and the clamor of many continental Europeans who look down on Americans as beings deprived of *Weltanschauung* and as incapable of formulating their attitudes philosophically need not impress us overmuch. The elites have long been stratified in Europe, and they have tended to close their ranks against those who do not share their educational or financial privileges. They are often tainted with snobbery, unmindful of the warning of one of the French intellectuals, André Suarès, that "the first condition for belonging to the elite is not to call oneself one of the elite." They are frightened by vulgarity and forget that vitality often must go with some lack of polished veneer. In literature and the arts, the self-styled elites affect always to choose a vanguard position, to cherish what is esoteric and obscure and therefore closed to less subtle minds than theirs. In politics, a tone of intellectual arrogance is wont to keep them apart from the masses or leads them to an excess of quibbling and a trend toward refined sophistry, from which even men of high mental stature like Mendès-France or Raymond Aron are not altogether immune.

It is no wonder that many an Anglo-Saxon thinker should recently have been wary of the seduction of continental European intellectuals for an America which, since 1933, has gained an influx of uprooted intellectuals, all adept at wielding philosophical concepts and often at wrapping their thoughts in barbaric English, but with little or no audience in this country outside a few reviews and university halls. Bertrand Russell scornfully defined the intellectual as "a person who pretends to have more intellect than he has," and an American President, angered by the foreignness of the very notion, mocked the intellectual as "a man who takes more words than is necessary to say more than he knows" (quoted in Eric Goldman, *The Crucial Decade*, 1956). A former college president who has always thought in-dependently and acted fearlessly, Harold Taylor, more reasonably indicted systematic anti-intellectualism, but rejected the extreme respect granted by some Europeans to their intellectuals; for this country refuses to accept "a class of political or social leaders whose function it is to think for the rest." More recently still, the most intellectual of American playwrights, Arthur Miller, in a thoughtful interview given to Henry Brandon (*Harper's Magazine*, November 1960), stressed the dissimilarities between himself and Beckett, Sartre, and other French representatives of the *théâtre d'idées*.

> Our culture resists knowing what it is doing. . . . In France, to a much greater degree, the people are aware that, if they don't know what they're doing . . . somebody knows what they're doing, and that this is a legitimate kind of work, so to speak. . . . Abroad, there are more people who have learned to tip their hats to the idea of an intellectual. . . . Here no writer would regard himself, as in Russia and France, as spokesman for the national spirit or something of the kind. . . . In a word, we are not so much persecuted as ignored. But everybody else is ignored, too.

The record of European intellectuals in public affairs or in their pronouncements during years of crisis is certainly not a uniformly admirable one: many are those who took a long time to discern the perils of Pan-Germanism, like Thomas Mann, or of Nazism, like Heidegger and scores of philosophers, scientists, and writers. Goebbels after all was an intellectual, and so was Gentile, and so were Henri de Man, and a number of French artists and writers who, flattered by the tribute of the enemy occupying their country, collaborated with him in wartime. There have been many intellectuals, like Ruskin and D'Annunzio, to sing paeans to war as a regeneration and to espouse rabid nationalism, and there are still a number of them who have successively sided with Trotsky, Lenin, and Khrushchev. Power and self-assertiveness can exercise a curious fascination on the feminine side of those creators who must apparently have something of a woman in them to be complete. Even Goethe did not escape the magnetism of Napoleon trampling his country under his horse's hoofs. "Some of the biggest swine in human history have been great intellects. Some of the weakest spots in Western free society are due to excessive preoccupation with intellect, with analysis," as another of the finest minds among our college presidents, Harry Gideonse, warned us. The failures of our sister countries in Europe may prove to us to be just as instructive as their success when that success is unquestionable. Too few of the Western European intellectuals in our century seem to entertain a dauntless faith in the future or to be willing to translate words and thoughts into deeds in order to bring about that future.

Faith, and a warm if at times naïve passion for fraternity, on the contrary, mark American culture as it is lived. These qualities are more than ever to be valued today. Behind much of the criticism (occasionally raucous and even rancorous) of this country voiced elsewhere in the world, there lurks a disappointed admiration for it and an inadequate comprehension of its goals, because they are all too seldom defined in broad, universal, and dynamic terms. The paramount issue in this country today is, in our eyes, to restore links between those who think and those who act, to turn more potential leaders away from the world of business, where they all too often become lost in routine, toward ideas and the problems of today, which are educational far more than economic, ideological even more than military. There will soon be four or five millions of young people attending American colleges: are they made to think independently about what they read and hear? Are they spurred to develop into leaders through an adequate realization of the challenges facing them?

Our faith in the effects of reason, or of more rationality, on mankind has been shattered: reasonableness has hardly made a dent on the emotional forces within us. Our faith in the effects of material comfort has likewise undergone deadly blows. Man is not evil merely because he suffers from inadequate housing, hygiene, or diet, contented or "good" because he is prosperous, well fed, and rich. Would that life were indeed that simple! Old-fashioned optimism is dead and gone, once and for all. We must put an end to colonialism, but that will nevertheless create a thousand more difficulties than existed before. We may reach an agreement on atomic warfare, but it will not constitute the end to our fears of world destruction. We may devise another agreement on Berlin or on Middle Eastern oil, but any agreement merges well-nigh insoluble problems into new or bigger ones; it does not solve them for good. Peace is not the absence of wars or the result of treaties. It is a continued and dynamic creation, far more challenging than war, and it should be proposed to the youth by our leaders as the paramount goal of the second half of the twentieth century.

It is sad to watch the leaders of the country which is now entrusted with guiding the free world, and also that part of it which we do not consider as free, to higher destinies, fritter their energies away in secondary matters and negative thinking. The panicky fear of Communism obsesses them; they are trapped by Russia into fighting for half-reluctant allies on the least favorable of terrains and into jeopardizing their moral superiority through an insensate fear of subversiveness. Meanwhile, their intellectual leaders allow the good men coming out of college to squander their ardent young minds on frivolities: the latter rush into business, work strenuously to find out what the public might want, and secretly knows it needs not. But who takes the trouble to awaken aspirations in a country where soon half of the adult population might be made up of college graduates? The genuine leaders would be those who might propose an alternative to armament expense as a cure for any prospect of a recession; other goals than an even higher dose of publicity to persuade citizens to purchase what will only clutter up their homes and dull their minds; and, what they do not even think of wishing, spacious thinking—not a hypnotized acceptance of the doings of other powers in the East.

The author whom we have quoted above and who is more familiar with American business life than most academics can be, Thomas Griffith, concludes his volume with words which may be endorsed:

> If a great effort must continually be made to provide against Russian assault, our real expenditure of imagination must be in lighting the chaos inside us, and recovering a clarity of purpose. Only in this way will we regain health as a nation, or hope to inspire others to admire us. The only competition that should matter to us as a nation is not with Communism, but with that best we ourselves might be.

BIBLIOGRAPHY

Amidon, Beulah (ed.). *Democracy's Challenge to Education.* New York: Farrar and Rinehart, 1960.

Anthony, R. "Le Rôle des hommes de pensée dans le politique et le social," *Revue Internationale de Sociologie*, XXXVII (1929), 41–47 (refutation of Julien Benda's *The Treason of the Intellectuals*).

Aron, Raymond. *L'Homme contre les Tyrans.* Paris: Gallimard, 1946.

Babbitt, Irving. *Democracy and Leadership.* Boston-New York: Houghton Mifflin, 1924.

Bergson, Henri. *La Spécialité.* Angers, 1882 (quoted in Algot Ruhe and Nancy Paul, *Henri Bergson: Account of His Life and Philosophy* [London: Macmillan, 1914]).

Bouglé, Célestin. *Humanisme, Sociologie, Philosophie.* Paris: Hermann, 1938.

Bogardus, Emory S. *Leaders and Leadership.* New York: Appleton-Century-Crofts, 1934.

Brown, Sir Lindor. *The Perils of Leadership in Science.* The David Russell Memorial Lecture. London, 1960.

Caillois, Roger. *La Communion des Forts, Etudes de Sociologie Contemporaine.* Mexico City: Quetzal, 1943.

Commager, Henry Steele. "Why Do We Lack Statesmen?" *New York Times*, Magazine Section, January 17, 1960.

Dautry, Raoul. *Métier d'Homme.* Paris: Plon, 1937.

Domenach, Jean-Marie. "Définitions," in *La Démocratie est une idée neuve* (*Esprit*, September 1959, No. 9, pp. 198–219).

Dugas, L. "La Pensée et l'action," *Revue de Métaphysique et de Morale*, XXXV (1928), 435–438 (discussion of Benda's *The Treason of the Intellectuals*).

Elizabeth Paschal. *Encouraging the Excellent. Special Programs for Gifted and Talented Students.* New York: Fund for the Advancement of Education, 1960.

Fayol, Henri. *Administration industrielle et générale. Prévoyance, organisation, commandement.* Paris: Dunod, 1920 (translated as *Industrial and General Administration* [London: Pitman, 1930]).

Ferry, Giles. *Une Expérience de Formation des Chefs.* Paris: Editions du Seuil, 1945.

Gardner, John. *Excellence: Can We Be Equal and Excellent Too?* New York: Harper & Brothers, 1960.

Gideonse, Harry D. *On the Educational Statesmanship of a Free Society,* New York: The Woodrow Wilson Foundation, 1959. Pamphlet No. 5.

Girard, Paul. *L'Education athénienne au Ve et au IVe siècle.* 2d ed. Paris: Hachette, 1891.

Goldman, Eric. *The Crucial Decade, 1945–1955.* New York: Knopf, 1956.

Grasberger, L. *Erziehung und Unterricht im klassichen Altertum.* Würzburg: Die Stahel'sche Buch-und Kunst-Handlung, 1864–1881.

Griffith, Thomas. *The Waist-High Culture.* New York: Harper & Brothers, 1959.

Hall, Sir Noel Frederick. *The Making of Higher Executives: The Modern Challenge.* New York: New York University, School of Commerce Publications, 1958.

Heidsieck, Patrick. *Rayonnement de Lyautey.* Paris: Gallimard, 1941 (Lyautey's essay, "Le Rôle social de l'officier," 1891, is ch. 3).

Huxley, Julian. *New Bottles for New Wine.* London: Chatto & Windus; New York: Harper & Brothers, 1957 (see "A Redefinition of Progress," pp. 18–40).

Jaeger, Werner. *Paideia: The Ideals of Greek Culture.* New York: Oxford University Press, 1939–1944.

Jennings, Eugene. *An Anatomy of Leadership.* New York: Harper & Brothers, 1960.

Keyserling, Hermann Alex von. *Menschen als Sinnbilder.* Darmstadt: Otto Reichl Verlag, 1926 (see "Schopenhauer als Verbilder," "Spengler der Tatsachenmensch," "Kant der Sinneserfasser," and "Jesus der Magier").

Lasswell, Harold D., et al. *The Comparative Study of Elites.* Hoover Institute Studies B, No. 1. Stanford: Stanford University Press, 1952.

Madariaga, Salvador de. *Anarchy or Hierarchy.* London: George Allen & Unwin, 1937.

Marrou, Henri. *A History of Education in Antiquity.* New York: Sheed and Ward, 1956.

Maurois, André. *Dialogues sur le Commandement.* Paris: B. Grasset, 1924.

Metcalf, Henry C. (ed.). *Business Leadership*. New York: Isaac Pitman & Sons, 1930.

Miller, Arthur. "The State of the Theatre in America," a conversation with Henry Brandon, *Harper's Magazine*, November 1960, pp. 63–70.

Orowan, Egon. "Our Universities and Scientific Creativity," *Bulletin of the Atomic Scientists*, XV (1959), 236–239.

Peyre, Henri. *Basic Education in French Secondary Schools*. Washington: Council for Basic Education, 1960 (pamphlet).

Roosevelt, Theodore. *The Strenuous Life*. New York: Century Company, 1900.

Steffens, Lincoln. *Autobiography*. 2 vols. New York: Harcourt, Brace, 1931. In vol. 2, p. 739, Steffens quotes a conversation with Woodrow Wilson in which the latter declared, "An executive is a man of action. An intellectual, such as you and I, is inexecutive. In an executive job, we are dangerous, unless we are aware of our limitations and take measures to stop our everlasting disposition to think, to listen, to—not act."

Taylor, Harold. "The Intellectual in Action," *Bulletin of the Atomic Scientists*, XIV (1958), 368–373.

Tead, Ordway. *The Art of Leadership*. New York: Whittlesey House, McGraw-Hill, 1935.

Toulemonde, Jean. *Essai sur la Psychologie de l'autorité personnelle. Etude d'interpsychologie et de pédagogie*. Paris: Bloud & Gay, 1929.

Urwick, Lyndall. *Management of Tomorrow*. London: Nisbet & Company, 1933.

Valentine, Alan. *The Age of Conformity*. Chicago: Henry Regnery, 1954.

Ward, John W. "Individualism Today," *Yale Review*, March 1960, pp. 380–383.

Whitehead, Thomas North. *Leadership in a Free Society*. A study in human relations based on an analysis of present-day industrial civilization. Cambridge: Harvard University Press, 1936.

Wilson, Woodrow. *Leaders of Men*. Princeton: Princeton University Press, 1952 (address first given at the University of Tennessee on June 17, 1890).

13 | THE CRISIS OF MODERN MAN AS SEEN BY ANDRÉ MALRAUX AND ALBERT CAMUS

THE WORLD and man have probably thought they were, and actually have been, in a state of crisis ever since the two have existed. Momentous periods of transition were lived by our remote ancestors when the ancient world declined and fell to give way to Christianity, and again when medieval culture became sterile and was replaced or reinvigorated by the Renaissance. The throes of death and pangs of birth suffered when the remnants of the feudal order and the absolute monarchies were swept away, in the Age of Enlightenment and of the American and the French Revolutions, were doubtless felt by the contemporaries as acutely as our anguish and our strange mixture of pride and of revulsion at having discovered how absurd is our world as experienced by us today.

The difference, however, lies in the universality of our modern crisis, which is no longer limited to a small area of the populated world but embraces the whole planet; it lies also in our having become aware of the terrifying acceleration of the pace of history, which brooks no pause and no respite. Our plight is made more laden with anxiety as it affects not just a few intellectuals specializing in the contemplation of history and in the wielding of philosophical concepts, but also statesmen, scientists, engineers, and those artists and writers who once might have been content with entertaining and charming their public. It is to men of letters that the people of many countries, those of France in particular, have lately turned in order to find a clearer definition of their predicament and the lineaments of a constructive solution.

French imaginative writers, even novelists like Stendhal, Balzac, and Proust, poets like Hugo and Baudelaire, were never content with telling a story, inventing characters, and singing their ecstasies or their gloom. All of them were moralists. No literature is in that sense more utilitarian, bent upon improving man's fate or sharpening his awareness of it, than that of the country which launched the doctrine of art for art's sake. Malraux and Camus are two of the most influential successors in our time to that long list of analytical and pragmatic spirits. Audiences, in and outside France, have turned to them as to representative men endowed with a longer memory than most men, accustomed to meditating on history but not paralyzed by the fetishism of tradition. In them they have also found a concrete and carnally vivid position of their problem: both Malraux and Camus, without ever having been encircled by any Existentialist creeds, have shared with the French Existentialists the determination to think the abstract concretely. Both also have been anticipators and prophets, "forgers of myths" as Sartre has called the new play-wrights of the France of 1940–1950. They cannot help remembering that their forefathers of the eighteenth century have been regarded as having, through their writings, prepared the French Revolution and created many of the myths by which the succeeding century fed its thought and its sensibility. They too want to help a new world be born. Their desire is less to think consistently than to live their thought, with dynamic unreason and often with perverse illogic. They think forward, heeding Kierkegaard's famous charge against the philosophers of his age that "we live forward, but we understand backward." Their novels, their maxims, their essays aim at nothing less than the redefining of man in his relations to the past, to other men, to the divine or its substitutes, to the future which provides them with the transcendence toward which the Existentialist "project" of many thinkers of today is directed. Like the Existentialists again, with less fanfare, and as a natural answer to what they consider to be the demands of our age, Malraux and Camus have, from the first, been "engagés." The cause to which they committed themselves may have varied; they have themselves evolved; some would even say that they betrayed their earlier allegiances, and more understanding observers would merely admit that they have matured. But they have not swerved from the dictum of one of the characters in Malraux's novels that "ideas must be lived, not thought." Taken separately and analytically, many of their ideas can be refuted; but the personality which animates them cannot be so easily. Since, unlike the neo-Thomists, the Marxists, or the Existentialists, neither Malraux nor Camus ever proposed a coherent doctrine, they recoiled from offering their fellow beings a panacea and from indulging the slight legerdemain which is required to swell a system to the point at which it may embrace the vast and complex reality. Like Maritain, Simone Weil, and Teilhard de Chardin among the French reinterpreters of religion, like Sartre among the atheists, Malraux and Camus (the latter, twelve years younger, proclaimed his affinities with the former and his glowing admiration for his work) have undertaken, in their soteriological literature, to point the way to man's salvation. Like other French agnostics or outright atheists, they have followed St. Paul's advice to the Philippians: "Work out your own salvation with fear and trembling."

Malraux's eventful career does not have to be narrated here. Malraux himself shows no interest whatever in his biography; he does not even take the trouble to deny the picturesque adventures which have been lent to him by biographers too prone to forget that an imaginative creator does not necessarily have to have lived the vicissitudes of his fictional characters. A scion of the middle class like most of those who have indicted the bourgeoisie, from Balzac, Karl Marx, and Flaubert down to Sartre, he has wasted little time assailing his class. He would probably find Sartre naïve in his assumption that one class alone is to be charged with the sins of selfishness, inauthenticity, greed, and colonialist exploitation. There is no sign of masochism in him and no nostalgia for the role of a martyr, as in the philosopher of Existentialism. He has fought alongside the people in the Spanish Civil War and in the Resistance; the episodes of his last novel, *Les Noyers de l'Altenburg*, breathe more tender sympathy with the soldiers imprisoned in the nave of a cathedral in June, 1940, and with the humble fighters of the tank corps than is perceptible even in the writings of Camus, who himself came from the least privileged layers of Society.

Early in his career, refusing to try for the traditional badges of appurtenance to the bourgeoisie, the baccalaureate and the admission to one of the Parisian Grandes Ecoles, André Malraux chose to work for a brief period in the world of publishing; he revealed there his taste for art history, for illustrated volumes, and for cubist poetry (Max Jacob, André Salmon, Pierre Reverdy), to which he was more strongly drawn than he was ever to surrealism. But he soon realized how little attuned he was to a regular career as a man of letters, laying the scene of family stories in some provincial setting, like Mauriac or Julien Green, or even, like his friend Marcel Arland, depicting the dreams and the self-centered meditations of an adolescent attempting to conquer Paris. The literature of the years 1919–1929 in France would gladly have forgotten the nightmare of Verdun and the Somme to recover the intellectual comfort of the prewar normalcy. Malraux, from the first, accepted the tragic element which was inseparable from man's fate. His affinities were, among the young writers of his own age, with Montherlant and Drieu la Rochelle and a whole spiritual family which cherished a feverish intensity, as had Pascal, Nietzsche, and Barrès. His spiritual kinship with those three personalities has not been adequately stressed as yet.

Above all, he knew that quietude and contentment were not to be for him, and that his vocation was to wrestle with angels or demons and to court a tragic folly which no serenity of age, no weary resignation would exorcize. In pregnant, elliptic book reviews and brief essays, never since collected into a volume, between the ages of twenty-five and thirty-five, Malraux (who was born in 1901) groped toward his own original expression of the crisis of the new "Children of the Century." In June, 1934, reviewing a volume translated from the Russian of Mikhail Matveev, the author of *La Condition humaine* declared peremptorily that there was no good war book written by "a novelist of peace," as he put it; for "man is an unknown animal which thought it could know itself in quietude. The drama opens, and he discovers his power of dream, his specific madness." Seven years earlier, in a revealing essay, "D'une Jeunesse européenne," he did not hesitate to speak for his whole generation. "Everywhere today men want to free themselves from their civilization, as others wanted to free themselves from the divine. . . ." But the West had to admit "the impossibility for it to part from the notion of the divine. . . . Of all the marks which we bear, the Christian one, inscribed in our flesh by our very flesh, like a scar, is the most deeply engraved." We are no longer Christian; yet we are forced to spell out the world with a code, or a cipher, which is Christian.

The determination of the young Malraux, in whom his elders like André Gide and Francois Mauriac, the first with unrestrained admiration, the second with some envy and regret that Malraux would not side with the tragic Catholics, hailed the most intelligent mouthpiece of the post-war generation, was to envisage Western Europe and its Christian heritage in a broad perspective. He set out to explore the art and the civilization of ancient Indo-China and soon allied himself with those who, in that French colony, yearned to be freed from colonial rule. After intense polemics against the official rulers from France and several mishaps, Malraux transferred his revolutionary activity to China. To him, the self-assigned mission of the least complacent among the young Western Europeans was to teach the Chinese what colossal potential force lay in ideas leading to action; such ideas were to be transformed into deeds, which would explode the serene order of the mandarins, rapt in their detached wisdom.

All the while, however, while he was trying to replace in its true perspective "that small advanced promontory of the Asiatic continent" to which Valéry's famous sentence had reduced Europe, Malraux remained concerned with the crisis of the modern world, which was centered in the West. The revolutionary and technological revolution occurring on the immense plains and peninsulas of Asia testified to the prestige and dynamic influence of Western Europe far more conspicuously than the moderate success of the missionaries had ever achieved through three hundred years. The first volume published by Malraux, *La Tentation de l'Occident*, in 1926, vibrates with eloquent pronouncements on the crisis which was then rocking the European man; long before Camus was going to popularize the word, life in Europe was termed "an essential absurdity." Western man had reached a state of weariness with all that had sustained him heretofore; he had thinned down his thought to a string of subtle negations. He was now searching for deeper reasons for living or for dying. God was perhaps dead, Malraux repeated, like all his French contemporaries imbued with the Nietzschean cry, as no Germans had yet been;

but man also was dying; and if the notion of man was thus imperiled, there would be no one to receive the legacy of the dead God. In a striking and very little known review of a volume in which a French conservative, Henri Massis, was attempting to denounce the lures of the East then imperiling the faith of the West in itself, *Défense de l'Occident*, André Malraux declared to the men of his generation (*Nouvelle Revue Française*, June 1927): "The modern world carries within itself, like a cancer, its absence of soul. He will not free himself from it; it is implied in its own law. And things will remain thus until a collective appeal of the soul wrings men. That day, the world in which we live will doubtless reel and collapse."

Many are the intellectuals in our century who have expertly diagnosed the symptoms of the crisis of our time, and proposed cures. Most of those, however, were content with lucid, sometimes profound, analyses: Paul Valéry, with his classical statements in "La Crise de l'esprit," then in several other lofty and negative essays on politics, was one of those. Others, like Anatole France, Jules Romains, indulged the French game of signing manifestoes, offering plans of a very theoretical character, and letting themselves be cheered by popular audiences which had never read the dilettantist banalities of *Jérôme Coignard* or unanimist odes to the crowd. Thought and an energetic commitment to action do not easily meet. Young Malraux was determined to prove true to Bergson's requirement that we should think as men of action and act as men of thought. He plunged into revolutionary action first, poured out fiery journalistic articles while in Indo-China, lent conflicting views to fictional characters dramatizing his obsessions in his early novels. The outcome of his meditations, which took place at the very time when he was immersed in political agitation, was first formulated in peremptory aphorisms, in which the conversations of his characters, like that of the garrulous protagonist in Camus' *La Chute*, abound. Only later, in a few speeches pronounced when he was fighting in the Spanish Civil War, then after he emerged from World War II as a hero of the Resistance and a champion of anti-Communism, did he formulate his diagnosis of the modern crisis of the West with some continuity, though never with dispassionate serenity. While attempting to rally friends to the Spanish Republican cause in 1937, he had spoken to American audiences, in 1937, on "the value, for men of letters, of an active political career," proclaiming:

> The pursuit of literature is no place for writers, who had in democracy a cause for which they could fight. If they lived, their writing would be all the better for the experience gained in the struggle; if they died, their deaths would make more living documents than anything they might compose if they stayed within their ivory towers.

Action, however, may also prove a facile means of escape from our mental anguish and an insidious poison; it invites us to pursue temporary, neatly defined, and limited goals, to abdicate our freedom of thought for the sake of efficiency and to submit to a discipline which may in time cramp our critical spirit. At the very time when he was fighting in Spain and nervously writing the fiery episodes and dialogues of *Espoir*, Malraux was living with anguish the plight of the intellectual in the midst of action. All action is Manichean and demands an "either-or," the drastic choice between yes and no, killing or being killed, obeying or disobeying, reaching a decision under fire and abiding by it with no room for hesitation or repentance. By nature, however, an intellectual tends to be an inveterate anarchist; he obeys reluctantly, prizes his own ability to criticize and to judge more highly than any forsaking of his free judgment. And the dilemma of "either-or" is often abhorrent to him; he relishes nuances and well knows that in them lies truth. If he has analyzed a situation lucidly, devised a theoretical and ingenious solution to the difficulties confronting him, he is likely to believe that his task has been fulfilled; others may see the application of his solutions through. The intellectual unwillingly forgets history and the ominous contemplation of precedents; he remembers how baffling and irrational the consequences of our decisions may turn out to be. None expressed it more strikingly than T. S. Eliot in the finest philosophical lines he ever wrote, in "Gerontion," on the cunning deceptions worked on us by history:

> . . . She gives when our attention is distracted
> And what she gives, gives with such supple confusions
> That the giving famishes the craving . . . .

It is to the credit of Malraux that, at the ages of fifty and sixty, having fought in two or three wars, taken part in several revolutionary movements, being now the most influential counselor of the President of France and the founder or organizer of many cultural establishments in France, he has not relinquished thought to espouse action solely. His greatest work as a man of letters is, in the eyes of many of us, his achievement as a writer on art or on philosophy of art and philosophy of history. In his contemplation of works of art, however, he does not seek oblivion of the harrowing concerns of the present, but a more lucid view of the crisis in which man is enmeshed today and the constructive path to a solution.

Any formulation of the solution envisaged by Malraux is bound to reduce to a few deceptively clear sentences what, in his fiery and elliptic prose, is imperious, obscure, disdainful of any prosaic links between blinding flashes of intuitions. But such must be the modest function of any criticism which wants to remain the handmaid to creation and the modest interpreter of the inspired inspirer to those less genial than he. The view of modern man held by Malraux since he bid farewell, in 1945, to the first and active stage of his career as a revolutionist and as a warrior, was first formulated in a remarkable lecture delivered, under the auspices of the UNESCO, at the Sorbonne in the fall of 1946, then developed in his sundry writings on art. Some day, a volume collecting the speeches and scattered articles given by Malraux to newspapers and magazines, none of which was ever perfunctory or lacking in significance, may well be regarded as one of the outstanding testaments of our age to future generations.

A crucial event which perforce controls the sensibility and the thought of modern man is the end of absolutes. Up to the end of the seventeenth and to the eighteenth centuries, man, Malraux likes to say, lived in a world of absolutes. There were agnostics and skeptics even in the Middle Ages, to be sure; there were even more during the era of the Renaissance. But those few dissenters swam, as it were, inside a Christian aquarium. Religion, in Western Europe, encompassed not only pilgrimages, the cult of relics, the building of churches, but also law, festivities, the whole organization of life and even the literature in which priests and monks were derided. Men and women were then firmly convinced that the order which they enjoyed was good for them and, at any rate, it was the only conceivable one. They had faith in their absolute. They conceived the ancients, the population, of whom they caught a glimpse in their pilgrimages or during the Crusades, as similar to themselves. They entertained little doubt that their own way of life alone was right and constituted the absolute standard.

Such a soothing conviction was undermined by the advent of a historical awareness (Montesquieu, Voltaire, Gibbon, Hume), by the observation of other peoples in other parts of the world, and by the growing realization that all was not well with Western man. Indeed, our religion, our ethics, our politics, they soon decided, were far from perfect and, in any case, valid only for us and relatively to us. But the populations observed in India and China, in Iran and in Peru were equally justified in behaving and believing as they did. The era of the relative then dawned. That substitution, as Renan was later to put it, of the category of the relative replacing the category of the absolute, was the most momentous revolution in the history of thought. The myth of the absolute had perished. New myths had to be proposed to soothe the harrowing self-doubts of modern men, questioning the validity of all that they had lived by, aware of something fundamentally false in their own moral conscience. "We are betrayed by what is false within," George Meredith was later to say, indicting the Victorian complacency, the last symptom of that belief that what was advocated, if not always practiced, in nineteenth-century England and in Adam Smith's Scotland, could well be imitated by the rest of mankind. Matthew Arnold, in his well-known essay on "The Study of Poetry," implied a similar meaning when he prophesied that "most of what now passes with us for religion and philosophy will be replaced by poetry." Literature, art, science have now and for some two hundred and fifty years ceased to be envisaged against the fixed background of religion, deemed to be a stable network of truths.

Ever since, the men of the West have been seeking substitutes, or, as Malraux calls it, "small change," "la monnaie" for the lost absolute. The myth which appeared at the time when the first momentous crisis of the European conscience occurred was that of progress. As reason applied to ethics and to politics would enlighten mankind, as men would know more and be liberated from superstitions, there would ensue an improvement in their material lives, in their institutions, and in their very natures. For a time, between

Turgot, Condorcet, Comte, and the early socialist thinkers, progress was conceived as inevitable, indefinite in its future expectations and irreversible. Then blows were dealt that new myth. Several flaws appeared in that alleged "law" of progress; for pauses, recessions, recurrences of barbarism also occur. The ghastly slaughters of World War I, the bombings and the extermination camps of World War II, the dropping of the atomic bombs over Japan in 1945 no longer make it easy for mankind to pay even lip service to that faith. Long before then, it had dawned on many a moralist that sacrificing the present to the inevitability of a better morrow, always striving for the latest model and for the latest doctrine also entail despair: the present becomes nothing but a stage toward the future and is corrupted by a flavor of death even before or while it is lived. Only a Nietzsche could exult in the thought that man is but a stage, soon to be transcended, toward the advent of the superman.

Another myth, a far less generous one—that of success—had lured the men of Western Europe and of America after the French Revolution and the ascent of the masses. "Pourquoi pas moi?" was the naïve, if natural, question asked by the children of the century of Napoleon and of Balzac, the brothers of Julien Sorel and of Rastignac, soon of Becky Sharp and of Horatio Alger. Individual success, often measured by material and social criteria, could hardly constitute a glowing myth likely to win the allegiance of men of today. It is to the credit of the youth of the twentieth century that it will not rest content in any intellectual isolationism. It is determined to stand up and be counted, in Keats' words in *The Fall of Hyperion*, among

> . . . those to whom the miseries of the world
> Are misery and will not let them rest.

International solidarity is perhaps the one creed of our age to be proudly set against the inhumanity of man to man which exploded in foreign and colonial wars since 1940. But individuals themselves set much less store by success than their ancestors did between 1820 and 1860. If literature reflects in some fashion the moods of a society, neither the literature of France nor certainly that of America (judged by Dos Passos, Faulkner, O'Neil, Arthur Miller) seems to nurture the cult of success and to encourage the pursuit of selfish happiness. The words "tragic," "anxiety," "anguish," and "absurd" have displaced "success" in the daily talk of college youth and even in the press. After all, as Robert L. Stevenson remarked with gentle irony, "the business of life is not to succeed, but to continue to fail in good spirits."

The severest setback to the myths of progress and of success, proposed as an ersatz for the absolute of old, occurred when Western man began to lose his faith in rationalism, or at any rate to subscribe to reason's claims to provide an adequate account of the world. The turning point may be assigned to the years 1910–1913. The full consequences of that turning back against Descartes were most severely felt by men who, like Malraux and Camus, reached manhood later. Camus' posthumous *Notebooks* testify to his crucial concern as that of reaching an ethics which could no longer rest on rationalism. The real is no longer automatically judged to be rational, as for Hegel; realism, as a means of understanding that which is minutely described, has perished in all but the very recent "new novelists" of France, and even among them, it is a visionary and phantasmal reality which is measured and catalogued. Existence is no longer based upon thought by modern Existential thinkers, who reject the Cartesian corollary of the "Cogito," divine veracity or truthfulness. Reason, and the spread of rationalism, of parliamentary democracy, of free elections, of political stability to the countries of other continents have ceased to fill the men of the second half of this century with pride and confidence. The crisis indeed runs deep.

We live, Malraux concluded after World War II and in conformity with what he had been experiencing and fearing ever since his earliest novel, in an age of violence, of wars and revolutions, and of the omnipresence of death. That truth has been concealed from many in English-speaking countries, the only ones, along with Scandinavian ones, in which violence and revolution are disbelieved in and considered as somewhat out of place in a world devoted to peaceful agreement to disagree, solidarity, and reformist evolution. However, the history of the world since 1940 cannot be said to have afforded much cheer to those who expected the spread of Anglo-Saxon values to prevail. The literary prophets of our age are Ernest Hemingway, William Faulkner (with some even Henry Miller, William Golding, and the Beatniks), Graham Greene, Arthur Koestler, Franz

Kafka, and a few French writers among whom Malraux and Camus, Sartre, Beckett, and Genet have won the broadest audience. In his lecture of 1946, his first public pronouncement after his years as a Resistance fighter and as a colonel, during which he had elected silence, Malraux recalled the shattered hopes of his generation. It, or we, had hoped for peace, dignity, and the benefits accruing to mankind from science. Instead, we have been ironically favored with the most murderous of wars, the deliberate destruction of dignity in the camps of torture and wholesale death, and the Bikini experiments with more bombs. The orator could point to the inmates of German concentration camps, recently released, still emaciated and as bewildered as reborn Lazarus, for whom seats had been reserved in the amphitheatre.

But Malraux was no Spengler, consenting to the decline of the West, not even a Toynbee resigned to the cyclical fall of civilizations one after the other. In *Les Conquérants*, the novel in which he had deserved the praise of Trotsky for first daring to write fiction about revolution, the gigantic phenomenon of our age, as Russia, China, Indonesia, and Africa have shown, one of Malraux's characters, Garin, had defied death with the words: "The only defense lies in creating." Such is also the creed proclaimed by Proust in the midst of his solitary gloom and later by the author of *The Myth of Sisyphus*.

The victory against nihilism and death and the lineaments of a solution to the crisis of modern man were, from then on, to be outlined in Malraux's speeches as a public figure, but even more in his volumes on art. No dry summary can do justice to the profusion of glittering diamonds which Malraux's imperious assertions resemble. His turn of mind is not analytical; nor is it historical, and little does he care about the borrowings of an artist from an earlier artist and about the succession of schools and the categorization of trends and movements. His concern is not to interpret the works of art in their own terms, but as the summation of the culture and of the metaphysical anxiety of the people for whom they were created. Unclear and defiant of logic as only a Frenchman can be when he has determined to repudiate what was taught him at school, Malraux leaps over intermediate links of his ideas and rushes upon us an avalanche of pregnant interrogations.

On the main directions of his thought, continuous and ever more deeply probed into from his early *Tentation de l'Occident* (1926) to *Saturne, Essai sur Goya* (1950) and *Les Voix du Silence* (1951), two of the greatest books of our mid-century and perhaps of our time there hovers no uncertainty. Our age stands primarily in need of great individuals: Malraux's Nietzscheism, parallel to that of Charles de Gaulle, has outlasted his fascination with Communism. He stands for the singular, today in danger, in Cocteau's phrase, of being persecuted by the plural. The very moving final chapters of *Espoir* had voiced Malraux's conclusions, reached in the midst of battles in the Spanish war, that it is difficult to be a leader if one refuses to seduce and to court cheap popularity; but to become one is probably the most melancholy fate, and also the highest, to which man may aspire. A similar thought will haunt Camus, torn between his double allegiance of an Algerian and of a Frenchman, of a liberal apostle of peace thrown into the dual war of 1939–1945: a war against Nazi Germany and a civil war inside every country. The highly complex world of today requires leaders, even more than the Renaissance or the Revolution did. Unfortunately, "the masses are very far from preferring what in them is the best."

Those leaders need not have anything in common with the arrogant and power-greedy elite chiefs which Fascist regimes hoped to produce. Malraux has been assailed by the Marxists as a turncoat traitor who once had been among them, if not of them, and had then recanted his former sympathy for the masses. In truth, even when he appeared to be closest to the Communists, in the middle 1930's when Communism attracted many, in Europe and America, who feared the alliance of the middle classes with Nazism, Malraux was very far from subscribing to their creed or from bowing to their Moscow-inspired dicta. Like his Garin in *The Conquerors* and the protagonists of *Man's Fate*, he was always a heretic. The words in which he outlined the goal to be pursued by Communism, at the 1935 Congress of Anti-Fascist writers in London, must have sounded strange in the ears of orthodox Communists: "To recreate the phantom heritage which lies about us, to open the eyes of all the sightless statues, and thus to shape, out of the age-old sorrows of man, a new and glowing consciousness of mankind."

To this day, the novelist and historian who is also the French minister of state in charge of cultural affairs points to his achievement in founding "maisons de la culture" in several French cities, in opening up "théâtres du peuple" and in acting upon his conviction that it is nobler to assert one's communion with other men than to stress one's differences. Already in 1934, at the Soviet Writers' Congress in Moscow, the young French author had boldly chided the narrowness of Soviet culture: "Beware, Comrades, of assuming that one necessarily creates a powerful literature because one expresses a powerful civilization. . . . Art is not a submission, but a conquest. . . . Marxism is the consciousness of the social, culture is the consciousness of the psychological. . . . The cultural motto of Communism must be that of Marx: more consciousness." No man is an island and no writer or thinker today can be satisfied with proclaiming his proud isolation from the masses as in the age of Byron and of Ibsen. Only through multiplying man by man can an attempt be made to assist man in living victoriously through the present crisis.

Man will also have to increase the force at his disposal through multiplying himself by marshaling all the possibilities opened to him by history and by culture. In art, Malraux contends, the citizens of several continents could discover today a common denominator and a language accessible to all. For, while religions have usually fought against those which preceded them in order to replace them (and since the emergence of a new religion is improbable in our age), arts have, despite controversies which usually only stirred the surface, inherited from each other. The credit side of history is to be read in the succession of masterpieces and in the cumulative cultural achievement of mankind. The unity of man in time, over centuries and millenaries, is proclaimed by the admirer of the Lascaux frescoes, "the Sistine Chapel of prehistory," as Malraux calls it, of the archaic sculpture of Greece or of the Greco-Roman-Buddhist art of Gandhara, of Romanesque, Khmer, and Negro art. That unity is no less conspicuous in space, over the motley array of cultures which, in Oceania as in South Africa, in Tibet and Scythian steppes as in Europe, have expressed the most lasting part of themselves in art. Rebelling against the mournful lament of tragedy which often asserted that life was "a tale full of sound and fury, signifying nothing," Malraux repudiates the temptation of nihilism and of absurdity which may have seduced him in his youth. He rejects the determinism of blood and tyranny, of murder, sex, and war, implicitly preached by many of our mass media. His motto is deliverance from fatality and triumph over destiny. At the end of his *Voices of Silence*, he lyrically offers his gospel to the men and women of today:

> The whole history of art, when it is that of genius, should be a history of deliverance; for history attempts to transform fate into consciousness, and art to transform it into freedom.

Albert Camus also started from the contemplation of the absurd. But the adjective, often misinterpreted, connoted for him a dissonance: the word is not clear and rational as man expects it to be; it cruelly baffles our endeavor toward a full understanding of it and it belies our naïve yearning for immortality. But life will be lived all the better for its having no meaning, the North African youth asserted in his early books, at the very time when a series of bouts with tuberculosis had blighted many of his hopes. He spurned all recourse to eternity, all acceptance of notions such as sin or hope in a beyond. "There are some words which I never understood, such as the word sin. . . . What do I care about eternity? I love this life with abandon and I want to speak of it freely. It fills me with pride at my human condition." Thus exclaimed that writer of glowing romantic prose in his early essays, all instinct with what another moralist, Joubert, had once extolled as "the most beautiful courage of all, the courage to be happy."

However, the conditions of this our life hardly make it easy to enjoy happiness long; even if personal threats to our health or to our security could be parried by the pagan hero that Camus wished to resemble, the mere contemplation of the world as we find it and of the millions who appear to be doomed to misfortune stand in the way of our thoughtless and selfish enjoyment. The character in *L'Etranger* who refused all links with any past and any future, all links with other men and their grossly imperfect justice as well as all links between sentences, has been caricatured by hasty readers into a hero for our age. Camus himself, in an infelicitous sentence such as he sometimes glibly threw to journalists and questioners, hinted that Meursault was perhaps the only Christ deserved by our times. In his more reflective moments, Camus went beyond the very elementary figure of that Algerian poor white who shot an Arab repeatedly, prefiguring some lighthearted murders similarly committed by thoughtless or exasperated poor whites during the Algerian revolt against the French government in the early 1960's. To be solitary and to disassociate oneself from one's fellow beings may appear easy to a youth in revolt. *La Peste*, a few years later, stressed, through an austere and moral allegory, that man is in fact solidary with other men and proposed as a goal to be a saint without God and to assist others without any regard for grace or for any ultimate reward beyond the grave.

In all that he wrote in the twelve years between *La Peste* (1947) and his untimely accidental death early in 1959, Camus pondered over the same anguishing issues: the order of thought and the order of things do not coincide; hence the absurd. But, from a philosophy of negation, modern man wants to derive a valid and workable ethics. Camus repudiated Christianity more forcefully than Malraux and even Sartre had done. "If Christ died for certain men," he insisted, "He did not die for us. But we refuse to despair of man. . . . We consent to do without God, but we shall not so easily dispense with man." Like Malraux, for whom his admiration was immense, he worked at rebuilding and ennobling the notion of man in our days of unrest and of wrath.

Revolt is our primary duty; for not to revolt is to connive at evil or to consent to present injustice for the sake of some imaginary progression in the future; it entails treating the oppressed creatures of today as means to be sacrificed to an ultimate end, be it the Kingdom of God or the rule of the proletariat. "To live is not to be resigned." Camus' symbolic hero, Sisyphus, belongs to the family of Prometheus. But in the midst of the complex problems which beset us today— technical, political, social, philosophical—and since we have renounced essentialist and transcendent values and must think and act existentially, it is difficult to choose revolt and not to commit evil. In the days which followed the liberation of France, in 1944–1945, Camus, engaging in polemics against the Catholic novelist Mauriac, had more than once to advise severity and the inflicting of capital punishment upon some who had betrayed their country to collaborate criminally with the occupying power. He then realized that the claim to punish, and even to kill, others, opens a door to fanaticism and oppression. The same man who has been more lucid, more prophetic, and also more courageous than his fellow citizens, at the head of an institution, of a revolution, of a country, the Prometheus among us, easily becomes convinced that he knows more and acts with sharper insight than other men. He has been a savior once, and he naturally wants to continue being one, imposing his own leadership, or seeking a renewed vote of confidence from the people, too easily prone to relinquish the burden of their responsibility, perhaps of their freedom. A Prometheus turns into a Caesar.

Nevertheless, the man of letters and the artist cannot abdicate and shrink their duty in a time of crisis. "It is not the combat which turns us into artists," said Camus, "but art which obliges us to be combatants." More and more, as he grew into middle age, Camus felt obsessed by the intricacies and the obscurities preying on the man of good will whose calling is literature. Camus, who felt like an ancient Greek, was fond of appealing, beyond Christianity, to the Hellenic wisdom which acknowledged that life has a facet of night and a facet of sunshine; a man worthy of the name, he declared in 1946 at Brooklyn College, must maintain his eyes fixed at the same time on that darkness and on that light. He himself, reproaching the Christian view of life with being pessimistic, wanted to cling to optimism about the future, through indicting, but redressing, the evils of the present. He had not shared the Germanic or Slavic fondness for "abysses." Yet a casual entry in his recently published *Carnets II* (1965) is revealing of his inner dilemma:

> The only effort of my life, since everything else has been granted me generously (except for money, which leaves me indifferent) has been to live the existence of a normal man. I never wanted to be a man of abysses. But that vast endeavor has been in vain. Gradually, I watch the abyss drawing near.

As Malraux contemplates the solution to our modern crisis through reinstating, through art, some unity to our notion of man and to mankind, Camus envisaged a solution as a man of letters and through the pursuit of his profession as a writer. One of his greatest pieces of writing was an address given at the Salle Pleyel, in November, 1948, before a writers' convention, "Le Témoin de la Liberté," translated in *Commentary* in December, 1949. In it, Camus proudly defended his calling, the artist's profession, as one "which, in the midst of a world withered by hate, enables every one of us to say in all peace of mind that he is no man's mortal enemy. . . . Artists bear witness to that in man which refuses to die." Eight years later, as he was solemnly bestowed in Stockholm the highest honor of literary life, the Nobel Prize, Camus again underlined the pitfalls which may ensnare any artist and writer: to blend in equal doses naturalness and art, to please, entertain, attract, move others, and yet not to forsake simplicity and sincerity. He added:

> Whatever our personal frailties may be, the nobleness of our calling will ever be rooted in two commitments, difficult to observe: refusal to lie about what we know, resistance to oppression.

Few men in our age have, forsaking quietude, laziness, the quest for popularity, and their own intellectual comfort, so courageously accepted and fulfilled the duties of men of letters who, today, have also to be prophets and committed leaders of their fellow beings, in Shakespeare's lines, "taking upon themselves the mystery of things/ as if they were God's spies."

ACKNOWLEDGMENTS

The author and the publisher thank the editors of the following journals for permission to reprint essays which first appeared in their columns:

Daedalus, Journal of the American Academy of Arts and Sciences, for "Excellence and Leadership: Has Western Europe Any Lessons for Us?", Vol. XC, No. 4 (Fall 1961), pp. 628–651.

Journal of the History of Ideas, for "The Influence of Eighteenth-Century Ideas on the French Revolution," Vol. X, No. 1 (January 1949), pp. 63–87.

Modern Language Quarterly, for "Romanticism and French Literature Today: Le Mort Vivant," Vol. XV, No. 1 (March 1954), pp. 3–16.

Publications of the Modern Language Association, for "Religion and Literary Scholarship in France," Vol. LXXVII, No. 4, Pt. 1 (September 1962), pp. 345–363.

The Texas Quarterly, for "The Responsibility of Mass Media," Vol. VII, No. 2 (Summer 1964), pp. 11–28.

Yale French Studies, for "English Literature Seen Through French Eyes," No. 6 (December 1950), pp. 109–119; "Napoleon: Devil, Saint, Poet," No. 26 (Fall–Winter 1960), pp. 21–31; "Romantic Poetry and Rhetoric," No. 13 (Spring–Summer 1954), pp. 30–41;

283

"Shakespeare's Women: A French View," No. 33 (December 1964), pp. 107–119; and "What Greece Means to Modern France," No. 6 (December 1950), pp. 53–62.

Thanks are also due Kalamazoo College for permission to reprint "The Crisis of Modern Man as Seen by André Malraux and Albert Camus," which was originally presented as a Scholars' Day address there in 1966.

INDEX OF PROPER NAMES

DATE DUE

MAY 2 '79			
GAYLORD			PRINTED IN U.S.A.